Servant of All

JOSEPH PARKER

Servant of All

A Commentary on
the Gospel of Matthew Chapters 8—16

AMG
PUBLISHERS
Chattanooga, TN 37422

SERVANT OF ALL

This edition originally published by
Richard Clarke, London, 1884.

ISBN 0-89957-241-3

Library of Congress Catalog Card Number: 98-70692

Printed in the United States of America
03 02 01 00 99 98 –R– 6 5 4 3 2 1

CONTENTS

FOREWORD

Servant of All is a superb collection of thirty-seven classic Joseph Parker sermons that were originally preached in a verse-by-verse series study on the Gospel of Matthew. *Servant of All* covers Matthew chapter 8 through the twelfth verse of chapter 16, and is AMG Publishers' second installment of Parker's three volume study covering the entire Gospel. Though Parker's study is very detailed, you will find no information on the Gospel here that is not relevant or insightful. While this study is a collection of sermons, you may find yourself thinking that you are reading an original commentary—a credit to Dr. Parker's writing style.

In our continuing effort to introduce modern readers to the classics of Christian literature, and to preserve their original clarity, we sometimes find it necessary to update spelling and some archaic terms in accordance with how our language has changed over the years. In some cases, unusual forms of punctuation are simplified in order to eliminate confusion. Brackets are also inserted where we have added scripture references. However, we at AMG Publishers feel that it is our responsibility to restore and preserve these classics for generations to follow by making as few changes to the original works as possible; therefore, readers should also note that points of current history cited by Parker are from the latter-half of the nineteenth century.

It is our hope that these compelling, yet colorful sermons by Joseph Parker, will inspire in readers an ever-growing love and appreciation for the Word of God.

r.a.s.

PREFACE

This life of Christ is not like any other with which I am acquainted—a fact which encourages the hope that it may form a humble companion to the truly great biographies which have distinguished the Christian literature of the current century. In this book the Evangelist is allowed to tell his own story in his own way, and I follow him in a strenuous endeavor to interpret that story so as to reveal the very heart of Christ to the men of today. Others have with competent learning and most noble eloquence traced the outer history of the Man Christ Jesus, and have thrown around that history the superb coloring of a high and reverent imagination; by their almost superhuman labors they have laid their age under obligations which can be but imperfectly discharged; and, therefore, if I venture to give another view of the sacred Life, I cannot but hope that the authors who have preceded me will see in my labor not so much a proof of my audacity as an illustration of the infinite fertility of the subject. I might indeed almost dispute the claim of precedence in some degree, inasmuch as my book entitled *Ecce Deus* is older by several years than the immortal work of Canon Farrar.

I have paid next to no attention to points of purely historical interest, as my one purpose has been to acquaint myself with "the mind of Christ" and with "the travail of his soul." Nineteen centuries do not separate between me and the Son of God; if they did, in any divisive and time-worn sense, he would not be the Son of God to me. He is the same forever. Today he walks with me; in many a sacred interview he makes my heart burn within me; and in all bread-breaking he reveals himself in new light and tenderness. I know not Christ after the flesh. Judea and Galilee, and the whole theater of action, have all practically disappeared; the sunset glow, the blue wave, the light wind sighing in the grove, all these have gone, and the poet can but recall a dramatic image of their effect; the Visible Teacher, too, has gone, and is no longer to be known after the flesh. But the Life is here; the Thought is immortal; the Love still holds out its redeeming offer; and the Cross gathers into itself the whole tragedy of life. Within this spiritual sphere my studies have been conducted in the hope of showing to some extent what Christ has to say to the present age. This purpose will account for the style of the book. Most of the book was spoken—spoken to men of business, world-weary, and sick at heart because of grief and loss and pain. Such men wanted to see Christ without delay; nor did they care for pomp of speech, or cunning art in literary structure; they were sick, and asked for healing only; or they reeled under strong temptation, and besought the Son of God to give them rest and hope. In comforting them I have comforted myself; and the comfort has not been a sentiment only, but a deep and complete conviction.

My supreme desire has been to reveal Christ to this age, and to show how he takes upon himself all the varying forms of civilization, and addresses every man in the tongue wherein he was born. I have not hesitated to repeat as one of the central truths of my religious creed that Jesus Christ is not only a historical character, but at once the forerunner and the contemporary of all ages. This is the sovereignty of the Son of God! The moldiness of time gathers upon every other name, and every other name is preserved simply in deference to the instinct of historical veneration, but the Name of Christ—the Jesus of Bethlehem, the Carpenter of Nazareth, the Emmanuel of the world—reigns by right of present power to break the dominion of sin, and bring the contrite heart into immediate forgiveness and ultimate sanctity. He is with us always, even unto the end of the world. For myself, his companionship today is as real as his historical identity is undisputed. Out of this glowing and thankful consciousness I have spoken much of this book, and so the heart will be seen in some workings which are not always so frankly disclosed. But why this dumb secrecy about our chief joy? If I have said much, I have left more unsaid, but have so left it for want of choice words and tones, rather than for want of thankfulness and courage. The "shout," the "loud voice," the "cry," have all been stifled, and every vibration has perished out of the temple walls. Is not Christ still worthy? Is he not worshiped with thunders of hallelujahs in the upper world? Do not the blessed ones cry day and night in the heavens praising him with infinite rapture, and with voices storm-like in their sacred energy? Jesus never discouraged the enthusiasm which was awakened by his own name. Never did he decline the smallest oblation offered by the hand of love; he took the box of ointment, the two mites, the cup of cold water, and I now offer him this attempt to reveal his character and to preach his gospel. Son of God, Lamb of God, Savior of the world, receive this morsel of bread, and break it for the satisfaction of the heart's hunger.

The Apostle Matthew

The following results in reference to the authorship of the first Gospel have been established by modern criticism—

(1) Matthew was the son of Alpheus, and probably the brother of James the less.

(2) Matthew is called Levi by Mark and Luke (Mark 2:14; Luke 5:27, 29).

(3) Some scholars think there is ground for believing that Matthew and Thomas were twin brothers.

(4) The old name Levi referred to his legal attachment and dependence; the new name Matthew may be interpreted as meaning "God's free man."

(5) According to a very ancient tradition, Matthew remained in Jerusalem for fifteen years after the Ascension of the Lord.

(6) Matthew does not observe the chronological order of events.

(7) "The very depth of St. Matthew's patriotism impels him to glory in the universality of the Messianic reign. The kingdom of God must overpass the limits of the Chosen race. Hence it is no matter of surprise that the Hebrew historian should alone commemorate the coming of the Magi and the refuge in Egypt, and that he and not St. Luke should tell the story of the Canaanitish woman."

(8) "We possess in the Gospel of Matthew, a delineation of the life of Jesus, which presents it in all the distinctness and fullness of a peculiar view. This Evangelist makes our Lord known to us in all the certainty and depth of his relation to history. Nowhere else is that golden thread which connects all history, the ever-advancing though secret progress of mankind, so clearly displayed; and nowhere does the Eternal appear so pure and bright in history, so free from all contamination of the corrupt and perishable, nay, in sharpest and most sublime contrast to all the pretensions of mere dead statutes."—Lange

(9) "From Papias, almost if not quite contemporary with the apostles, downwards, we have a stream of unimpeachable witness to the fact that Matthew was the author of a Gospel; while the quotations which abound in the works of the Fathers prove that at least as early as Ireneus the gospel received by the Church under his name was the same as that which has reached us."—*Kitto's Cyclopaedia*

one

ELOQUENCE SUPPORTED BY GREAT BENEFICENCE

Matthew 8:1–4

"WHEN HE was come down from the mountain." The great *speech* had been made, the grand propagation of new ideas had begun, a wondrous intellectual apocalypse had been opened, charming and dazzling the inner vision with all its mystery of separate yet blended colors, and now the great *action* is commenced. Herein you have the hemispheres of Christianity: it is a great speech, and it is also a great healing: it is an eloquent *word* and it is an eloquent *practice*. It requires the mountain from which to project its great deliverance of an intellectual and spiritual kind: it does not exhaust itself by that exercise, it has not only strength enough left to come down the mountain, but having descended from the mountain and entered into the city, it has strength, sympathy, patience, tenderness, and every other requisite for the healing and the redemption of man.

Wonderful is that word in the sixty-first chapter of Isaiah, wherein Christ, forecasting the ages, says, "The spirit of the Lord God is upon me, because he hath sent me to preach the gospel to the meek, he hath sent me to the broken-hearted, to them that mourn, and to those that are in captivity." Jesus Christ did not come to the Scribes and to the Pharisees, the Son of man did not come to our intellectual capacity and self-contented sufficiency; he came to the meek and lowly and broken-hearted and mourning and captive, and unless we be in one or other of these conditions the Son of God will speak to us an unknown tongue; we shall not recognize one syllable in all his gospel; it will shoot over our heads as a light not meant for our darkness. But if we be in the condition described in the words given in the prophecy of Isaiah, then every word

1

he speaks will be a word to us, the very word we need, the only word as it would seem that the heart could possibly understand. We determine by our moral condition what the gospel is to be to us. Given a right state of heart, and every hymn will lift you to heaven, every petition in the prayer will broaden and gladden your life, but given a wrong state of the heart, proud, self-sufficient, self-contained, unconscious of guilt, lacking in contrition and compunction, and God's own word would be to you an idle tale, ill-pronounced and pointless.

"When he was come down from the mountain, great multitudes followed him, and behold there came a leper." What is the meaning of this startling distinction? Why not have included the leper in the multitudes? Why this broad plural and this sharp singular together? It is always so: both these relations to Christ are right; man never knows himself really and truly till he has been both part of a multitude and set aside in his absolute and untouched personality. You say you can read the Bible at home and therefore need not come to church. No. There is a church-reading, and you cannot have it at home. There is in you a multitudinous element which can only be recognized and satisfied in the great congregation. There is also another side to your nature: you must separate yourself from the multitude and be nobody but yourself, frightened of yourself, so much yourself as to be a fear and a terror and a distress, because of the pressure of your need and the infinite hideousness of your personal transgression. It is good sometimes to be in the religious crowd; we are then dispossessed of some littleness that cling to the best of us. The mere friction, the subtle sympathy, the feeling that man is larger than any single individual—these have a peculiar influence upon the rightly-constituted mind, giving it solemnity, nobility, dignity, setting it in its right relation and perspective and color. "Forsake not the assembling of yourselves together as the manner of some is" [see Heb. 10:25].

Yet there came a leper. The leper always makes room for himself. There are some men that cannot be pluralized, they have a whole corner to themselves. It is marvelous into what little bulk even a great multitude can shrink when a leper comes near. You thought there was no room before; let a leper come, and the space on which the multitude can stand is much lessened. Everyone of us is a leper, but not yet known to be such. You would not be allowed to sit where you are now if your real character was known. Every man must feel his own leprosy and go with his own prayer, and pierce the multitude, and get through it to have his own interview with the Son of God. We are not saved in great swelling crowds; we must go one by one, and each state his own case in his own words to the only healer of human life. I need not teach you a prayer: lepers are mighty in prayer. Leprosy kindles wit, leprosy sharpens a man's tongue into a keen accent, leprosy teaches brief speech, but ringing and telling, without one waste word, ear-piercing and making God himself hear. Leprosy batters upon heaven's door with a violence that God never neglects.

A sweet prayer, a full, tender prayer is the leper's—"Lord, if thou wilt, thou canst make me clean." Go and stand beside the publican, that other leper, and hear his prayer—"God be merciful unto me a sinner" [Luke 18:13]. Go beside that cross where the better thief dies, and hear his prayer—"Lord, remember me when thou comest into thy kingdom" [Luke 23:42]. A prayer in a sentence you have in each case; not a long argument, and yet you could sooner add a beam to the sun than you could add one touch of beauty to this prayer. The leper was no literary man; he was not skilled in phrase-cutting, and in word-setting; he was no clever lapidary, cunning in giving facets to words, that they might catch the light and throw it back again most beautifully—his only teacher was his heart. When will men listen to that great teacher, the hot heart, wild in misery, mad with despair, almost in hell because of self-compunction? There are times when our life does not sharpen itself into this most leprous necessity, and at those times we need longer prayers. Then we may need the help of our friends to write prayers for us or to pray with us. There are times when we want longer communion with God; when he says, "Come up to the mountain early in the morning and meet me on the top." And when we do not leave the mountain till the sun has just light enough in it to light us down the long stairway again, then we may need many words, and beautiful, quivering with sacred life, glittering with celestial beauty, musical with heavenly tunefulness—wondrous words, almost divine, as if they would totalize themselves into one verb. You have had such experience, you have been part of a multitude, and you have been suddenly turned out of it and made to stand alone before the Christ. Forsake not the assembling of yourselves together, let me say again; and let me further add, have hours and half-hours in which there is nobody with you in the sanctuary, when you are alone in it, yet not alone, for the Father is with you.

The leper teaches us a beautiful prayer. We will omit his own personal petition and put in our own—his introduction will do for any prayer. "Lord, if thou wilt." Every man has to fill up the form with his own cry. Lord, if thou wilt, thou canst make me *strong:* I am weak, I am a child of infirmity; my bones ache, my knees smite one another with feebleness and terror; I hardly live, my life is a burden or a pain—if thou wilt, thou canst make me strong. Lord, if thou wilt, thou canst make me *happy.* I am hardly ever happy; I dare not be happy, for fear a moment's gladness should bring back the pain with increased poignancy. I am as those who are afflicted and who dare not sleep because the waking again is intolerable agony. Lord, if thou wilt, thou canst make me *rich*—nevertheless, not my will but thine be done.

Sorrow turns instinctively to the supernatural. I would not listen to a strong, robust, rude man talking to me about the supernatural. He knows nothing about it; he never needed it so far as his bodily sensitiveness or necessity is concerned. Go and argue with the leper: tell him that the supernatural is not accessible; tell him to go to the ordinary physician; reason with him upon the vanity and the uselessness of religious expectation. Will he hear your prating? What is it that breaks through every argument in the time of its intolerable fire, its pain, its agony, its heartache? Go and tell the mother who is just lowering her one little child into the grave not to be religious, and not to say, "My God, my Father"; tell her to turn away her tear-filled eyes from the blue heavens, for there is no one there who cares for her agony: fill her ear with atheistic polysyllables, and drag her back from the altar—and see what intellectual conquests you can win. Feeling is sometimes the very inspiration of life. Argument can touch but a very little portion of me. Whatever leaves the *heart* untouched is barren, vexatious, and worse than useless.

Herein is a lesson to the young and strong of a kind that cannot now be very persistently urged. A child, thank God, is all laughter, and I would not punctuate its laugh with a single tear. Let the child laugh. The strong man, who never had a headache or heartache, who never knew what it was to toss upon the bed hour by hour, calling and crying for sleep— what can *he* say to anybody? Ask the fat ox the way to heaven, and it will tell you as soon as can such a man say one true word about things that are above the clouds.

Sorrow never came into the world with the will of Christ. Lord, if thou wilt, thou canst make me clean. Certainly. Then leprosy never came with his will, sympathetically. Whenever you see a grave dug in the cold earth, it is something done against God's will. He never meant this green earth to have its bosom ripped that his children might be thrust into its darkness. We have put the earth to new uses; we have spoiled God's garden, and we have grown his flowers to decorate our dead. No tear ever comes into our eye with God's will. And yet observe that I put in the word *sympathetically*, and did so with a very distinct purpose, because leprosy, sorrow, death, are here with God's will *judicially*—they are all his servants. He says in his kind heaven, where the summers are all stored for the earth, "I must not withdraw the leprosy, or they will go mad. I must not kill the fiery flying serpent, or they will swear with a more determined loudness. I must not withdraw the plague, fever, cholera, smallpox, blight upon the wheat fields and olive yards, or they will curse the night through as well as the day. I must keep the constables on the ground, I must thicken my policemen as to their numbers or quicken them as to their vigilance, or that crowd of men upon yonder little black earth will all go to perdition."

So these afflictions, leprosies, and divers diseases are God's constables, God's judicial sentences, God's safeguards, part of God's disciplinary forces. Do you suppose you can drink every night and awake in the morning with a clear head? God puts something into your cup to prevent that. Do you suppose you can plunder and defile and then be as much at rest as if you had sacrificed and prayed? God takes care to put a dart through your liver, to touch you with an argument, and with the only argument you can understand. He does not meet you in the morning as your mother does, with a remonstrance, he meets you with a dart, he transfixes you with a spear, and says, "He that sinneth against me wrongeth his own soul, spoils the fine membrane, twists the holy aspiration, diminishes the divine capacity, debases the noblest elements of his manhood." You wondered how it was that your hand shook so when you wrote the letter. It was because of the debauch. It is not because you are growing an *old* man, but because you are a *bad* one!

"Jesus put forth his hand and touched him." Who else dare touch the leper? The touch was death. "And the leper in whom the plague is, his clothes shall be rent and his head bared, and he shall put a covering upon his upper lip, and shall cry, 'Unclean, unclean.' All the days wherein the plague shall be in him, he shall be defiled: he is unclean, he shall dwell alone—with the camp shall be his habitation" [Lev. 13:35, 36]. In the light of these old words read the text—"He touched him." The sunbeam can touch contaminations without defilement—who can touch pitch and not be defiled? Blessed Savior—when did he say "No" to any prayer of the leprous, the blind, the broken-hearted, the bereaved, the penitent? It was not in him to say "No" to any of these. Many a "No" he gave in reply to Scribe and Pharisee and pompous suppliant who brought his own answer as well as his own prayer: he never said "No" to me when I said "God be merciful to me a sinner." He always gave me a new sheet of paper, and said "Try again: do not blot this one, or you may never have another." I have taken it and blotted it all over and gone back with the old prayer, and got another sheet of paper, pure as the holiness that gave it. These are my reasons for believing in Christ. He is not the Son of God to me because some *grammarian* has forced him to that high eminence; he is God the Son because he has healed a heart no other physician could touch, and cleansed a sin which would have defiled and polluted every river that ever flowed through the earth. When the soul has these experiences of the Savior he does not need to have his Deity buttressed by any grammatical patronage.

Mark the wonderful consistency in this Man's procedure. We find him saying in his sermon, "It hath been said by them of old time, but I say unto you." Now in his action we find him repeating the same form. "It hath been said by them of old time, Thou shalt not touch the leper, but I say unto you, I will touch him." He separates himself from others, yet he is consistent in the reasons of that separation.

"Tell no man." Jesus Christ did not think any miracle worth preaching. We trouble ourselves about the miracles, we ask ourselves hard questions about them, we go to the length of writing expensive books about them. Jesus Christ made nothing of them. Christ says to those he worked miracles upon:

> As for the miracle, do not name it. If you mention it at all, tell it in your own house, and do not let the news get beyond your own circle. I came not to convert the world by miracles; do not encourage the idea that salvation is part of a romantic scheme, one of a set of marvelous phenomena. I have come for other work: not to dazzle the imagination by the performance of miracles, but to charm and save the heart by the proclamation of the kingdom of heaven. See thou tell no man so far as the *miracles* are con-

cerned; so far as the *doctrine* is concerned go ye into all the world and preach the gospel to every creature [see Mark 16:15].

We have taken hold of this kingdom of heaven by the wrong end. We meet in classes to discuss the miracles—we poor cold pieces of iron in which there is no fire, have met to consider the constitution of the sun. When will we be wise, and think not of Christ's miracles but of Christ's doctrines? When will we think of what he came to do with regard to the poor *heart?* That is the central business and that is the supreme joy of the Church.

So then the sermon is already being turned to advantage by the people. "Ask, and it shall be given you." Did the leper overhear that? Was it told to the leper by some kind friend? Did he say "I will put this great Speaker to the test—he said 'Ask, and it shall be given,' I will ask him"? He asked and he received. Now the other side must also be consistent. Christ also said, "Think not that I am come to destroy the law or the prophets. I am not come to destroy, but to fulfill." Jesus Christ says to the leper, "You have asked me in effect to prove the words, 'Ask, and it shall be given you'; now I must ask you to prove the words, 'I am not come to destroy the law but to fulfill': so go, show thyself to the priest, and offer the gift that Moses commanded" [Matt. 5:17; 8:4]. A wondrous and self-confirming consistency marks this whole revelation, and those who have studied it most profoundly and lovingly are most deeply impressed with the perfectness of the literal and moral consistency of God's book.

A wonderful revelation, then, is now before us. This suffering and its removal are to be looked at in the light of two antagonistic wills. "Lord, if thou wilt, thou canst make me clean." There the creature's will becomes right. The moment the will of the creature becomes right, Jesus says "I will: be thou clean." Your will is wrong—trouble not yourselves with little intellectual inquiries and difficulties and enigmas; it is a waste of time, it is a mortal delusion on your part to suppose that you would be a good man and a holy saint if some little intellectual cobwebs were taken out of your head. Your *will* is wrong. "Marvel not that I say unto you, Ye must be born again" [John 3:7]. When your *will* is right, you will find that God's will has always been on your side, on the side of your redeeming and healing and perfecting. He waits to be gracious: he can do nothing with a crooked will, he can do nothing with a perverse will, he can do nothing with a corrupt will, he can do nothing with a selfish will. When we come to him and say, "Lord, if thou wilt, thou canst make me clean," thus putting ourselves into his hands simply, lovingly, absolutely, his answer is immediate and complete. It is not therefore your intellect only that must be illumined and rectified: the word must be deeper; you must be born of water and of the Spirit; you must be washed in the laver of regeneration: "Marvel not that I say unto you, Ye must be born again."

This redemption is not a question of mere intellectual satisfaction, still less of intellectual excitement or delight: it is a question of the will, the heart, the very source and spring of life. The work is not superficial, but profound: the work is not artificial, but vital: the work is not external, but internal—after being internal it expresses itself in all exterior dignity and loveliness.

two

THE HUMAN SYMPATHY
OF CHRIST

Matthew 8:5–13

"And when Jesus was entered into Capernaum, there came unto him a centurion, beseeching him." Towns are differently excited by different visitors. If Beethoven were to come to London, all the music of the metropolis would vibrate with delight and expectation and hope. If some great athlete were to visit the metropolis, all persons interested in athletics would be instantly filled with a desire to see the performance. When Jesus Christ went into a town all the sick people, all the broken-hearted, the helpless, and the weary felt a thrill of expectation and hope, and they were almost bettered by the very news that he was coming. Think of a man entering a town whose very presence sends a gospel to the broken-hearted—that is the man I want to see. I could listen to the musician for a while, I could applaud the acrobat for a moment or two, I would withhold the palm from no man who had won it, but when I had passed through the whole rank and file of those who had entertained, instructed, and amused me, I should want everyday to have with me the man that could touch my afflictions, and bear my diseases, and heal my wounded heart. I would say to him, "Abide with me, the day is far spent, but it cannot die while the light of thine eye is in the house; abide with me" [see Luke 24:29].

This is how Jesus Christ endears himself so much to my heart, and how it is that my love for him is a love passing the love of women, and how it is that I cannot be torn away from his side. It is not that I am puzzled by his genius, thrilled by his mighty miracles, astounded by much that is wondrous in himself and his works, but because he himself took our infirmities and bore our sicknesses, and goes up into the sick-chamber

9

though a leper be in it, and though a pestilence too foul for my mother to face be filling the chamber with its fatal contagion. This is the Christ to whom I call you. Know him by the depth and tenderness and incessancy of his sympathy and love, and fall down before him, not because forced to your knees by some grammatical and exegetical pressure, but because constrained to that worshipful act by an infinite understanding of your own *heart*, and an ineffable and redeeming sympathy with every emotion and passion of your life.

"There came unto him a centurion, beseeching him, and saying, Lord, my servant lieth at home sick of the palsy grievously tormented." A servant at home—what an extraordinary and antiquated conjunction of terms, "There came a centurion, saying, Lord, my servant lieth at home sick of the palsy, grievously tormented." That is not a prayer—there is no request in that form of words, it is a mere piece of intelligence. See the character of the man in the form of his approach. Is there no prayer in the *eye*, is there no agony in the *look*, is there no supplication in the *tone?* What can the printers do but catch the bare words and put them into cold black ink? This is how it is that the written page is not the spoken discourse; it lacks the fire that glowed in the face, the inquiry that sharpened the vision of the eye, the music and the eloquence that made the tone pierce the hearer's heart like a prayer. Why you, man of few words, gifted with rare silence, often complaining that you have no language, could pray like this! Prayer is the lifting of an eye, prayer is the falling of a tear, prayer is the outdarting of an arm as if it would snatch a blessing from on high. You do not need long sentences, intricate expressions, elaborate and innumerable phrases; a *look* may be a battle half won. "According to thy faith, so be it unto thee." You may pray now, or in the crowded street, or in the busiest scene—you can always have a word with God—you can always wing a whisper to the skies. Pray without ceasing [1 Thess. 5:17]. Live in the spirit of prayer, let your life be one grand desire, Godward and heavenward, then use as many words or as few as you please, your heart is itself a prayer, and your look a holy expectation.

Beautiful is it to see the pagan come into Christian worship. He does not know what to do. A trained soldier and a man in authority, he wishes to be respectful and yet he does not know what is proper to the new situation. He therefore pleadingly states the case. It is beautiful to see one unaccustomed to the form of worship in any place, enter into the strange sanctuary and look inquiringly around to see what has to be done next. There is no wish to come into collision with the established usages of the place. There is, indeed, a lingering liking for the way at home, but a willing disposition to accept new forms and methods. There is something pathetic in such ignorance, and something instructive in such inquiry. But see the centurion, a man, a stranger, a pagan, one far off, coming to state his servant's case, and to leave it with a beseeching look and a beseeching tone—why that is to receive education in an uncertified school, it is to receive a hint from lips uncircumcised—that is to learn from those who themselves are ignorant of the subtle and peculiar methods adopted under new circumstances.

Jesus will be puzzled by this new form of approach. Having heard about the servant at home sick of the palsy, he will say, "Well, what then?" He will teach this man how to pray, he will say, "If you want any favor from me you must approach me in certain form or I cannot hear you." He understood the heart—he meets the suppliant half way. Do you suppose that your ladder-prayer can reach the stars? It only touches God because God comes down to let it touch him. Heaven and the heaven of heavens cannot contain him, yet he comes down to the habitations of men and listens for their prayers as if those prayers filled the universe.

How does Jesus Christ adapt himself to this man's approach? He meets the man in his own spirit. Without hearing the request he says, "I will come and heal him." That verse makes me a believer in the deity of Christ: I need no other proof. If he said *that*, he is God enough for me. Not "I will come and inquire into the case, I will come and see whether anything can be done to mitigate this awful mischief: I can sympathize with you, if I can go no further," but with the calmness of the fiat that arched the heavens and lit its lamps, he says, "I will come and heal him." The people were astonished at his doctrine, because he taught them as one having authority. They are astounded at his word, for he speaks of disease as one having infinite power. Last Sunday we saw him touching a leper, and heard him saying, "Be thou clean"; today our lesson brings before us a man sick of paralysis, grievously tormented, and Jesus Christ says, "I will come and heal him." Then he was no *specialist*. Properly we have amongst ourselves now special studies of special cases. One man undertakes the brain, another the heart, another the blood, it may be, another the bones and joints. This is right, amongst ourselves; for probably hardly any one man has the time, even if he had the capacity, to master with sufficient adequacy all the details and necessities of our wondrous bodily frame. But Jesus Christ said to the leper, "Be thou clean," to the paralytic man, grievously tormented, "I will come and heal him." When he went into Peter's house and saw his mother-in-law laid and sick of the fever, he touched her hand and the fever left her, he put out the fire with his touch. He is no specialist, he has not a necromancer's power over any *one* department of human life or human suffering. His healing was fundamental and all-inclusive. He made the well-head pure, and the flowing stream was as pure as the fountain whence if flowed.

It is so in spiritual matters. There is not in the Church a doctor who cures lying, and another who makes a special study of drunkenness, and a third who is gifted with peculiar ability in dealing with persons of felonious disposition. There is one Mediator between God and man: he makes the *heart* right, and then all the accidental and local diseases, with all their train of ever-varying symptoms, are cleansed and utterly expelled. Thus in the Church of Christ we have no special means for special cases, as contra-distinguished from the general means at our disposal for the universal disease and apostasy. There is one word for all, one healing for all. When you talk of your follies and peculiar sins and characteristic slips and individual passions, these are but symptoms of a grand moral ailment: the whole head is sick, the whole heart faint, and the remedy must be vital and fundamental, not a successful playing with accidental symptoms, but an appeal to the heart, a cleansing of the inner nature. "Ye must be born again."

Whatever your complaint is, of mind, body, or estate, you may take it to Jesus Christ. If you are not doing well in business, go and tell him about it: if you are afflicted in any bodily way, go and state the case to him and leave it in his hands; if you be possessed with devils and grievously tormented in your heart, go and state the case to the Son of God. Go and tell Jesus *everything*. Do not tell him what answer to give in return. I like everyday to have a long talk with him in the streets, or in the house, or anywhere, just telling him what I did yesterday, and what a fool I was for doing it, and asking him to keep me this day without sin, and putting my whole broken life into his care, that he may teach me that the part is not the whole, and that there are purposes in his will and providence which I can neither comprehend nor control. He always heals me with rest and with added faith. The thorn remains, the cruel sting goes deeper, the fire licks up further blood, and yet there is an *inner* healing, a sacred rest, and loving trust in God.

The centurion having heard the reply of Jesus Christ, said, "Lord, I am not worthy that thou shouldest come under my roof; I am a man under authority, having soldiers under me: and I say to this man, Go, and he goeth; and to another, Come, and he cometh; and to my servant, Do this, and he doeth it." He was a man under authority, and his word was law; then why did he not command his servant to be healed? It is thus we always come to our limit, it is thus that the scepter we lift touches the end of its dominion, and shrinks back into a common walking staff. Said the centurion, "I have authority." Then why did he not use it in new directions? Within our own lines we are mighty; beyond those lines we are captured as trespassers or slain as mean spies. When men learn to keep within their own proper boundaries, intellectual and other, they will attain fullness and the most satisfactory fruition of their power, but the most common of us can ask questions that may vex and trouble the heart of God. Happy is he who knows the length of his scepter, and who lays it down at the right point, who says, "I am a man under authority, but there is a point at which my word has no force: I am silent at that point, and I begin to pray where I cease to rule." That is the true law of life.

Yet what wisdom the man had! He said, "But speak the word only." He little knew what he was saying. "The word"—that would have been beautiful and complete—"the word *only*," there he falls into softness and weakness; he shows the stoop which proves him to be but a man. "The word *only*." The word is the authority, the word is the power, the word is the soul, the word is the incarnation. "In the beginning was the Word, and the Word was with God, and the Word was God" [John 1:1]. Your word is *yourself*: do not imagine that your speech is something independent of your individuality; your speech is your soul in utterance. When a man speaks earnestly, the word is the very fire and flame of his heart. Jesus Christ could not but speak earnestly, so his quietest word held the thunder, the lightning, as the dewdrop holds it, for there is force enough in that one dewdrop, if rightly touched, to rend the mountain and throw down the altar stair that faced heavenward. Let your yea be yea, and your nay nay [Matt. 5:37]—let your word be your true self, and it will always be, according to the degree of your capacity and influence, with authority and power.

Now it is Jesus Christ's turn: O that we could have seen that marred and sorrow-ridden face when he lifted it up and marveled. He himself had seen a miracle: his own miracles, viewed as mere expressions of power, fell into insignificance before the miracle performed by the centurion, the miracle of all-trust, living, loving, simple, unquestioning, undisputing trust. "Verily I say unto you, I have not found so great faith, no, not in Israel." A great wave of emotion swelled his heart; forecasting the ages, he saw the crown already rounding into shape that was to sit upon his own head, and though the cross lay between him and that crown, he endured the cross and despised the shame.

We have it in our power to gladden his heart. How pleased he always is with faith. If a man looked trustfully at him, he said he was a son of Abraham. Sinner, others called him, and publican; Jesus called him Son of Abraham. How pleased he is, let me say again and again, with faith; a woman touched the hem of his garment and he called her daughter [see Matt. 9:20–22]. He had never seen the woman before, humanly, yet he called her by endearing names and sent her home with his peace. Her house was never so rich as it was in that sunset. He does not ask our intellect, our pomp, our power, our grandeur; what can these be to him, who thickly inlaid the floor of heaven with "patines of bright gold"? What can our treasures be to him who spoke the sun into being, and rolled the stars along? But when we look up to him and say, "Lord, I believe," it fills his very soul with joy. He keeps back nothing from *faith*, he says if we had faith as a grain of mustard seed, the mountains would be at our bidding and the earth would be our slave.

What can we say now but "Lord, increase our faith"? We are full of questioning and speculation, and cleverness and metaphysics, and we are keen at suggesting difficulties, and clever in the creation and piling of obstacles. I would God I could say always right in the devil's very face when he is grinding at my weakness most, "Lord, I believe."

three

WORKING ALL DAY

Matthew 8:14–17

"AND WHEN Jesus was come into Peter's house." The centurion would not hear of the Lord Jesus Christ going to his house: it was beneath so great a worker and teacher: it was a humiliation not to be permitted by the sense which the centurion had of Roman dignity and Roman majesty. Said he, "Speak the word only, and my servant shall be healed" [Matt. 8:8]. Jesus Christ appeared to the centurion to be in his right place when he was upon the mountain, when he was upon the sea, when the great blue sky was the only roof over his head. It did not enter into his mind that Jesus Christ could enter a little human habitation. Do not let us make the Lord Jesus Christ too *dignified* in our social and conventional sense: there is more in Christ than what we should limit by the word *dignity*. I am afraid that some of us keep a long way from God, because his dignity, as we falsely and vainly interpret it, keeps us at a cold distance. We must get to an appreciation of his mind by such words as love, grace, sympathy, condescension, pity. It is in that region that our imagination and our love must move if they would realize all the higher blessings and all the tender benedictions which are associated with the Divine name.

"When Jesus was come into the house." We have been with him at the *river*—there he was baptized; we have been with him in the *wilderness*—there he was tempted; we have been with him as he walked by the *seaside*—there he called disciples to become fishers of men; we have been with him on the *mountain*—there in soft and musical thunder he addressed the ages. He came into Capernaum, the *city*; he is getting nearer. Today he enters the *house*, and thus completes his relation to all points

15

of human life and human need. He would come into your house if you would let him; he would come nearer still, he would come into your heart if you were willing. "Behold I stand at the door and knock; if any man hear my voice and will open the door I will come in" [Rev. 3:20]. He cannot force his way into your heart-house—he could take the slates off your roof, pour down his rain upon your little fire until it was quenched, but he cannot force a child's love; the feeblest life can mock him with bitter taunting and keep him outside. Know your power: it is a mischievous strength, but know, O man, that it lies within your power to smite God in the face and to mock him with every throb of your heart. Know your power, realize your strange weird majesty—that you are almost God!

When he was come into the house, he found a shadow there.

There is a shadow in every house, there is a fever in every family.

> There is no flock, however watched or tended,
> But one dead lamb is there;
> There is no fireside, howsoe'er defended,
> But has one vacant chair.

If we could find a house in which there was no fever, no death, no pain, no sorrow, no poverty, we should all want to live in it.

But Peter was a *disciple*, he was an incipient apostle, he was the senior disciple; great honors were in store for his name in the ages, and yet the shadow was in *his* house. You would think that God would send all the shadows upon the atheist, and would pile night on him so thickly as to make him mad with darkness. Yet it is not so in the Divine government. "For whom the Lord loveth he chasteneth, and scourgeth every son whom he receiveth. If ye endure chastening, God dealeth with you as with sons; for what son is he whom the father chasteneth not? But if ye be without chastisement, whereof all are partakers, then are ye bastards, and not sons" [Heb. 12:6–8]. Doubt your sonship if you never feel that you are chastened.

Who would not have spared the senior disciple—who would not have made him the focal point on which should have converged all the rays of the Divine approbation, so that he might have been like a light seen afar, blazing forth the excellence and the wondrousness of the Divine election. The thief that lived next door had less fever in his house than Peter had. Sometimes the bad man's ground brings forth plenty, sometimes the pampered and overfed Dives has wealth upon wealth, while the praying soul is outside with dogs for his companions and crumbs as his portion. All this cannot be reconciled within the narrow limits of time. We want more field: the line that appears to be straight is only apparently straight, because of the limited points within which it is drawn. Extend the line and it partakes of the shape of the world upon whose surface it is drawn. So within these narrow points of time, the rocking cradle and the deep tomb, there is not scope enough to reconcile all the divine purposes and actions and mysteries; we need more field, a more ample horizon. We shall get it by-and-by, and then we shall know how God has been dealing with us in forcing rivers out of our eyes and in making our heads a burning pain. O child of God, much praying man, wearied almost with crying at heaven's gate, proceed, persevere, the sigh of your weakness shall be far mightier than the thunder of your strength. Do not despair, do not yet give up; while there is one dying ray of light in the sky, hold on.

Who would be without affliction at home at least sometimes? Affliction unites the family. Given great prosperity and great wealth, and you may possibly find along with these great vanity and great tendency to self-assertion and to mutual contradiction and contention: but given affliction, and there is something in it that touches every heart and constrains every energy, and focalizes all the resources of the house, so that the sick-chamber is often the *church* of the habitation. It would be a fool's hiding-place if not for the sick-chamber; that sick-chamber makes the young pause, the impetuous take time, the thoughtless set down his foot quietly lest he should give needless shock and pain in the quiet place of suffering. It sets wits to work—not the intellectual wits only, but the heart's wits—to find out new delicacies, new tones, new music, new expressions of gentleness. It makes women of us all.

You would not be half the man you are but for your sick child; your tendency is towards self-assertiveness, aggressiveness of speech, sternness, harshness. You have a magisterial cast and bearing in your life, but that little sick child has softened you, and been like a benediction upon your life. Men now take notice of your voice and say, "What new tones have subtly entered into it; how different the kind grasp, how noble the new bearing, how impressive the sacred patience, how touching and pathetic the sadness of the face!" Afflictions do not spring out of the dust: do not be impatient with them; we need something to soften this hard life.

O, if it were all buying, selling, getting gain, outrunning one another in a race for wealth in which the racers take no time to recover themselves—there would be no gardens on the face of the earth, no places consecrated to floral beauty, no houses built for music, no churches set up for prayer. But affliction helps to keep us right, affliction brings us to our knees. Poverty says, *"Think, fool, think."* Affliction opens the Bible at the right places. If you, strong man, with the radiant face and the full pocket, were to open the Bible, it would open upside down, and at nothing. But you, broken-hearted mother, you child of sickness, you orphan and lonely one, your Bible falls open always at the right place. Give me your family Bible, and I will tell you your history. The Bible of the strong, prosperous, rich man—'tis like himself; well kept—too well. Hand me yours, man of the broken heart and the tear-stained cheek, and the reddened eye and the furrowed brow. Ah, all marks and thumbings, and corners turned down and marginal notes and pencil indications— twenty-third Psalm, fortieth chapter of Isaiah, a hundred places in Jeremiah—including the Lamentations—why, I need no concordance to this Bible, if I want to seek out the promises. I see your guest has been sorrow, and the hospitality you have offered him has been patience. If you would know the value of the Bible in the house, consult those who have needed it most, and abide by their sweet reply.

"When the even was come." What even? The astronomical evening. It brings its own beauty with it. Do not be sorry when the sun westers and glows with solemn pomp in his dying hour. When the even was come *astronomically*, the sun rose redeemingly. Jesus came with the sunset, and when he comes the sun rises. It was a wondrous conjunction, the old, old sun of the heavens, faithful servant of God, lamp too high to be blown out by man's breath—when the sun had done all he could for the earth, he was going away, and then arose the other Sun, the Sun of Righteousness, with healing under his wings [see Mal. 4:2]. See what a busy sunset was this. They brought unto him many that were demon possessed, and he cast out the spirits with his word, and healed all that were sick. Mark, this work of Jesus Christ was twofold: it had to do with demons that held the dominion of the mind, and it had to do with diseases that held the dominion of the body. What wondrous ease is in these words—"He cast out the spirits with his word, and healed all that were sick," and it is written as if he had merely looked up or breathed, so consummate, so infinite, so deific the ease. It is always so that God must work;

he can do nothing by an effort; if it were an effort it would not be divine. Power is in the *ease:* the ease is the signature of deity.

In all great life the same thing is exemplified. The painter does not paint with difficulty, if he be heaven-born; he paints because he *breathes.* The poet does not struggle with a long and painful agony to write his verses: he writes because he breathes. All this, of course, has its limitations in human life; it reaches the fullness and the last touch of its infinite sacredness in Christ, who spake and it was done, who commanded and it stood fast— because he planted the heavens and set the earth upon nothing.

Observe, not only was the word twofold, but it was complete—it was finished. How is it with us in regard to our human helpings and healings? We speak in this fashion, and not inaccurately or unwisely, namely, "The doctor did me much good; the physician did me some good; the medical advice was in some degree just what I wanted; the relief was palpable, and I was glad of it." Do you ever find that word recorded of Christ? Did he ever *almost* heal a man? It is a curious thing of those uneducated and demon possessed men who wrote about his life, to have set down this, so consistently, as if they had been working upon a plan of mutual and collusive deceit and fraud. Did he ever come into contact with a devil-ridden one and say, "I can almost heal thee, but not wholly"? His disciples have come into conflict with such a possessed individual, but Jesus was not there. He came down and found the crowd around the disciples and said, "What is it?" It ennobles us to see him in that hour; his face has a transfiguring effect upon our commonness. "What is it?" and a voice said, "I brought my child to thy disciples that they might cast out the devil that has seized and ruined him, and they could not" [see Matt. 17:15–18]. Did his face darken with fear? Did his persona contract with shame? Did he postpone the controversy? He said, "Bring him unto me," and he said, "I command thee come out of him," and he came out like a scourged hound that knew the master's voice, a voice that fell upon him like a thong of scorpions, and he came out.

Did Jesus Christ ever *almost heal* the crippled? Did he ever *almost open* the eyes of the blind? Did he ever give only *partial* relief to the deaf? He said, "Go, tell John the things ye see and hear; the blind receive their sight, the deaf hear, the dumb speak, the lame walk, and unto the poor the gospel is preached" [see Matt. 11:4, 5].

Yet he who can work omnipotently in all these directions which are indicated by demon possession and direful disease, cannot work faster in your heart than you will *let* him. It is there that he must work partially, and incompletely. He would make us without spot or wrinkle or any such thing, but we will not *let* him. We know our power and we use it. He can drive out the devil—but how does he bring the angel in? He can banish our disease and restore our bodily health—but how does he make the soul well? "Behold I stand at the door and knock" [Rev. 3:20]. It has pleased him to make us so, that we can keep him knocking. There is no force in the *moral* direction: God works by consent of the human heart. "Behold I stand at the door and knock." No other god dare take upon him such humility. We keep our mythological gods in courtly pomp, we keep them well up in the smoke and the cloud. It takes *truth* to search in the mud, to light a candle and seek for the lost man; it takes *God* to die that man may live. Let us give our hearts to him.

Jesus Christ's work was *continual.* We have been impressed with this as we have come along the story. It presents him with opportunities, and he accepts them as they come. The multitudes were gathered—he opened his mouth and taught them. There came a leper—he said, "I will, be thou clean" [Matt. 8:3]. He entered into Capernaum, and there came unto him a centurion, and he healed the centurion's servant [8:5–13]. He came into Peter's house and found a fever-stricken woman—he touched her hand and the fever fled from that touch. When the evening was come, they brought unto him the demon possessed, and he healed all that were sick. Jesus Christ's ministry was a great effort; it was a great life. O you preaching man, do not spend your time in preparing your *sermon,* but in preparing *yourself,* and the sermon will be right, not perhaps artistically and technically, and according to the wooden standards of the self-made schools, but there will be in it subtle flame, subtle sympathy, magnetism, divine flashing and gleaming that will help men to the mountains. The Savior never gathered himself together for a great occasion—he *was* the great occasion. He created the opportunity, he ennobled the chance of the day, he found a wilderness and built a tabernacle in it; he found a needy humanity, and he left the blessing of heaven where he found the trace and signature of the devil.

Apply all this to ourselves. Jesus, come home with us and see what a shadow is there; come upstairs with us and see the daughter who has not been well these twenty years, and the son whose life is an almost daily weakness, and often a sharp and crying pain; come and see the child-grandmother that has been groping for heaven's gate many a day, because in her heart there is a longing to go home; come and see *all* of us, upstairs and down: the birds will sing the blither for thy coming in, they will find their cages enlarged in your presence; come and look into the poor man's cupboard and turn his one loaf into five and his little dinner into a feast for a king. Come into the shop, the accounting office, the bank, the marketplace, the office, and see how we have huddled things together, and straighten out these crooked things for us. Come into our hearts, and see how we have demons in them, demons of ambition, demons of falsehood, demons of vanity, all kinds of demons, and cleanse the defiled heart. We are all sick; there is not a life that has not its pain, not a hope that has not its shadow, not a prayer that has not its fierce temptation. O thou Healer, thou Father and Mother of us all, dear Jesus, Thou art womanly and manly, a Man, a God, Son of Mary, Son of Man— enter every heart and make it beautiful as heaven!

four

THE CONDITIONS OF DISCIPLESHIP

Matthew 8:18–22

"He gave commandment." There was always in him some sign of lordship. He did not *receive* instructions, he *gave* them; though in one moment more his mouth was to be opened in a confession of the fact that he had no place to lay his head, yet he gave commandment. This kind of writing does not come of the uninspired human fancy, nor is it held together with sufficient artistic cohesion, to be the child of the mere imagination. Yet there is a rugged and vital unity about it, which is the seal of truth. A peasant and the son of a peasant and without any signs of power about him such as are reckoned of consequence by earthly judges, he yet "gave commandment." Why this imperative tone? Why this subtle claim to dominion? Why this quiet assumption of supreme power? When he concluded his discourse the people were astonished at his doctrine, for he taught them as one having authority [Matt. 7:29], not as one *being* in authority, not as one who had on an official cloak and must be respected for his clothes' sake, but as one *having* authority, breathing it, holding it, originating it, directing it; and this same authoritative speaker of doctrine, gave commandment, issued a royal precept, told the people about him what to do. Truly the parts do hold together, not with any mechanical contrivance, but because they belong to one another by the law of a reconciliation which does not come within the technical sphere of the mere fancy. His look was law; his tone admitted of no qualifications; his word was prompt, complete, authoritative, final. He never recalled a sentence to amend it; he never requested permission to add to his own doctrine an explanatory or emendatory note. Show me a single instance in which he ever corrected himself. Our writings are

23

blotted all over with erasures and disfigured by a thousand interlineations, but his writing is straight on, no sentence interfering with any other sentence, any more than any star clashes with any fellow planet in all the sea of the heaven.

"When he saw great multitudes about him he gave commandment to depart." We should have thought it would have been an excellent reason for staying where he was. What more could he need than great multitudes? He came to teach, to preach, to heal, to bless, and to save, and behold here are great multitudes, and yet he gives their presence as a reason for leaving them. Why did this Son of man leave the great thronging, sweltering multitudes? Because the true spirit has left them. They were a mob: it was a great gathering of curious gazers, of persons who wanted to be satisfied with mighty works and wondrous signs. They were swollen with their own wonder, moved by the bad inspiration of their own love of amazement. To such people Jesus Christ never has anything to say. To the miracle-loving Herods he answers never a word; to the merely curious inquirers regarding doctrine or history he preserves a stony silence. It is not the crowd as a crowd he wants or seeks, it is the needy heart, the conscious poverty, the piercing, pleading pain. Do not suppose that we can attract him by anything of a merely multitudinous or formal or ceremonial character. To this man will I look—*which* man? The crowned one, whose shoulders are decked in purple, whose feet are plunged in soft velvet and down? To this man will I look. I long for the answer to that statement. "Which man?" my heart inwardly cries. To the man that is of a *broken and a contrite heart and who trembleth at my word* [see Is. 66:2]. Fill your churches with multitudes and with eloquence and with incense and with color, till the eye is weighted by its oppressiveness, but if the waiting, panting, broken heart be not there, Christ is miles away, yea, on the other side of the horizon, with his back to us. "The Son of man is come to seek and to save that which was lost" [Luke 19:10]. He comes to our poverty, weakness, and self-renunciation, not to our wealth and strength and self-assertion.

We now see him as about to move to the other side, and while he is in the process of going, a certain scribe came and said unto him, "Master, I will follow thee whithersoever thou goest." This man represents the ardent and hopeful side of human nature. He sees no difficulties, his heart is swollen with a new and glad impulse, and he says he will follow that impulse, whatever the event may be. Could consecration be more complete? Could any promise be less reserved? The Son of man will leap towards this man as towards a friend: he will fall upon his neck and cry tears of joy upon his shoulders. What was his reply? Cold as ice. The hot heart came to him, and he dropped into it a great load of polar ice. The reply in letters was this: "Foxes have holes, and the birds of the air have nests, but the Son of man hath not where to lay his head." What became of the scribe? The text does not inform us.

Jesus Christ treated the ardent temperament by always presenting the dark side of the case. It is in this way that he balances us. To the low in heart, the fearful and timorous in spirit, he speaks a promise, and so lifts up the mind on the depressed side until a happy equipoise is established. To the bold, enthusiastic, romantic disciple, who is going to walk upon the wind, he says, "You are going to a land where you will not have a pillow for your head." It is thus that men see different sides of the Christian faith: it is thus that men are measured by different standards in the Christian sanctuary. It is thus that perhaps no two Christian experiences exactly coincide. Christ is to us what we are to him. He fills the great mountain with light, and he fills the little daisy, too, with light, and never a beam too much to bear down its weak little neck. He that gathers much in this field has nothing over; he who gathers little has no need. How foolish, then, and utterly vain is any attempt to reconcile men's thoughts in mere letters and words. You cannot write Christian experience once for all. It varies, it carries a thousand different colors and tints and hues and mixtures of color, and utters itself in innumerable tones, complete, strong, tender, weak, whining, valiant, glad as the utterance of a trumpet, and sad as the moaning of a heart that is stabbed. Do not, therefore, be looking out for uniform standards and unanimous opinions and coincident experiences. Christianity will answer you so as to bring up the side of your character that needs elevation.

This is beautifully illustrated in the case of the next man. Another of the disciples said unto him, "Lord, I will go with thee to the other side, but suffer me first to go and bury my father." How filial, how tender—a plea to which the Son of God can have but one reply. What does he say? He speaks in a most soldierly tone. He hardens himself into most inexorable discipline, and says, "Follow me, and let the dead bury their dead." A hard tone, without one pulse of human feeling in it: how unloving, how unsympathetic, how chilling, how calculated to alienate human affection! This answer was to a particular person of a particular temperament, and was meant to redeem that man from a false conception of Christian doctrine and Christian duty. It does not apply to all cases; it had a distinct and limited application, and was the only message fitted for the kind of man to whom it was delivered. He could not hand the message indiscriminately to others; it was a gospel spoken to his own heart; it was bread intended for the satisfaction of his own hunger.

This man, however, has many representatives in all ages. Let us understand him a little. He is the kind of man who always has some *arrangement* to make. He is the sort of person who can never do the next thing that is to be done without precedingly doing something on one side. There are persons who, when we call them, say, "Coming—*presently.*" A broken obedience, a reluctant reply, a mixed answer! Who can tell how far that "presently" stretches over their life? "Presently" is a word that cannot be described by the dictionary, and that cannot be measured on the face of the clock. Are you not acquainted with some friends who are always quite willing to serve you, but first must go down the road or up the hill, to the post-office, or upstairs, and then. . . ? Such arrangements may be permitted as between man and man, such little slaveries to the matter of convenience may be permitted on the social scale, but when it becomes a question of following *Christ,* we are called upon for absolute self-surrender. That is the very essence of Christianity. There is nothing double in Christian consecration; the true Christian servant has one eye, one hand, one end, one heart, one prayer, one desire. Have we attained this? Not a soul amongst us has come within a million miles of its attainment, but if we *desire* it, hope for it, and struggle towards it, God will take a broken column as if it were a pillar completed to a glittering point.

The answer of Jesus Christ to all the temporizing and arrangement-making people is an answer of unreserved and absolute surrender. Do you suppose that we have given Christ everything? I have not. If you have, I have nothing to say to you. I am still burying my father, I am still completing my bargains, I am still adding to my estate, I am still studying the ways and tricks of a perverse world, I am still hushing my breath, so as not to awaken the sleeper. I am going after Christ, but I must first quaff this cup, inhale this fragrance, and breathe in this cloud. I am coming—*presently.* This is what you said to me when I asked you to join the Church, to surrender to Christ, to become an out-and-out Christian. You did not say to me, "No!" you said, "Thank you, I will come—*presently.*"

These answers of Jesus Christ are exaggerations in the sense of having *another side* to them which would have shown their true meaning. There are some persons who do not understand the law of exaggeration: to them an exaggeration is a lie; they do not know that we have to paint very broadly, to be seen afar. There are those who do not understand that we have to infuse into some utterances an emphasis beyond the immediate literal requirement of the case in order that the detonation may be heard. They do not comprehend Jesus Christ when he utters those sublime exaggerations, yet nothing but such exaggerations would have met the cases in question. Now let us qualify them.

Peter once said to Jesus, "We have left all and followed thee." Jesus Christ replied, "No man has left father or mother, sister or brother, houses or lands, for my sake and the gospel's, that has not received a hundred times more in this present life and in the world to come—everlasting life" [see Mark 10:28–30]. That was not the answer which he made to the scribe: to him he set forth the *severe*—by-and-by he would enter into the *gracious*. His gospel does not *tempt* us; the kingdom of heaven is not a bribe, it is first a cross, a discipline, a pain, an agony, and afterwards a sweet quiet heaven. In the case of Peter the great act had been *done*, in the case of the scribe it was *about* to be done. The scribe would have been misled if the great promise had been held out to him; he therefore had revealed to him only the darker aspect of this great adventure.

Jesus Christ never lets any man really go after him and be disappointed with the result. He keeps his grace for daily revelation according to the daily need. He gives more grace [James 4:6]—he gives grace upon grace. He will not tempt you as with a bribe, but he will feed you with an eternal satisfaction. I do not ask you therefore to come into the Christian sanctuary that you may get rid of your distresses, and your debts and burdens, your pains of body and your clouds of mind, but I call you and tell you that it is a cross you have to take up. That was the message of Jesus Christ to another of his disciples—"Follow me, quench every other love, fix your undivided vision upon myself, beware of wandering desires and divided affections and broken resolutions and imperfect vows. If any man will follow me, let him take up his cross" [Matt. 16:24; Luke 9:23]. A great teacher, truly, and not less gracious than severe.

From these two instances two false inferences might be drawn. First that *Jesus Christ did not care to make disciples.* He had the chance of making two disciples here in the superior sense (for probably they were both disciples in the merely literal interpretation of the word), and yet he discouraged both the men. When did he ever appear anxious to increase his numbers? When was it a matter of personal consequence to him to make two into four and four into twenty, and when did he send forth a statistician to schedule the numbers of his flock? Truly this kingdom is not a new miracle, mystery, or arithmetical surprise or success. Arithmetic has nothing to do with it. Christ works slowly but he works continuously, and the end shall come and he will deliver up the kingdom to God his Father, and God shall be all in all, for he must reign till he hath put all enemies under his feet. The last enemy that shall be destroyed is death, then in all the universe there shall be nothing but radiant, joyous anthem-singing, life and immortality. He did not like men to go away from him, but still if they wished to go, he did not hinder them. Jesus said to his disciples when many turned away and walked no more with him, "Will ye also go away?" He was accustomed to loneliness, he had trodden the winepress alone, and of the people there were none with him. We do not flatter or patronize Christ by the multitudinousness of our number; he asks not for many only, but for much—for the very life and loyalty of the heart.

A second false inference that might be drawn from these answers is, that Jesus Christ had *nothing to offer to his disciples.* He told one man that he would have no pillow for his head, and he told another simply to follow him and let the dead bury the dead. Again and again are we taught that this kingdom of heaven is not a bribe; we are not to go after it for the sake of the loaves and fishes. Jesus Christ never promised a downy pillow: he has many a time darkly hinted at a crown of thorns. Jesus Christ never promised honors and delights and satisfaction of an earthly kind: he always said, "The cross is heavy, and it must be laid upon the weakest shoulder." O thou severe One, what is the meaning of all this? The meaning is in a sentence. He seeks for truth in us which shall correspond to the truth that is in him. My profession must not be a personal luxury—it must be truth to truth, reality to reality, Christ and his disciples one, as he and his Father are one.

Tell the mocker that Jesus Christ does not bribe his disciples: tell the taunting fool that in this warfare every man is to be a soldier, trained by the most severe discipline, whose delinquencies are to be punished with the highest penalties, but tell them also that are without and who mock and taunt and wonder, that there is no such bread as that which comes down from heaven.

five

CHRIST'S INWARD PEACE

Matthew 8:23-27

"HE WAS asleep." Think of the sleep of the *bad* man; tired with doing evil with both hands, weary in the cause of wickedness, having done his last bad trick, having worn out his last energy in following that which is evil and also forbidden, he falls asleep. Who will talk to him in his dreams—what images will he see in the visions of the night? Suppose he should never awake, and men should come in the morning to see how he left his work—with a bad purpose broken off, with a program inscribed to the devil half wrought through—who would care to bury him? Would it not disgrace a horse to carry such bones to the grave? Is it not a prostitution of human decency to touch so foul a thing?

Think of the sleep of the *good* man; weary in his work of noble benevolence, the spirit willing but the flesh giving way, with the tear half dried that he was just going to cleanse utterly from the eye of sorrow, with the word almost broken off at the middle syllable that he was just speaking in the ear of great distress—overcome by weariness he falls down into a dead sleep. Suppose he should never wake again—who then could tell the world's loss—who could add up in figures the deficiency that would come upon the average of the world's intelligence and piety and beneficence? When some men die, they make the world poor, they leave such great gaps behind them: it is as if altars had been broken down and ways to heaven had been shut up, and light that lighted the darksomeness of life had been put out with a rough hand suddenly.

Do not account too much of the bad man's sleep, or of the good man's sleep—no argument is to be founded on the sleep of either. The murderer has slept on the night of his crime, the condemned criminal has slept on the night before his execution, the good man has lost many a night's sleep by anxieties which he could not control. We are not therefore to make any moral use of sleep or of sleeplessness in the case of particular persons, but all men do sleep, and many may never awaken out of their slumber, and I ask you whose sleep would you like to have, the bad man's sleep—a weariness that comes out of evil practice, the high and venturous pursuit of forbidden and disastrous prizes, or the good man's sleep—weary *in* his work but not weary *of* it, only going down into the depths of sleep that he may come up as one refreshed, to renew all that was sweetest, noblest, and best in his life's toil.

"Let me sleep the sleep of the righteous, and may my slumber be like his" [So say we all, but if we would sleep well, we must work well, if we would have the angels at night we must have God during the day. If the darkness is to be jeweled by stars, then must we toil with filial love and ever-heightening delight while the sun lasts, to make men wiser and truer and altogether better. Sweet is the sleep of the laboring man, blessed is the slumber of the soul that does its utmost to please God; it is prefigurative of that rest which remaineth for those who are the servants of the Most High. Look on the bad man's sleep—it is as a beast getting ready for further blood. It is as a man whetting his instrument that he may commit deadlier havoc on society. Who would not pray that such strength might never be renewed? And if any man have strength to say openly, "God forbid he should ever awake again on earth," it would take much piety to keep back the "Amen" from those who heard the supplication.

We have now therefore to deal with the sleeping Christ. He told us that he had no place to lay his head, but the head that is weary is not particular about its pillow. He told the scribe that he had no place to lay his head, and yet in a verse or two farther on, we find him asleep. If on a pillow, it was a borrowed one. He does not contradict himself; whether he have pillow or no pillow, he must sleep. Behold him then in the rear part of the ship, behold him who said he had no place to lay his head, laying down that very head on a borrowed pillow and sleeping as if he nestled in the heart of God.

What occurs during his absence in sleep? "Behold there arose a great storm in the sea, insomuch that the ship was covered with the waves." A storm always rises when he is absent. His turning away from us means the opportunity for a storm. We are only at peace while he is with us;

everything depends upon his nearness. It is not a merely negative condition of things which he leaves behind him—not only is the light withdrawn, but the darkness is seven-fold; not only is the wind troubled, it is troubled even to the point of tempest; not only does the tide roll as usual, but it foams into infinite billows and our little life-ship is tossed upon it as with scorn, and we are threatened with mortal danger. It has always been so in my life. A sleeping Christ will do me no good, a painted Christ will not be of effective service in my life, a wooden crucifix or even an ivory cross will not help me—it must be the wakeful Christ, with every energy astir, power pouring out of him in every look, and in every movement, the actual, positive, real, personal, living Christ. We are mocked by his figure—we are saved by his personality.

What did the disciples do under these extraordinary and exciting circumstances? They came to him and awoke him, saying "Lord, save us: we perish." They came to him, they did not go to one another. For a long time we may seem to be equals; we speak about the average of human strength and human intelligence; we say all men are tolerably much the same, it is a long broad line of equality stretching over the whole human sphere, and human nature may have its ups and downs, but as a whole it is almost upon a level. Then there are great crises in the family when the chief man is sought out in a moment. We know him, he cannot be disguised; he may be asleep, but he is the chief; he may be out of the house but he must be sought for. I thought we were all equal? So we are, when we are all cold, when there is no immediate necessity, when there is no wolf with open mouth and gleaming teeth and eyes of fire standing at the front door. But let a *crisis* ensue in the family and the least child in the house intuitively turns its eyes in the right direction. The servant seeks the master, the weak calls for the strong, there is always a point of *supremacy*.

So in the nation: when there is nothing particularly stirring, we are all about equal, we lay down the great democratic doctrine that one man is as good as another, and constitute ourselves into a mutual commendation society, and speak of one another as if we were of one height, of one compass of mind, of one common integrity of heart. Suddenly a great crisis arises; then our little and comfortable doctrines all depart; then the man of stature stands up; then we know to whom to look, or, not knowing, we divine and guess, and by force of conjecture we create the man and make him the king of the hour.

If anything should occur in your business of an extraordinary nature you will soon find out who the principal is. If your business should proceed in the ordinary course little or no notice will be taken of you. People will not know, perhaps, whether you are in or whether you are out; if out, how long you will be in coming in, but let any particular crisis arise, and you will be named, you will be the necessity of the hour, and there will come into your heart by the grace and presence of God the energy that will meet the hour and stamp it with conquest.

The disciples not only came to Christ—they came in the *right spirit.* "Lord," said they—how is it that we give the right names when we are in the right mood? How is it that we create terms to meet necessities? Suppose you had met those men on the road in a quiet hour and had said to them, "Now, doctrinally, who is this man you are following?" Probably their answer would have been superficial, or ambiguous, or inadequate. You might easily have led them in the direction of doubt; it would not have been difficult to have troubled their incipient faith with many a dash of skepticism. But perishing, in trouble, near their last breaths, they seize him and call him "Lord." It will be this way with a great many, perhaps with some too late. Many will say to him in that day, Lord, Lord; and he will profess unto them that he never knew them [7:23]. Some confessions come too late; some homage destroys itself by its tardiness. Why should we not use our calmness, our self-possession, our faculties at their richest and best, and make recognitions of Christ's relation to us while we are in a fit state of heart and temper to make them with intelligence, and breadth, and cordiality? Do not believe the cold-blooded tempter or evil speaker, or septic, or infidel; he is a mighty man when there is nothing to fear. I do not know how far some mockers will be able to carry their mocking when grim death with bony grip seizes their flesh. We shall hear of them *then*—till then we do not touch them.

Not only did they come to the right man in the right spirit, but the disciples came with the right *request,* saying thus—observe the completeness of that word and its marvelous moral emphasis—not "Help us," not "Join us in a common endeavor to save the ship"; not the address made to Jonah, "Arise and take thy share, and call upon thy God as we have been calling upon our gods" [see Jon. 1:6]; not, "Let there be a common appeal to the distant heavens," but "*Save* us: take the whole case into thine hand; we fall back and are nothing—go, thou mighty One, almighty One, to the front to save us." We cannot do without that word *save*. It gets around the whole compass of our necessity; it touches with a marvelous pathos all the pain of our moral distress. Jesus Christ, the Son of man, came "to seek and to save that which was lost" [Luke 19:10]. His name was called Jesus, because he should save his people from their sins [Matt. 1:21]. He is mighty to *save*: he is called the Savior, the Man with the long arms, the Man with the infinite strength, whose touch is emancipation, whose look is benediction. "He saved others— himself he cannot save" [Matt. 27:42; Mark 15:31]. Thank God! If he could come down from that cross, morally, he would ruin the world.

With what prayers have we come to Christ? Have we asked him to enter into co-partnership with us in the doing some business in life? Have we said to him that we should be pleased if he would make out what is lacking in our own strength, that we might with two-fold power address ourselves to some difficult engagement? I wonder not that the prayer lies in the air somewhere, a wasted thing, a bird with wings too weak to get beyond the cloud line. We must go to him with our emptiness, we must have nothing in our hands, we must have nothing but a great distress to hurl upon his ear, and we must use words that will show him that our self-renunciation is complete and hopeless. If you had uttered big prayers, you would have had big answers. If you have nibbled at the heavens—I wonder not that their dignity has been offended. Let us go to Christ with nothing to recommend us, with our blindness, deafness, dumbness, our complete necessity, then we shall see how he will answer the mute appeal of our helpless condition.

What answer does Christ make to those perishing disciples? "Why are ye fearful, O ye of little faith?" The quiet soul always brings quietness. You say of certain persons in your own house, when they come into the chamber of affliction, they seem to centralize and to quiet everything; their composure is so serene, their self-possession is so complete, that they bring with them half a deliverance from the distress that was overwhelming you. See the *physician* in excitement, and everybody in the sick-chamber goes down; see his face quiet, hear his voice untroubled, feel his grip firm, and at once everybody in the sick-chamber takes heart again. The doctor does not know how his face is being search by eager eyes, and if there be a flush in it or a wave of suppressed feeling, it is interpreted to mean disaster of the most appalling kind. The quiet soul brings quietness, the Son of Peace brings peace—he creates peace.

There is only one storm to be feared, and that is the storm of unbelief. Why are ye so fearful, O ye of little faith? There is only one loss to be deprecated, the loss of faith. "Simon, Simon, Satan hath desired to have you that he may sift you as wheat, but I have prayed for thee, that thy faith fail not" [Luke 22:31, 32]. I may lose health, money, friends, power, but if I have not lost my faith, I have lost nothing. I shall come up again. Destroy this body and in three days I will raise it again. Blessed are those whose faith is greater than the power of destruction that lies around them.

Lord, increase our faith. Faith is power, faith is peace. Pray only for faith, for that wondrous ability to trust which he exercised and manifested who said, "Though he slay me, yet will I trust in him" [Job 13:15]. My last look shall be a prayer, my last heart-throb shall be towards the heavens: if he has torn me, he will heal me; if he has wounded me with all his instruments, on the third day he will revive me, and in my greater joy I shall forget my lesser woe. Lord, increase our faith—our heart's faith; we do not mind so much about our intellectual faith—it is here and there, and any fool can twist it—but see thou to our heart's faith, that deep inner trust that lays hold of thee with pertinacity that cannot be shaken off. Lord, increase our faith.

I cannot give up the miracles, because I should be giving up the great doctrine that *mind* is greater than matter, and without that doctrine we should be poor indeed. I hold to the supremacy of mind; my belief is that the spirit is the mightiest force in creation. GOD is a Spirit. If we had less body and more spirit we should be quieter, mightier, wholly grander. I will not have it that the sea is mightier than man: I would cling to the belief that there is a fire in man that can astound the sea and awe it into submission. The time will surely come when mind shall be acknowledged to be supreme, when the Book that speaks what are now romances because of our coldness will be proved to be speaking words of truth and soberness. "If ye had faith as a grain of mustard seed ye would say to this mountain, 'Out of the way,' and it would be cast into the depths of the sea" [see Matt. 17:20; Luke 17:6]. I am not content to dwell in the lowlands of the merely material and measurable, in a kind of conscious imprisonment. I would say to the sun, "I am greater than you: you could fall and crush me, but I should be conscious of defeat, while you would be unconscious of victory."

Be careful how you allow *mind* to be displaced from its *regal position*. It is a reflection fraught not only with supreme intellectual grandeur, but with the most exquisite moral pathos, that the *word* shall be mightier than the difficulty external, that the "I will" shall abolish death and fill up the grave and plant its face with the flowers of victory. Do not too readily yield to those persons who would snub your mind and magnify the mountain outside of you. The mountain is but huge mud, the sea but infinite water, the body but an invention for the moment, but mind—God is mind: God is a spirit. There are difficulties from the other side of the case, but they are nothing compared with the extreme difficulties that would suddenly be created by the displacement of mind from its royal elevation.

Jesus gave commandment to depart unto the other side, and a storm arose. Learn that storms may arise even while we are in discharge of plain and divinely commanded *duty*. If these men had taken the ship at their own suggestion, and attempted to cross the sea for their own convenience, we should speedily have visited upon them the penalty that they were worthy of the storm which overtook them. Let us learn the brighter lesson and encourage the grander faith. Storms may arise even in discharge of duty. Do not create your own difficulties. You are a child of God, and you have great sorrow to bear. Do not reason that if you were a child of God you would not have any sorrow—that would be faulty, not high and correct reasoning. You have a great difficulty in your business; do not reason that you have missed your providential way because you are encountering this terrible obstacle. The disciples were actually obeying Christ at the very moment the storm seized their vessel—so it may be with you. These things come not for the deepening of your fear, but for the quickening, the enlargement and the completion of your faith.

Danger will always move men to prayer—I will not guarantee that their prayers will be answered: the prayers of the wicked are an abomination unto the Lord. There are some of us who never pray but in danger—I dare not pledge that God will be present to hear. He may be—his mercy endures forever, but if he were less than God, he would not be. Your own mother would not be; you have worn out the last filament of her love. Your own father would not be: his eyes have been cried out with tears that boiled. If God were less than God, you would not lay hold of him even in the bitterness of your agony. You may do so—it will be because he is God and Father.

The upshot of the whole was that the men marveled. A poor outcome, a miserable *dénouement*—they marveled. We are like them, we are great at wonder, we are geniuses in the matter of being open to surprise and amazement. We can do any amount of wondering. There is a wonder that is legitimate, there is a wonder that is akin to worship, there is a surprise that may lead to faith. With such surprise may we be well acquainted, but beware of the round eye and the open mouth of vulgar wonder which stares at a miracle as at a show, and encourage that holy amazement which looks, then shuts its eyes, and then falls down in prayer.

six

THE SUPREME MIRACLE

Matthew 8:28–34

THIS IS decidedly the worst case that has yet come up in the sacred narrative. There is always a *testing* case in every ministry. There are critical hours in every life. Jesus had been with wondrous placidity dealing with diseases of many kinds, touching them, and healing them, and driving them away, but most of the cases appear to have been what we should term of an ordinary kind, though there was nothing ordinary in them from any point of view but his own. That which is commonplace to him is a miracle to us; that which is a miracle to us was commonplace to him. We do not occupy the same ground, we do not look at things from the same angle of vision. Here is a test case, and it makes me tremble. I have never seen Christ confronted like this before.

The men were exceeding fierce, so that no man might pass by that way. There was no mistake about the terribleness of this possession. The devils had been in the man a long time: he was naked; no house could hold him; he dwelt in the tombs; he was driven of the devil into the wilderness—the case was extreme; it makes me tremble; it turns all other incidents into ordinary events. How will Jesus Christ do *now?* We have put that question regarding one another in critical circumstances when great distress has come upon the life, when a loss of property has been threatened, when particular audiences have assembled for the purpose of giving judgment—in many other varieties of human experience we have asked concerning our friend, How will he carry himself *now?*

While we are wondering what Jesus will do there is a cry of fear from the other side. He was working when we did not suppose he was doing anything; he was giving one of those silent *looks* which eloquence cannot follow in descriptive terms; he was troubling the hidden devils with light which they only could see. The cry of distress comes from hell. Is there something in Christ's face, that troubles the evil one? Is there anything in that calm, serene, majestic look which makes hell afraid? He alone was quiet. By-and-by it will be seen that this is the exact relation between parties in the universe: the good triumphant, the wicked cowardly and afraid. It does not look so now, because the wicked are too demonstrative to show their real character: they make a noise to keep their courage up, they fill their ears with their own vulgar din, and imagine that there is no other voice appealing to them. If I look at society from one point of view I am utterly disheartened—my hope goes out of me: it is evidently devil-ridden and hell-bound, and nothing can stay it in its awful course; perdition must enlarge its borders to receive our enlarging civilization. When I gather into one all the evil thinkers and evil doers that are in the world I feel that evil has the upper hand, and that God himself is but a theological term.

Then, again, we come upon incidents that give a new point of view and a new reading of human events. We see that God is not dethroned: when the true collision comes the result is won by a *look*. God is to do wonders by the brightness of his face: the silent glance is to be as a sword before which absolutely nothing that is evil can stand. The ever-speaking but ever-silent face, gleaming with light, glowing with fire, is to make its way through the universe, and to leave heaven behind it. Oh, you speaking man, and book-writing man, evangelist, apostle—call yourself by what name you will, this conquest is not to be won by *our* noise, or fuss, or high demonstration of religious zeal—all this is right enough in its own place; it is part of the plan; it has pleased God to do certain things by the foolishness of preaching, but *the devil is to be burnt out with the divine look.* Hold your little light aloft; speak mightily or gently, in thunder or whisper as you will, and do what little lies within the scope of your little power, but understand that the final deposition of the devil, and the ultimate setting up of the dominion that is divine and beneficent, is to be done by the breath and the power and the glory of God. A nation shall be born in a day, the light shall fill the heavens in a moment, and the earth shall lose her cold shadows, and in the new warmth that shall penetrate her veins she shall give up her dead, and be scarred and seamed no more by tombs and sepulchers and sanctuaries of death.

Read the histories as given by Matthew and by Luke, and regard them as completing one another, and as forming substantially the same incident, and you will see from its graphic coloring what man may become. Do not make little local anecdotes of these divine histories; do not let the years grow between you and the Book of God till they separate you as by a thick wedge from all that is venerable and true in history. This incident is occurring today. If I have to wander over a wilderness of eighteen hundred years to get at it I shall tire on the road. It occurs next door—tomorrow it may occur in our own house.

See here what man is, what man may become—what man really is in the sight and estimate of God. If you would profit by this incident see yourself in it. It is an evil temptation, one that will deplete you of every true sympathy and right conception of history and of the future, which leads you to think that this incident occurred once for all, and became an exciting and romantic anecdote in the neighborhood in which it took place. *You* are the demoniac: *I* am the one possessed with devils: they have never awakened yet altogether, but some of them are beginning to open their eyes, and to turn in restlessness, as if about to rise. Why will you put the Bible away from you thousands of years, and talk of Moses as if he were a dead man, and of the evangelists as though they lived only in epitaphs? These things are around us *now!* When John Newton, the celebrated clergyman, saw a man being taken away to the scaffold to be hanged, he said, "There goes John Newton but for the grace of God." You cannot tell what you are; that is no merely earthly fire that burns in your blood. If you want to see what you may become go to the madhouse. It is an awful church, it is a terrible sanctuary, but if you want to see what you are made of—go to the madhouse, into its very vilest and most appalling quarter, where no wise word is spoken, where no noble look ever illuminates or elevates the human face, where no prayer to heaven is ever spoken, where there is violence extreme, cruelty only kept from its proper issues and outcomes by iron and granite, and all the forces of the most watchful civilization. Pick out the worst specimen of that madness, and see yourself in those eyes of fire and those cheeks livid with excitement, and in that whole frame shaken and torn by passions that cannot be controlled. I am afraid you have been too daintily reared; I tremble lest you are the victims of your own respectability. There is no respectability in the sight of God. We see the contrast between the madman and the philosopher. That contrast is nothing as compared with the contrast between the sinner and what God meant him to be when he made him a man, and that appalling contrast is forever in the light of him that made us.

When I take this view of human nature, which is the only fundamental and profound view, all others being shams and tricks of an inventive immorality, I see our need of Christ. The doctor can heal my skin, the nurse can cool my brow, a friend may be able to lull me to momentary sleep in which I may forget my troubles, but when it comes to the point of agony, and I see the heart as it really is, and feel it as if it were on fire of hell, then I know that no water can quench it, but only blood can answer the great distress. You may whiten the sepulcher, you may make the outside of the cup and platter clean, you may look good to the eye that rests upon the skin, but to the eye that reads the inner life and sees every filament of your heart—to that eye we are wounds and bruises and putrifying sores [Is. 1:6].

The physiologist tells me that in every two square inches of the human brain there are two hundred million fibers, each of which can receive a mental impression. I am lost in these astronomical figures. A hundred million fibers in one square inch of the human brain! No *theologian* told me that, but the *physiologist*, a man whom everybody is ready to believe. That these should be kept for one hour is surely the supreme miracle of heaven. That these should be wrong and think amiss, and move the whole life in a forbidden direction, what is it but a tragedy that might make all heaven rain oceans of tears? It is a terrible thing to live; it is an appalling thing to be a man; there is but a step between the best of us and madness—yea, they who make psychology a study tell us that thin is the veil that separates genius from insanity.

There are people who would rather have demons in the land than have Jesus Christ. The whole city came out to meet Jesus, and when they saw him they besought him that he would depart out of their coasts. The demons have to ask their places at Christ's hand: their power of trespass is great, but it never impairs the divine dominion over them. "Do not drive us out of the country, suffer us to go into the swine, tell us where we have to be"; and he says, "Back." He orders them behind: like hounds that are afraid of his voice they make way for him. No man had passed that way before; when the Son of man passes that way he clears a space for himself. Have you seen *Christ leaving the Praetorium*? The dominant idea of that grand picture to me is that as he comes down the steps the whole space enlarges to let him through — nothing comes within touch of him. Somehow the great painter has thrown back the space and given him room enough to show the King in.

Now that his great conquest is completed the people who had lost their swine came to him and besought him that he would depart out of their coasts. It was not impiety; it was a great fear. There are some people who can only live in the commonplace; who hide themselves in the cellar when it thunders and lightens. They could deal with a great excitement in the neighborhood if it were far enough off, somewhere among the tombs, with a noise now and then caught in the wind that made them get closer together, but the great fear that came into their hearts when Jesus came was too much for them, their commonplace lives were rudely shaken, and they could not live in the excitement of such a presence. It is one of two things with this Christ when he comes into a place; it is deadly fear or infinite rejoicing: he is a savor of death unto death, or of life unto life. He never comes in merely as a respectable citizen a few inches higher than his neighbors: when he comes the land cowers in great fear or lifts itself up in jubilant delight and religious rapture. Do not believe in your Christianity if your hearts are cold. Christianity is nothing if it be not the supreme passion of life. If Christianity does not put everything else down and set its regal foot upon them, you have only entered into the letter, you have not come under the inspiration and blessed dominion of its spirit.

Are there not those who ask Jesus Christ to depart out of their coasts because of the effect of high religious conviction and noble Christian sentiment? Are there not persons who put trade above man? What is a man compared to a good balance sheet? What does it matter what becomes of the *man* if the *master* is all right? What do I care what becomes of my servant if I am happy? Of what concern is it to me what becomes of the weak so long as I am strong? There are cases which come before me as a public man which cannot come before you in your strictly private capacity, which makes me weep with sadness, and I blame some of you for some cases of oppression and distress which disfigure and debase our civilization: I include myself in the waiting curse. That women should be sitting and making twelve of your carpet bags for eighteenpence, that women should be standing day by day behind the counter till their limbs swell and blacken and they can stand no longer, that women should be made to decorate your apparel at wages which will not give them one single hour of relaxation or wholesome country air—what is this but preferring demons to Christ? I do not know where the wrong is, altogether: it is not a wrong you can lay your fingers upon and throttle; it is a widespread wrong, and nobody is responsible. Doesn't he that ponders the heart consider? When he makes inquisition for blood will he not identify this and that man and yonder fine lady and demand the price? It is not an easy question; there are faults on many sides, and probably the whole fault cannot be accumulated and set down at any one man's door. Therefore I would speak with forbearance as to the direct application of these doctrines in particular instances, but do not let us run away from the solemn fact that there are people in the world who would set *trade* above *man*.

There are those who calculate the expense of social regeneration, there are journals that calculate how much the missionary societies have expended, how many conversions they can trace, and they have divided the one set of figures by the other. What can you expect from such men? Incapable of religious enthusiasm, they are incapable of social justice. There are those who would ask how many swine there were and how many men were cured, and they would divide the one set of figures by the other, and talk about the statistical result. I hold that if one soul can be converted in this house, it was worth building the place for, if it should be burnt down today. We should work for men; our whole passion should be *human*; if one poor little child could say to me, "Till your church was built I never knew Christ: having come to it I see him now to be fairest among ten thousand and altogether lovely [Song 5:16], and I give myself right to him, if he will take so unworthy a thing"—if *that* could be the result of this ministry, it was worth all the trouble and all the money, ten thousand times ten thousand over and over again, and multiplied by the number of all the stars of heaven. Let us take this view of our work. It is something to enliven a human heart, to lighten one human burden, to dry one human tear. If I could have the joy of thinking that this had been done by any exposition of this narrative, whatever might be set upon the other side would be less than the small dust of the balance.

The people besought Christ that he would depart out of their coasts. They accorded him a negative treatment: they did not violently thrust him out, they courteously begged him that he would go away. I have more hope of those who violently treat him than of those who politely decline to have anything to do with him. You are sitting there today saying of yourself, "I have never made any *profession* of religion." The greater your shame. You have begged Jesus to depart out of your coasts: you have no high feeling against him, you never profaned his name by vulgar desecration; you attend a religious place of worship, but you make no profession of Jesus Christ's name. You, on the other hand, say that you leave all religious questions *alone*. You have asked Jesus to depart out of your coasts intellectual, speculative, imaginative, practical, ideal. He is not within your coasts at all—you have begged him to go away.

Read the next verse in the next chapter. "And he entered into a ship and passed over." He may go then? Truly. We can get rid of him? Yes, yes. He will not be an eternal torment? No, he will not always strive with me—I can shake him off? Yes, you can—*will* you? I can banish him? Yes, yes—you can stab him to the heart, you can spit upon him, you can smite him on the head, you can crucify him, you can get rid of him— but if you do get rid of him do not come at last and beg to be admitted into the heart that you have wounded. Be consistent throughout. Will you get rid of him? Come, say, "My Lord, my God, cast the devils out of me, make me a sanctuary, a living temple—abide with me." That is the better course. "Now is the accepted time, now is the day of salvation" [2 Cor. 6:2].

Come into our house, Jesus, and dine there, and sup there, and stop the night there, all the night, the life-night, till the day dawn and the shadows flee away.

NOTES

Verse 8—*Not worthy.* "The proud hilltops let the rain run off; the lowly valleys are richly watered."—*Augustine.*

Verse 14—"Peter's wife was still living twenty-five years afterwards, when St. Paul wrote his first letter to the Corinthian Church (1 Cor. 9:5). Probably all the apostles were young men, not much over thirty"—*Conder.*

Verse 21—*Suffer me first.* "These words imply, what Luke expressly records, that Jesus had laid on him the command to follow him, which accounts for the subsequent rebuke. The command, moreover (Luke 11:60), *to go and preach the gospel,* implies that this was not his first call, but that he had been a disciple for some considerable time. Some special occasion, therefore, is indicated— perhaps that of the news being brought of the father's death. The explanation, that the disciple wished to *go and reside with his father until his death,* though ancient, is plainly wrong (as *Stier* and *Alford* show); the father was just dead, and he wished to postpone obedience to Christ's command to filial respect.

Had this brief delay been granted, another hindrance, equally pressing, might have presented itself. The Lord's reply, though at first sight it surprises us by its sternness, simply carries out the principle that no plea whatever can bar Christ's claim to immediate obedience: no 'first' can take precedence of that"—*Ibid.*

Verse 26—Rebuked the winds and the sea. "This seems to have been almost, so to say, our Lord's formula in working miracles; the fever (Luke 6:39), the frenzy of the demoniac (Mark 9:25), the tempest, are all treated as if they were hostile and rebel forces that needed to be restrained. St. Mark, with his usual vividness, gives the very words of the rebuke: "Peace, be still"—literally, *be dumb, be muzzled,* as though the howling wind were a maniac to be gagged and bound"—*Ellicott's Test.*

seven

CHRISTIANITY MORE THAN AN ARGUMENT

Matthew 9:1–8

"AND HE entered into a ship and passed over and came into his own city." That does not tell us half the truth. A reference to this verse will show you the necessity of reading the Scriptures through, and of paying attention not to the text only, but to the context. Anybody would think, from reading this first verse, that Jesus had, upon his own will and motion, returned into his own city: we should have no hesitation in coming to the conclusion that Jesus did this because he wanted to do it or had willed so to do. Is there not a cause? Refer to the verse which concludes the previous chapter if you would find the key of the verse which opens the ninth chapter. "Behold the whole city came out to meet Jesus, and when they saw him they besought him that he would depart out of their coasts, and he entered into a ship and passed over." Now the whole case is before you. You thought he came away spontaneously, whereas the fact is he was driven out. He never leaves the human heart of his own will; he never said to any one of you, "I have been here long enough, I must now leave you to yourself."

But you tell me that Jesus Christ is no longer with you, you say you sigh to think of happier days, you recall the hour when Jesus Christ was the only guest of your heart, and now you mourn that he is no longer present in the sanctuary of your consciousness and your love. He never left of his own accord. I cannot allow your mourning to go without one or two sharp and piercing inquiries. How did you treat him—did his presence become a shadow in the life—was his interference burdensome—did he dash some cups of pleasure from your hands—did he call you to sacrifices which were much too painful for your love? Search

45

yourselves and see. I never knew him to leave a human heart because he was tired of it, weary because he had expended his love upon it—but I have known him to be whipped out, scourged away, entreated to go, banished.

"And he entered into a ship and passed over and came into his own city." How he looked as he did so! No picture can ever tell us how the eyes fell upon the dust in shame for those who had desired his banishment. How his heart quivered under a new and sharp pain as he realized that he was indeed despised and rejected of men! How he felt as his good deeds became the occasion of a desire on the part of those who had seen them to send him away from their coasts! This is a mystery on which there is no light. Do not imagine that you began the story with the first verse of the ninth chapter. It is true that Jesus entered into a ship and passed over, but it is also true that the people demanded him that he would depart out of their coasts. So when my heart is empty of his presence and I wonder whither he has gone, I will revive my recollection, I will command my memory to be faithful and to tell me the white truth, the candid fact, and when it speaks it will shame me with the intolerable reminiscence that I *begged* him to go. Let us be honest, or we shall never be healed, let us face the stern, fierce facts of life, or we shall make no progress in purity or in spiritual knowledge.

"And behold they brought unto him a man sick of the palsy, lying on a bed, and Jesus, seeing their faith—" Is it possible for *faith* to be greater than the *palsy?* Are such miracles wrought in the consciousness of man? Does the soul ever rise in its original majesty and put the body down? Sometimes. Is it possible for the will to be so inflamed and inspired to rise above paralysis and to say, "I am master!" I like such flashes of the divinity that is within us. We are too easily cowed; our physicians complain that our will does not cooperate with their endeavors, so that we too easily go down. There is something in us that can conquer paralysis. I cannot gather together all the subtle influences which make up the present economy of things, but again and again in the history of others, and now and then in my own history, I have seen such a rising up of the inner nature as has said to the body, "I am master." I magnify these occasional revelations of the latent force of a kind of suppressed divinity, until I see death dead, the grave filled up, and the whole universe full of life.

Magnify all the *best* hints of your nature; be ready to accept suggestions of new power; never take the little and dwindling view of your life.

If now and then your heart leaps up like sparks of fire in prayer seize every one of them. *That* is where your grandeur is; that is your true self. Caught in some mean conception, conscious of some unworthy fancy—know that this is the *leper* that has to be healed. Caught in some rapture of worship, some sweet desire for heaven—know that this is the *angel* that is in you, and that by-and-by nothing shall be left in you but the angel, the true spirit, conqueror through him who wrought its redemption.

"And Jesus, seeing their faith—" That was just like him. He always sees the *best* of us; he never takes other than the greatest view of our life and its endeavors. "And Jesus, seeing their faith." Shall we amend the text? "And Jesus, seeing their—sectarianism." That would fill up a line better than *faith*; it is a longer word; it has more syllables in it; it fills the mouth better—shall we put it in? "And Jesus, seeing their—denominationalism." There is a word that would almost make a line by itself. That word ought to have something in it; polysyllables ought not to be empty. "And Jesus, seeing their—congregationalism, their attachment to Episcopalianism, their deep love of Roman Catholicism." I fancy we cannot amend the text. We can take out the little word *faith* and put in the long words I have named: these would not be amendments: they would be spoliations; they would be blasphemies; they would belittle the occasion; they would taint it with a human touch. Let the word *faith* stand; it is universal; it is a cord that stretches itself around the star-lit horizon; it touches those of you who belong to no sect, the dumb, the groping, the wondering, as well as the clear-minded and the positive as to religious principle and conviction.

Jesus Christ always startled his hearers by seeing something *greater* in them than they had ever seen in themselves, and always seemed to credit his patients with their own cure. He said, "Daughter, thy faith hath made thee whole" [Matt. 9:22]. He gave the woman to feel as if she had all the time been her own healer. And the broad and everlasting meaning of that assurance is that you and I have it in us at this moment to get the healing that we need. The physician is here; his prescription is written in syllables clear as stars, and in lines open as the heavens. What he waits for is our faith. "Lord, I believe; help thou mine unbelief" [Mark 9:24]. "Lord, increase our faith" [Luke 17:5]. "Believe on the Lord Jesus Christ and thou shalt be saved" [Acts 16:31]. "Be it unto thee according to thy faith" [see Matt. 15:28]. "Believe ye that I am able to do this?" [Matt. 9:28]. There is something then for *us* to do. Find it out and do it, and God will be faithful to his word.

"And Jesus, seeing their faith, said unto the sick of the palsy, Son, be of good cheer, thy sins be forgiven thee." But this was a question of the *palsy*: the man had not come as a *religious* inquirer, had he? I was not aware that Jesus was sitting down somewhere for the purpose of holding religious conversation with people. This man is sick from paralysis; he cannot move a limb; it requires four people to carry him; and Jesus Christ gives a *religious* turn to the event. We want this sick man healed; we do not want to hear anything about *sins*; we are not religious inquirers, we are afflicted men. How we do belittle everything we touch—if we pluck a flower it dies! Jesus Christ said, "All these afflictions have a common root: sin is the explanation of every scab on that leper's brow; and look at the trembling in that paralytic; sin drove the sight from those eyes, and the hearing from those ears, and the strength from those ankle bones. This is the accursed work of sin." He is a fundamental Teacher; he does not treat symptoms; he treats the central and vital *cause* which expresses itself in symptoms so patent and so distressing.

This is the great lesson which the world is so unwilling to receive. Give us Acts of Parliament, give us better houses for this class and for that class, give us better drainage and larger gardens and better ventilation, and we shall cobble the world up to stand on its rickety legs ten years longer. All these things are in themselves right enough: no sane man has one word to speak against them. If they be brought in, however, as *causative*, they must be rejected, they are collateral, they are cooperative, they are helpful, and in that sense they are necessary, but the world's stream will never be pure till the world's fountain has been cleansed. We think we can cure the world by officialism and by small sanitary pedantries, by congresses and conferences—all these things have their place and their use, but until we get at the root, and core, and center, and heart, we are as men who are throwing buckets into empty wells and drawing them up again. The world will not believe this, so the world has not yet risen and taken up its bed and walked.

"And, behold, certain of the Scribes said within themselves, This man blasphemeth." There again is the belittling which man does in all his interpretations. O, if the sermon could be equal to the text in all cases, what preaching we should have and what hearing! Christ said, "Thy sins are forgiven thee." The Scribes said, "This man blasphemeth." We always drag down what we touch: the day of rapture is gone, the sacred hour of enthusiasm has withdrawn itself, because we have besought it to depart. Men never speak in fire now: we have fallen upon an age of prudence and word measurement, and we are tricksters in the uses of syllables and in the adaptations of phrases, and never get beyond the poor range of little speech, or utter as with the heart those sentences which are revelations. We like to hear the little mincing voices that dare not utter one word louder than another; we like to hear the multiplication table repeated every Sunday from the first line to the last; we like to keep within statistical proofs and references that have been scheduled and that can be verified. The great prophet of fire, Elijah, is gone—were he to come again we would take him by the throat and thrust him into the dungeon.

The Scribes were right from their own point of view. It would have been blasphemy in any one of *them* to have spoken a noble word about anybody. There are some throats that were never made to emit one noble sound. There are men to whom prayers are lies, and revelations are delusions, and prophecies are but the witness of the weakness of their speakers. A man cannot hear above his own level. "He that hath ears to hear let him hear" [Matt. 11:18ff]. Every *dog* has ears—yes, but not to *hear*. Men carry the standard of judgment within them; from the little man the little judgment, from the great man the noble criticism, from the most divine, the most divine love. It is better to fall into the hands of God than into the hands of men.

"And Jesus, knowing their thoughts—" See how he never relinquishes the *spiritual* line in all this incident. Jesus seeing their faith—that was a spiritual perception: Jesus seeing their thoughts—there is the same power of working mental miracles. He reads our minds; there is no curtain made yet by human hands, however so cunning, that can shut out those eyes. He understands every pulsation of the heart, he reads every motion of the will, all things are naked and open to the eyes of him with whom we have to do. The eyes of the Lord run to and fro throughout the whole earth [2 Kgs. 4:35; Zech. 4:10]—sometimes the universe seems to me to be all eyes; I am surrounded by eyes of fire. All speech seems to sum itself into one pregnant sentence—"Thou God seest me" [Gen. 16:13].

Do not lightly pass over these words, for they open the great sphere of the *mental miracles* performed by Jesus Christ. We are accustomed to read about his physical miracles and to doubt them. Any Scribe can doubt. It is no great thing to doubt. The doubter never did anything for the world; the doubter never put one stone upon another. The world is indebted to its faith for its life and for its progress. Jesus not only cured paralysis, he read *thoughts*: already he begins to forecast the day when physical miracles shall depart, and the miracles that shall astound shall be heart-readings, and heart-companionships and spiritual revelations, and moral opportunities and destinies. We live in that dispensation now; miracles of an ordinary and outward kind have all gone, but the miracles of the Holy Ghost are being performed everyday.

"For whether is easier—" It would appear—for I regard this statement as elliptical—that some thought had occurred to the mind of the Scribes that it was easy enough to say, "Thy *sins* be forgiven thee," but the thing to do was to cure the man of the *palsy*. It was easy to talk blasphemies, but what about performing the *cure?* There was a kind of self-gratulation as they suggested that Jesus Christ had taken the easy course of talking blasphemies and letting the substantial thing that was to be done alone, so he says, "Whether is easier to say, 'Thy sins be forgiven thee,' or to say 'Rise and walk'?" The Scribes committed the mistake which the whole world has ever since been repeating. Where is there a man who does not think of every intellectual effort as quiet easy? It is very difficult for a man to walk upon a tight rope across a river—that is something amazing— worth a shilling to look at, but for any man to preach—why, of course that is easy enough: any fool can do that: everybody knows that anybody can preach a sermon! To suggest a *thought*, to flash an idea upon the intellectual horizon—any man in a family who is good for nothing else can do that.

We always send the imbeciles into the Church. To go into the army requires a man, and to go into the navy requires a kind of man and a half, and to go into the law requires a good many men, but to go into the *Church*—why the soft sap of a family will go into the Church. This is possible—possible in relation to all the communions into which the great Christian Church is broken up. There are no doubt soft men and im- becile men in every pulpit in Christendom—that is to say in every sec- tion of the Church in Christendom—but do not understand that the intellectual is always so easy. It is sometimes hard work, even to *preach*. There are those who think the spiritual worthless. It is easy to give ad- vice: nothing could be easier than to address oneself to spiritual necessities, and such service is worthless. Whoever thinks of paying a schoolmaster or a preacher?

There are those who think of religion as merely sentimental, as having no practical value in it: yet there is not a man amongst us who does not owe his social status to religion. You would never have had the customers that flock around your counter but for religion; you would never have got your debts collected but for religion; you would never have been saved from the gutter and the workhouse if an angel of religion had not come after you and brought you in. Religion is not a colored cloud, an evaporating sentiment, it is a most practical factor in the creation and redemption and sanctification of human life.

"And when the multitude saw it, they marveled and glorified God." Trust the great broad human instincts, and do not ask the Scribes what they think. Take your case to the Scribes and say, "Gentlemen, what is your learned opinion about this man's cure?" and they, having rolled themselves round and round in the thickest bandages of the reddest tape, begin to consider. I have faith in broad human instincts: I will not altogether withdraw from our proverbial sayings. I know the crowd has been wrong, I know the mob has been out of the way again and again (I am not speaking of mere crowds or mere mobs: I am speaking of the average human instinct all over our civilization), yet it answers the true voice in the long run, it knows the right man, it knows the right cures, it knows the right books. That human instinct is the next best thing for our guidance to divine inspiration. Make friends of the people, and let little cliques and coteries rot in their own isolation.

Observe the course which Jesus Christ takes, "But that ye may know that the Son of man hath power on earth to forgive sin. Arise, take up thy bed and go into thine own house." We must sometimes prove our religion by our *philanthropy*. Sometimes a man can understand a loaf when he cannot master an argument; sometimes a man can understand a kind action done to his physical necessities when he cannot comprehend or apply the utility of a spiritual suggestion: you do not relinquish the ground that the spiritual is higher than the material when you accommodate yourself to the man's weakness and say to him in effect, "You cannot understand this spiritual argument, therefore I will come down to your ground and do what you can understand." Thus the Church must often prove its religion by its philanthropy. The world cannot understand our creed, but the world can understand our collection. There are masses of men in London today who could really not understand what I am endeavoring to expound: it is beneath them, or above them, or beyond them, but they will be perfectly able to ascertain what we have done for cases of necessity that may now be appealing to our liberality.

This is God's method of proving his own kingdom and claim. "The goodness of God," the Apostle says, "should lead us to repentance" [see Rom. 2:4]. Every good gift given to the body and given to society is an angel that should lead us in a religious direction. God says to us everyday, "That ye may know how to care for your souls, I will show you how to care for your bodies." Now what has he done for the body? Look at that lamp he has lighted, now shining as the southern zenith: look at the meadows he has spread and the gardens he has drawn around our habitations: look at the loving air, the hospitable summer, the abundant autumn, the restful sleep of the winter—and if he had done so much for the body, he says, "But that ye may know what I would do for your mind, for your soul, for your higher faculties, I give you these witnesses, that you can lay your hand upon and examine for yourselves."

It is an argument I cannot refute, it is an appeal I would gladly obey.

eight

CALLING TO DISCIPLESHIP

Matthew 9:9-13

"AND AS JESUS passed from thence, he saw a man, named Matthew." This is a man's account of *himself*. Matthew is the writer of these words. Surely he was most modest, for I know not how his self-description could have been shortened. He simply describes himself as "a man named Matthew," and he says that Jesus saw him as such. There he understated the case. Imagination turns these sweet and modest words into great and noble enlargements of meaning. Jesus saw a *man*. Was he a registrar, numbering the people in ones and twos—was he a mere statistician, putting down the human family in arithmetical figures? He saw a man—he saw more than we mean by that term, he saw that term in all the fullness (shall I say in all the tragedy?) of its meaning. He saw the *ideal* man, he saw the *possible* man, he saw the undeveloped acorn, he saw the germ out of which might come whole Bashans and Lebanons of strong growths.

How easy to pass a man—and how readily it comes to our tongue to call some persons *nobodies*. We are given to the black art of contempt, we take pride in it, we say, "This man is little, and that man is contemptible, and yonder man is nobody," and we hurl our depreciatory adjectives at all and sundry whom we do not care for. Therein we show the little side of our nature. Every man is of some account, every man is somebody; it takes a Christ to warm us into our best consciousness, it takes a look from those eyes in which the summer shone to warm us into encouragement. Some are soon snubbed, they are easily put down—a frown will send them away backward for a whole week: they can only live in approbation, in the sunshine of kind judgment. When Jesus Christ looks upon a man, he looks him into a nobler manhood. He wants to look at you—why do you avert your face? Turn to Him, let your faces meet, and you will never forget his look.

He was a man named Matthew: that name is the only foothold which the writer of this gospel claims for himself in human history. We cannot tell what we write when we write a man's name; it is nothing to us but something to go by, a mere handle or convenience, a sound that is an identity, pointing to a particular individual. But the giving of that name took a whole day in the family long since: it was canvassed, it was made matter of reference, it was carefully balanced with other possible appellations, it was prayed over, it was something snatched from the grave that superior excellence might be remembered, that kind memories might be vivified through the generations to come. Yet how foolishly people name their children, and with what utter ignorance they send them forth with appellations the most misleading, and sometimes involving the most cruel irony or the most laughable burlesque!

It would be an interesting study to collect the Bible names and to go into the reasons why those names were given, and then to show the contrasts and discrepancies between the names and the characters of those who bore them. Our mother Eve said, "I have gotten a man from the Lord: call him Cain." He was gotten from the Lord, but did he ever go back to the Lord? And it is difficult to think that the Lord ever had anything to do with some men. Who can tell? The times are sadly out of joint: there certainly be ironies in our individuality that would seem to exercise the hand of providence from our formation and direction. Yet "the Son of man is come to seek and to save that which was lost" [Luke 19:10]. We are lost, he is in quest of us—can we help him to find us?

"I will," said the daughter of Pharaoh, "call him Moses, because I drew him out of the water." So are our names given: they are monumental names or memorial names: they represent affection, interest, kindness. No child was ever purposely called by the name of a *bad man*. The wicked have no real friends: there be many eagles that pluck them, there are no angels that bless them. Did you call your child by his name because it was the name of a *drunkard?* Did you reason thus with yourself, saying, "My little girl shall bear the name of a woman who was notoriously bad and because she was notoriously bad"? Have I not heard you reasoning just to the contrary by saying, "We will call this child after his good old grandfather, we will call this little girl after her sweet mother, we will call this boy after the name of some illustrious character in history"? When did any man ever go up to the upas tree and pluck one of its deadly twigs and put it into his child's hand to be known by through the handful of his days? O bad man, nobody likes you: they may smile upon you because they have not yet got the last shilling out of your pocket: they may give you guest room in the house because they cannot decently thrust you into the appropriate kennel—but nobody *loves* you. The memory of the wicked shall rot, the candle of the wicked shall be put out. Only goodness would we immortalize. There is still left in this poor nature of ours that strange instinct to preserve the beautiful: we would crush the poisonous adder; who would willingly slay the singing bird, so blithe, so modest?

"Saul, who is also called Paul" [Acts 13:9]. Thus men like to shuffle off the old name, because they have put away the old character. It is in our power, under the blessing and special call of God, to put away our old names. It is the prerogative of God to give each of us a new name, not the name that was sprinkled upon our brow in the baptismal drops, but a name written on the forehead by an invisible finger and visible to none but the Giver. Have we received the new name? Do we carry the new white stone? Is our brow sanctified and ennobled by a writing not to be read by vulgar eyes, but to be seen by every angel flying in the midst of heaven, is a solemn question. Every man must give his own reply.

"And as Jesus passed forth thence, he saw a man named Matthew, sitting at the receipt of custom." In other words he was going about his daily business. He was found, he was sought out, he represents a special class of the Christian elect, of the Christian believer and worker. He was following a despised occupation. There are despised occupations now, there are occupations which never can be forgiven, and that can be said in free England, in republican France, and in democratic America. There are some trades we recoil from, and yet we are Christian professors and citizens of no mean city. But there are some occupations we would not mention if we could help it. A man who is a chimney-sweeper; who would like to be a relative of his?

There are some of you who do not like to see your brothers when they are in their working clothes. You can do with them on a Sunday, when they have got their best garments on, but to think of your walking with some fine person, and to see your brother come up with his fustian jacket on, what an outlook you take upon the universe, what an inquiry flames into your face as if you were most astronomically disposed! There are no *inferior* occupations, but there are some very inferior occupants! I do not say that this occupation or that is the best possible in the world. I am not called upon to give any opinion as to the conflicting merits of occupations and professions, but I want to see the man through all the circumstances, as Jesus Christ never failed to do. The Pharisees called Matthew a publican, a tax-gatherer, a sinner, an alien. So was Zacchaeus called, but when the turn came of Jesus Christ to speak about Zacchaeus, he said, "He is a son of Abraham," and the little man stood up a like a king. He talks the same way about everyone of us. When he sees the very least and common of us give a homeward look, he says, concerning such a looker towards the heavens, "He also is a son of Abraham."

"And he saith unto him, Follow me." Is that all? That is all. Is it not imperative? It is most absolute. When do kings say, "If you please"? Who ever goes to see the Queen by her special and humble desire? I have always noticed that when the Queen sends for anyone, she *commands* them. Why, Jesus Christ seemed to have caught the trick of that high royalty. "Follow me," said he. Abolishing every mood and tense fancied and projected by the fertile brains of grammarians, he shut up human speech into the imperative mood. I like to hear his commands; they were softly spoken, but they were commands at the root and core of them.

He commands you and me just as absolutely today. "Follow me, come unto me." That is his gentle command, his imperial but compassionate edict. He never says, "Follow me, to do me any service that I cannot do without." He uttered the word, "Follow," with a tone which meant, "and you shall have all heaven for the following." The very imperativeness of the tone hides a gracious intent. This is no scourging tone that would drive men before it; it is the tone of a complete assurance and a sublime and indestructible purpose, an assurance of his own sufficiency to meet the need, and his purpose to cover all human necessity with the infinite fullness of his unutterable grace. Will you come?

He did not go to Matthew and raise him from the seat; he did not employ any mechanical powers for the purpose of drawing Matthew: he launched his word. It is an old way of his, it began with, "Let there be light, and there was light" [Gen. 1:3], as if light had been standing behind the chaotic mass, waiting for the word and could not move until that word was spoken. The Bible is full of commandments, but the commandments are not grievous, they are not the utterances of an arbitrary will, but the subtle pleadings of a heart that lives for us, and that would seem to be unable to live without us.

"And he arose and followed him." How *easy* it is for some men to rise and follow Christ, as compared with others. They seem to fall into the way of faith: it is like bringing the sun to bear upon a bud that wants to open, and that is just waiting for light in order that it might unfold its deep and sacred beauty. It is so easy for some men to pray, they seem to be walking up a gentle green slope to meet God at the height of it. When other men try to pray it is like climbing up a rugged steep rock, some of the stones loose, and if you put your foot upon them you will fall. It is so easy for some men to do the act of benevolence; there are some persons to whom I dare not state a case of necessity, because while I am stating it they are putting forth the hand to relieve it, and others need long pleading and much pressure and detail, the utterance of which becomes a sheer cruelty to the man who has to speak it, before they can advance the smallest testimony of their regard for human suffering.

It is so easy for some people to go to church: they like it, they wait for Sunday; when they open their eyes upon the Sabbatic light they say, "Thank God, this is the King's day."

> The King himself comes near,
> And feasts his saints today.

Other men have to be dragged to church, and the "Amen" of the preacher is like the utterance of an amnesty, so quickly and cordially do they run from the sacred roof. But God is able to conquer our perversity, and to subdue our obdurateness, and to bring the most reluctant to his throne in pious and loyal homage. He will have some of you yet. It was difficult to bring you here this morning, but already your hearts are warming towards him who is the Lord of the house and the King of the day. Perhaps you are saying, "He was certainly kind: he surely took a noble view of us; his utterances were great and splendid gospels; if they were dreams, they were not gilded, they were of real gold." So far so good: he will have you yet: help his conquest by your consent.

This act of obedience is to be done with all the spontaneity and impulse of love. Christ never drags a man after him: he is no tyrannical God that says, "I will bind you hand and foot, and take you captive." We run with the feet of love, we follow with the credulity of intelligent obedience. My Lord calls me, I must go; I know his voice, its infinite sweetness, its tender pathos—it fills me like a gospel. Do not suppose that Christ lays a mighty arm upon you and takes you against your will. He never hurls his omnipotence against the sinner: his commands are inspired by love. Hear them: "Rise, he calleth for thee. The Master is come and calleth for thee" [see John 11:28]. No other man ever wanted to see you, no other person ever cared for you. Here is the infinite solicitude, the unmerited and ineffable grace.

"And it came to pass as Jesus sat at meat in the house, behold many publicans and sinners came and sat down with him and his disciples." It was probably in Matthew's house. Matthew was, by all historical accounts, not a poor man, but one who could show hospitality of the kind indicated in this passage. The publicans and sinners came and sat down with Jesus: that was an unconscious tribute. How is it that we are drawn to some people, how is it that we know certain persons whom we never saw before in our lives, what is that singular mystery of kith and kin which we all realize when we have spoken to certain people five minutes? I have watched the eye of poverty and the eye of grief and want, and I have done so this very morning. A poor creature was waylaying a few travelers, and one after another passed, and her keen and hungry eye saw nothing in them to which she could appeal. Then one I saw pass, and she said, "Pardon me, sir—do not be offended—" How did she know to whom to speak? Is there a masonry of hearts? Are there signs in the face, is there gleaming in the eye, is there something in the walk, are we revelations to one another? Did any poor soul ever stop you to tell a tale of grief? Yes. Thank God for that interruption: it meant a great deal, such woe, hunger, pain and want as stopped you have eyes that can read the heart.

The publicans and sinners got around him as cold people get around a fire. They need no welcome in words; they are cold and here is the fire. If you felt the cold you would draw near to the great fire of Christ's love, and until you do feel it I can do nothing with you or for you but declare in ardent speech the excellence of One who would do you good if you would allow him.

"When the Pharisees saw it, they said, Why doth your Master eat with publicans and sinners?" This is a narrow criticism: it abounds in every time. All men have at least got thus far in the tormenting art of criticism—they are able to find fault. He is indeed a remarkable imbecile who cannot find fault with somebody; he is indeed much neglected in his education who cannot find fault with any sermon he ever heard or with any person he ever saw. Of all the shams that ever were performed in this insincere world, though the sham of hypocrisy be the worst, the sham of criticism is the most tormenting.

How did Jesus reply to this narrow criticism? When Jesus heard that, he said, "They that be whole need not a physician, but they that are sick. But go ye and learn what that meaneth, I will have mercy and not sacrifice—I will have the reality and not the sham, I will have the thing meant and not mere words and tricks about it. God is a Spirit, and they that worship him must worship him in spirit and in truth" [John 4:24]. So Jesus Christ lived in great principles, and so he lived above public opinion, he never lived in defiance of it. It is a poor criticism of our Lord's habit and manner amongst men to say that he defied public sentiment. The true criticism would be that he lived *above* it, he dwelt in the sanctuary of great principles, he worshiped in the temple of universal benevolence. Any fanatic can *defy* public opinion, it requires the most divine of saints to enthrone himself *above* it and to move in his sublime course, impelled by divine inspirations and undegraded by human tempers or social flatteries.

nine

THE SPIRITUAL LAW

Matthew 9:14–19

JESUS CHRIST was always pestered by little questions. It is very seldom, if ever, that you hear a great inquiry propounded to him. Why do you eat with publicans and sinners? Why do you eat with washed hands? Why do you heal on the Sabbath-day? Why do you not fast more? These were the small inquiries by which those who were immediately around him and were observing him critically or in partial sympathy belittled every occasion. A man is known by the questions he asks. Whoever asks any great question concerning the Bible? Be assured that he who asks the great question gets the great answer, and be not surprised if, in reply to our little and superficial inquiries, we receive shallow and disappointing replies. What is our question when we open the sacred book?

The persons who put this inquiry were honest men. They were not Pharisees, they were the disciples of John, and their question was, "Why do we and the Pharisees fast oft, but thy disciples fast not?" These people represented those persons who have only got so far as the gospel of abstention. Many of us are at that point, the very first and lowest in the Christian life. Our Christianity consists in *not* doing things. It is a necessary point in our higher culture: no man can work up the line which has upon it the grim rough words, "Thou shalt not." Yet the purpose of Jesus Christ is to lead us away from the negative gospel and virtue of abstention into the glorious gospel of ample and life-long liberty.

You find people whose virtue consists in abstention from vice: it is a kind of negative quantity, it is the mere negation of wrong. They will not eat, they will not drink, they will not pursue this pleasure, nor will they follow after that delight, they will not be seen in such and such

61

company—that is their lean and most puny virtue. It is necessary, it is part of the education, but a man ought not always to rest there. Virtue is positive, religion is emphatic, the true spirit is one of liberty. The question, therefore, which we should put to ourselves everyday is, how far are we yet in the prison of the letter, and what advancement have we made into the kingdom of liberty? True virtue would, of course, consist in being able to go around the whole circle of legitimate pleasures and yet to keep that circle in its proper place. He has grown up into the fullness of Christ who can sit down with publicans and sinners, who can touch pitch and not be defiled, who can take up serpents and play with them, and can drink any deadly thing and it shall not hurt him: but who has attained that height? That is the grand liberty that is yet to be realized. They shall take up serpents, and the serpents shall have no power over the hand that grasps them, and if they drink any deadly thing it shall not hurt them—the soul shall be so much better than the body, the mind shall have lofty lordship over that which is physical, and the spiritual shall triumph over the material. That is the line along which our education has to proceed. Do not scourge it unduly, do not hasten it with the impetuosity which is not wise. The majority of us are yet virtuous simply because we are not so vicious as we might be.

"Why do we and the Pharisees fast oft, but thy disciples fast not?" Religion is enjoyment, religion is associated with wedding bells and wedding feasts, and wine-drinking, and high delight, and infinite liberty, and cloudless sunshine. He who binds it down to other ideas forces an eagle into a mean cage and bruises its noble wings with iron weapons. He, of course, would be the grand Christian who made everyday holy alike, whose Saturday was so holy that his Sunday could not possibly be holier. But we have not yet attained that spiritual excellence, therefore some of us are obliged to set apart one day in the week and to say concerning it, "This day is sacred to religious purposes: we will call it a day of rest, a day of prayer, a day of hope." When we have completed our Christian education, there will be only one day in the week, and its name will be the Sabbath day, the Lord's day, every moment a jewel, every breath a waft from heaven, every exercise nobler than prayer, even as noble as praise.

Sometimes this high ideal of religion is unduly forced upon us by thoughtless people, as if it were attainable and realizable here and now by every professing Christian. Let me protest against such undue urgency. We are travelers, and therefore we go one step at a time. We are mounting a ladder, and the rule is, one rung at once; when we get to the top the ladder may be burned, for we have mounted to the very sanctuary of infinite liberty, but while we are climbing let no man cut one rung out of the ladder; every rung is part of the trying, solemn, but most salutary discipline of life. When we have attained the fullness of Christ's purpose, and are all shut up in the wedding chamber, eating and drinking with him from morning till night at the great festal board, then all our money will be sacred, but just now some of us are obliged to put away into God's basket God's portion: we are so thievish we should steal it if we did not seal it up on the Saturday: our fingers have got the felonious movement, and they would take that money if we did not seal up and stamp it as God's. Do not despise, therefore, the man who is yet in the narrow gospel of abstention and whose virtue consists in not being vicious. He has undertaken a great lesson: the pages are very long and the print is very small, and therefore it is not often that we have to turn over. The great question we have to put to ourselves is whether we have got hold of the right book, whether we are animated by the right spirit in its perusal. If so, we shall come to its finish then as great and perfected scholars, we shall lay hold of the great liberty and shall be enfranchised among those who have no need of candle, or sun, or moon, for the light is from God, and it needs no intermediate atmosphere through which to come to us. That is our resting point: it is afar off, we are on the road, faint yet pursuing—in that pursuit find your rest and hope.

If the disciples of John ask a little question, Jesus gave a great reply. He was not answering them only, he was answering the spirit of all coming time. Herein you have the reason why sometimes a great answer was given to a small inquiry. The individuals who put the question spoke for themselves alone, expressed their momentary fretfulness or surprise, but Jesus Christ in every little question saw the inquiries that would fall upon his cause and kingdom through all time, and therefore he spread out his answer beyond the immediate occasion that elicited it. Hear this marvelous answer, struck from him in a moment.

> Can the children of the bride-chamber mourn as long as the bridegroom is with them? But the days will come when the bridegroom shall be taken from them, and then shall they fast. No man putteth a piece of new cloth into an old garment, for that which is put in to fill it up taketh from the garment, and the rent is made worse. Neither do

men put new wine into old bottles, else the bottles break
and the wine runneth out and the bottles perish, but they
put new wine into new bottles, and both are preserved.

Christ's replies were all extemporaneous: never did he retire to consider any question that was put to him: the answer was plucked out of
his eternity, it was always ready. If he could have paused for one moment
he would have lost the crown of his deity. In the instancy of his replies
was the fullness of his light: you had but to touch him with right fingers
and you drew from him the healing virtue.

What then is his own notion of our union with him? The figure is beautiful. We are children of the bride-chamber, and he is the bridegroom,
and we are gathered around a wedding table, and the air vibrates and
dances under the thrill and shock of the wedding bells. "Fasting?" saith
he; "it is a stranger to a scene like this, it is an anti-climax, it is an alien
that cannot speak the language of this fair land." We are not called to
gloom and mourning and falling of the head, nor are we summoned to
take the bulrush and sackcloth and ashes. My Father's house is a bride-
chamber, the sanctuary is a place where the wedding guests assemble,
the temple of the Lord is the place where the life-wine is poured out in
rivers for the soul's ample drinking. Child, young one, spirit of delight
and hope, you thought the church was a gloomy place: if there is any
gloom in it, blame the human fingers that brought it to the place. The
high ideal of the church is joy in its keenest accent, pleasure without
alloy, the very ecstasy and rapture of gladness. Christianity—tell the world
that her ways are ways of pleasantness and all her paths are peace.
When Zion is looking around and considering what keynote she shall
take, say unto her, "Rejoice, rejoice greatly, O daughter of Zion!"

Yet the Lord keeps us on the right lines for one swift moment, quicker
than the twinkling of an eye. In this passage he directs attention to the
highest point of joy, and then he descends to the common average
line of life, and says, "But the days will come when the bridegroom shall
be taken from them, and then shall they fast." Then they will base
their ceremonies on reason, then the ceremonial observances of the church
shall not be priestly tricks, for they shall come out of the heart's wound,
out of the life's bitter grief; they shall not be calendered for punctual observance, according to the movements of the clock, but they shall express an inner, real, secret, profound, unutterable grief. When that

black grief seizes you, you need not turn to some man-written diary to know whether it is fast-day or not. Every heart will be its own calendar, every life will keep its own fasts, and no man needs ask the meaning of the dejection which shall then picture itself on the worn face. It shall bear so clearly the autograph of the heart, that no man, wayfaring or foolish, can misread such writing.

There are those who ask questions about fasts and feasts and new moons and special days—mechanical scholars, mechanical Christians, technical purists, persons who need to go to ink-written paper to know what they have to do next. Is the bride-groom with you? If you can say "Yes," then eat and drink, eat and drink abundantly indeed, and let your soul delight itself in fatness, whatever the calendar may say. Has the bridegroom gone—is his chair vacant—is his sunlike face no more the center of the feast and the security of its delight? I need not exhort you to grief and mourning, the heart will know what to do: follow the intuitions of the heart in these matters, and then your ceremonies will not be tricks of the hand, but expressions of the inner life, your fasting and your feasting shall be accounted sacraments in heaven.

Nor was the answer parabolically beautiful only, it was philosophically broad and true. "No man putteth a piece of new cloth into an old garment, for that which is put in to fill it up taketh from the garment, and the rent is made worse." You are not to be partly one thing and partly another, the left hand is not to be a Jew and the right hand a Christian. That is not Christ's idea of his own purpose and his own kingdom. We are one thing only. There are those that are least in the kingdom of heaven, and there are those that are greatest, but they are all in the kingdom of heaven; and he that is least in the kingdom of heaven, is greater than he that is greatest outside. You cannot be both Jew and Christian, both believer and unbeliever, both infidel and worshiper. You are the one or you are the other, and if you are trying to unite the two, then you will know by experience and loss that men who put new wine into old bottles lose both the bottles and the wine. What are you? Under whose banner do you come? Whose name do you bear? I ask not whether you are giants in the kingdom, but whether you are little children in the house, just breathing, crying, cooing, laughing, wondering, looking with eyes that are all wonder and but little vision. Let your hearts reply, and according to their answer let the exhortation come, for no other exhortation can touch the reality of the case.

Do not fast by rule, do not go to church because of mere custom, do not read the Bible according to the measurement which you have laid out. If you are still in the state of pupilage which requires such mechanical help, far be it from me to deny you the advantage of such assistance. Some of you will need to say you will read so much Scripture today and to-morrow: if any of you have grown away from that mechanical arrangement, as I trust most of us have done, do not visit with severity of criticism your opinions upon those who have not attained your height of excellence. I cannot bind myself to read so many verses in the day, nor can I bind myself to fast on this day of the month. I must let the day bring its own religion, I must let the day deliver its own letters, I must let the day bring its own angels. I cannot forecast my religious doings and observances: tomorrow the bridegroom may have gone, and I shall not need you to tell me to fast: my head will sink, and in the chamber of the heart there will be a great vacancy and a fatal gloom. Tomorrow he may come back, and this hand will thrust itself out to find the rope that rings the loudest bell. God make us all read, for reality is the glory of piety.

I am surprised that I find so good a stopping place in the seven-teenth verse, yet the eighteenth verse opens in a way which constrains me to go on. "While he yet spake these things unto them—" Christ was a speaker that was often interrupted. Some of us simple talkers cannot bear interruption; to be broken in upon is fatal to our lame speech, be-cause we are not speakers, we are reciters or readers of a lesson, or per-formers of a trick. If we talked right out of the temple and sanctuary of our life, we could bear to have our speech punctuated by various kinds of interruptions, and especially by those interruptions which called us to beneficent labor. "While he yet spake these things unto them," while there was wonder on the face of those who received the answer, while the air was still stirring with the vibrations of his sacred and revealing voice, while the question was yet under consideration, "behold there came a certain ruler and worshiped him, saying, My daughter is even now dead, but come and lay thy hand upon her and she shall live." We began with a little question, we come into a tragic prayer. Such, indeed, is the sharp transition of life. Now the great Teacher has to answer the tech-nical inquiry, and now to recall the dead, and now to redeem the world.

The ruler's little child was twelve years old, and she was dead, yet he said, "Come and lay thy hand upon her and she shall live." "*Thy* hand—

are not all hands alike? Is there a science of palmistry—are there those who read the man in the hand—are not all grips of the same intensity? Why say, *"Thy* hand"—could no other hand be found? We are sometimes shut up to the help of one man, even in our lower life. "O for our own doctor: his very voice would do the patient good. O for our own physician; he knows just what to give when the sufferer is in this crisis of agony. O for our old mother: there was healing, there was comfort in her gentle hand. O for the old father—if he had been here he would have found the key to open this gate. O for the old pastor that first showed us the light and brought us to prayer—he would know what to say to us just now." We have, therefore, analogy to help us in this matter. In the great crises of life there is often only one hand that can help us. Thy right hand, O Lord, is become glorious in power. The right hand of the Lord doeth valiantly. In Thy hand is both honor and might. The good hand of my God be upon me. Out of whose hand do you take your daily food? Thou openest Thine hand and satisfieth the desire of every living thing. Lay Thine hand upon us even when we are dead, and we shall live again. Dear hand, wounded hand, mighty hand, hand of the Loving One, lay it upon us, before us, behind us, around us—keep us in Thine hand and let our names be written on its palm.

See the life of our Lord—the bridegroom making all the children of the bride-chamber happy, intoxicating them with the sacred wine of his own joy, answering a little technical question and rushing to recall the dead to life: for we read, "And Jesus arose and followed him, and so did his disciples." When did he ever refuse the request of a broken heart? When did he ever say "No" to the contrite spirit? When did he ever pierce the upturned eyes of contrition with sharp darts of rebuke? He arose and followed him—like a servant. He made himself of no reputation, he took upon him the form of a servant and became obedient, obedient unto death, obedient unto the death of the cross [see Phil. 2:7, 8]. Not obedience in any of its reluctant forms or manifestations, but the utter, complete obedience that left nothing undone.

What is there in your house today—is death there? Ask Jesus to go home with you, and you will have light at eventide. Is there a great grief at home today? Take Jesus with you and he will sanctify the bitter grief. Is the house very empty today, and cold, and lonely, and are you afraid to hear your own footfall within the unsympathetic walls? Take the guest with you— he can break the bread, and make a feast of it in the breaking, and he will fill up every vacancy and make you glad, if not with immediate restoration, with a great hope that shall be more precious than any satisfaction that is possible within the bounds of time and space. With Christ in the house we have companionship, sufficiency, rest, thankfulness, hope — and there is nothing else in heaven.

ten

AFFLICTION IN THE HOUSE

Matthew 9:18–26

"WHILE HE SPAKE these things." We need not critically inquire whether any interval separated between what is written in the seventeenth verse and in the eighteenth. No doubt such an interval did occur, yet it would have been quite in accordance with the habit of the great Teacher and Sufferer if he had interrupted any speech in order to do good to a broken heart. It did not shock the writer when he wrote, "While he spake these things unto them." It did not occur to him that he was indicating a point of interruption, nor did it occur to him that he was violating any probability of the case. Christ himself was the one improbability, the one impossibility of human history, and therefore we must not bring little rules and standards by which to measure anything that he did or said.

He was answering a question put to him by the disciples of John about fasting, and Matthew writes, "While he spake these things unto them," before the answer was yet fully given, or while the last word was being uttered, or while he was in the act of pausing for some rejoinder either by way of comment or inquiry—just then a great, solemn, heart-laden prayer burst upon his startled ear. "My daughter is now dead, but come and lay thy hand upon her and she shall live." Elijah taught us that other gods might be so busy that they could not hear the cry of their devotees: Elijah spoke so in irony and mockery, bitter and severe, telling us to cry louder, that the other gods were talking or pursuing; he told us that we got no answer because our voice was too low, that the gods were on a journey or sleeping—nobody knew what he was doing; he must be called for by a louder and more shrill cry. Jesus Christ was never so busy that he could not answer any question put to him, and in

69

proportion as that question was acute, arising from the heart's sore distress and burning agony, would he interrupt even a miracle of minor kind, to accomplish a miracle of a superior kind. These are the things that prove his quality, these are the elements which, being brought together into one complete mass, establish his claim to be something more than I am. I go with him so far, and in a moment he shoots beyond me and stands alone on the solemn elevation. Up to a given line he is a good man simply, extremely kind and sensitive, answering every emotion of the life that is around him steadily and truly; then in a moment he leaves all examples and precedents and parallels behind, and stands before us as God, so much like God that were a man to say to him, "My Lord and my God," not a heart in all the listening assembly would feel the shock of an irreligious or painful surprise. The cry would accord with the circumstances, and would establish a sweet though pensive rhythm. The two words, the word of Christ and the acknowledging word of man, would form a balance to one another, and establish between them a consistency that would grow into an argument.

Yet he appears to be Servant as well as Master, for we read, "And Jesus arose and followed him," as if he had no alternative. He never has an alternative when the heart really wants him. It is the heart that shuts him up to one reply. He can tell your intelligence to wait, he can rebuke your eager ingenuity or your impetuous fancy, but when the broken heart needs him, if he were to delay, then it would be but to come with some richer blessing on the third day. Sometimes he does put off until the third day; it is his favorite day, he typified it by instances in his life, he crowned it by his resurrectional return. "Come, let us return unto the Lord: he hath bruised us, and he will bind us up again: he hath torn us, and on the third day he will revive us." But he always answers the cry of the burdened and broken heart. He arises like a servant, and clothed with humility as with a garment, he walks after the man that wants him as a slave might go.

Yet you say you have never seen him and never known him. I can tell you why. You have had no trouble in your life. You have always sought him by the lamp of your intelligence; you have always invited him into the cunningly arranged chambers of your fancy and imagination; you have always endeavored to tempt him by your intellectual curiosity. To all these Herods and Pilates he answers nothing. To this man will I look, the man whose eyes are upon the dust, whose accusing hand is upon his heart, and who sobs rather than says his eager prayer. You will send for him someday and he will come.

This is an instance of a man praying for *another* and yet praying for *himself* at the same time. "My daughter is even now dead." That is all we hear, but there was an unspoken prayer, for there was a subtle undertone, there was an aside in the action that touched the heart of Christ. If the child is dead, why call her back? Who would call back a friend from summer to winter, from the land where the moon is as the sun, and the sun is bright seven times beyond himself, to the land of night and coldness and ice and bitter desolation? He could have said, "Jairus, I congratulate thee: is she gone, is she at home, have the angels taken her?

> Let the angels take her
> In God's acre
> > Dust to dust
> Must thou thus forsake her?
> > Ay, thou must,
> Will the stronger wrong her?

I bless thee: thy twelve-year-old child is an angel now."

But there was another prayer: not only was the little girl dead, but the living man was dead too. He answered the prayer not for the child's sake, but for the *man's* sake. The house was no longer worth going into, the house had become a ghastly tomb, the house had shaped itself into its ghost's faces, and miserable spectacles—Jesus went for the living man's sake. "When such friends part, 'tis the survivor who really dies"; so wondrous is the way of mercy, so subtle and incalculable are the methods and issues of divine providence, that sometimes they who are in heaven have to be called back again in order to make up our life, or we shall fall right down in the pit of despair, and our lamp shall go out in total and perpetual darkness. Selfish man—still not wholly selfish. If a man has lost one of his wings and cannot fly, he may surely ask to have it returned to him. If the lame man has lost his one crutch, surely God will not account it inexcusably selfish if he should ask to have it given back to him.

My daughter—in another place, my little daughter, my only daughter—is dead. Does death go into *great* houses? This man was governor, a ruler, a man of station and social influence. Does death go into the house of the ruler, into the dwelling of the magistrate, into the habitation of the judge, into the palace of the monarch? Is he not frightened by the great gates gilded at their tops like pinnacles? He makes others fear, he knows no fear himself. Let us proceed with the narrative, for it is full of action. There is no rest in the outward life of this Christ: He has to cut out days and nights in which to rest, for the world's necessity would never allow him even to sleep. He had to create a Sabbath sometimes in the night that he might go to church and sing and pray. This portion of the chapter is full of action, it moves, it trembles with a strange energy, divine and human.

"And behold, a woman—" Yes, I will, and I know she will develop something in Christ that no man could ever touch. I will behold this woman; I have known Christ to appear bested by a woman; I have never known him to appear beaten really in his own field but by a woman. He once told a woman that the meat was not for the dogs, and she said, "Truth, Lord: yet the dogs eat of the crumbs which fall from their masters' table" [Matt. 15:27]. And he could not stir one step from that spot till he had given a great "Yes" to her great prayer. Let us then in very deed observe this woman. She has been diseased twelve years, which was exactly the age of the little girl that was dead. The little child had twelve years, let us hope, of joyous life and daily dreaming, much laughter, high glee; and this poor woman, all the time, year by year through every one of the twelve, had been suffering much. No physician could treat her case successfully; she never grew better, but rather worse. She came behind him. There is a touch of modesty and a touch of something more than modesty and nearer divinity still—if there be nothing nearer divinity than downright, healthy, real humbleness. She was going to entrap him, she was going to perpetrate what centuries afterwards was known as a pious fraud, she would steal a blessing. She had a speech in her heart—who has not? You are going to face some difficulty tomorrow, and you have told your nearest friend what you will say, or you have kept it altogether in your heart, and turned it over and over with many an amendment. You will begin so, and continue thus, and then you will wait. What secret preparations we have, what speeches gotten by heart, what prayers stored up in the silent chambers, to come out someday and surprise heaven!

What would this good old mother say? She said within herself, "If I may but touch his garment I shall be whole. I need not trouble him with any speech or with any form or ceremony of restoration, I am one that need not go to him in trouble—if I may but touch the hem of his garment, the dusty hem, the hem that is trailing on the ground. I need not ask to touch his dear hand, nor need I pray for that dear hand to be laid upon me. I will go behind him and watch the train of his dress as it goes along the ground, and if I can but touch it for a moment, I shall be whole." That was faith, that was religion! A soul that could burn with such spirituality must cure any body which it tenanted for a few frail years. Your bodies would be better if your souls were stronger.

Does Jesus Christ permit any theft? Jesus turned about, and when he saw her, as no other eyes had ever looked upon her, he said, "Daughter." We are all his daughters, we are all his sons, he is our Father and our Brother; all relations in marvelous contradiction represent themselves in him, just as we put ourselves in relation to him. "Daughter, take heart again, be happy: thy faith made thee whole." He asks no questions regarding her disease, or the time of its continuance, or the peculiarity of its symptoms, or the keenness of its pain. He knows us altogether.

> He knows what sore temptations mean,
> For he has felt the same.

We have not a High Priest that cannot be touched with a feeling of our infirmities, for in all points he was tempted, tried, searched, as we are, yet he kept sin at bay, and was conqueror always.

But how kind to make this little speech as well as to give the healing. A flower is all the better for having fragrance as well as beauty. How sweet to say something to her, to make a whole little speech to the woman herself! Sometimes he made the speech to the multitude: he said, "I say unto you I have not found so great faith, no, not in Israel." He took, so to speak, her little birthday book, which we give to our friends to write their names in, and he writes a little speech with his own dear hand, and it is all the woman's own. "Daughter, be of good comfort, thy faith hath made thee whole." He almost made the woman feel she had cured herself. He takes no glory—he needs none. He does not say, "Behold the virtue of my clothes, see what can be done by this oversoul that flows into the hem of my garment." He tells the poor woman that she healed herself. He loads us with benefits!

And then these people came to Jesus, not because of their richness and health and strength, but because they wanted something of him, because of their helplessness and pain, or poverty of some kind. That is just what we do if we come to him in the right way. Sometimes you mock us, and when you see us going to church you say, "There go the good ones, there go the patterns of society, there go your pious ones. We poor creatures do not go to church or to the sacrament of the Lord's Supper—we leave that for you patterns of high virtue and noble piety." There is no sense in your mockery, you are altogether wrong in your conception, and therefore wholly unjust in your criticism. We come to Christ because we are *bad*. If you could say to us, "There go the bad ones," you would speak with some justness. "There go the cripples, there go the helpless ones, there go those that cannot make up their own life and redeem their own soul, there go the paupers, the dependents, the helpless ones." Say so and you touch the reality of the case. I do not remain to partake of the sacred bread and wine because I am good, but because I am the chief of sinners [see 1 Tim. 1:15]. I never knew any man come really and truly to Christ who did not come because he was helpless, because he was suffering from mortal distress, because he was conscious of an emptiness and powerlessness of soul which nothing can touch but the divine hand of Christ.

Think of us, therefore, as *worse* than you. You can do without him, we cannot. You want to wait till you have washed yourselves and appareled yourselves and made yourselves fit for his presence.

> All the fitness he requires
> Is to feel your need of him.

Think of us as the worst men in society, the vilest, the meanest men, those who are utterly conscious of being self-helpless, and who want someone to rest on, and spare your bitter taunt and heartless mockery.

Now we resume the story that was interrupted by this woman, and beautifully interrupted. Such parentheses are the very glory and blossom of the history. It would be poorer history but for these interruptions. Jesus Christ does a great deal of good *on the way* towards doing some other good. He preaches as he is walking down to the church. His very passing by the house of the people leaves a blessing behind it. He is as a flower carried through the quiet air that breathes its fragrant blessing, that all may receive it and be made glad. This is an aside in his ministry which does not lie on the direct line as part of one continual purpose: it is something that happened intermediately.

Now he comes to the ruler's house. "When he saw the minstrels"— for heathenism had made some incursion even into Jewish habits—"when he saw the minstrels and the people making a noise (an artificial noise;

hired mourners made to create a sensation), he said unto them, Give place, for the maid is not dead, but sleepeth." Thus he would always reduce his own miracles. He did not say, "She is seven times dead"; he always made light of his miracles; he said, "It is only the death swoon, she is asleep"; and they laughed him to scorn. They knew better—so did he, if it came to a merely literal interpretation, but he includes death itself in sleep. So he will strip death itself of all its terrors and stings, and make it at last into a child's slumber. They laughed him to scorn—they had seen a thousand children dead, and they knew that this child was as dead as any child that had ever been buried in rock or in pit.

"And when the people were put forth, he went in." I see his stoop as he passes under the door and takes her by the hand. She could not touch him, and therefore he touched her. He will have it either way, only the *touch* must take place. He does not care whether it be your touch or his touch, but the hands must meet, the lives must impinge, there must be a beneficent collision. The woman had strength enough to touch on the ground, as it trailed along, the hem of the simple garment; the little girl lay there stiff and cold, and motionless, she could do nothing; he therefore did it all. "He took her by the hand, and the maid arose."

These miracles must not be blotted out of human history. They set *mind* in its right place; they set the moral forces of creation in their true position; they will not let death have all its own rude, violent way in the world; they put life on the throne; they elevate soul above body, spirit above matter. That is the grand interpretation of the miracles, that mind is regal and matter slavish, servile, and wholly helpless under the dominion and beneficent sovereignty of the soul. If you have been trying to reconcile the miracles with your little laws of nature and partial conceptions of the universe, no wonder that your heads are dizzy and in the whirl of skepticism, but if you see in these miracles types of the supremacy of mind, the royalty and divinity of spirit, the right relation of the universe to the King and Creator, then these difficulties become as the small dust in the balance, as a drop in the bucket. They are not to be accounted of. When you come into this spirit of high, loving, pure, sublime, and noble criticism, then all these miracles wrought by Jesus Christ will no longer be the surprises of such a history but the commonplaces of a life so divine.

eleven

THE WORLD THROUGH WHICH CHRIST PASSED

Matthew 9:27–31

WHAT A WORLD our Lord Jesus Christ passed through! He was always surrounded by the deaf, the dumb, the blind, the poor, the broken-hearted, the weary, the hungry, and those that had no helper. Herein was the realization, and most vivid and happy fulfillment of prophecy: it was foretold of him that he was to be the Apostle to the meek, the captive, the broken-hearted, and the mourning. *Every man creates his own world.* You can find a tolerably comfortable world if you please. Shut yourself up in your own parlor, enjoy your own honey, warm yourself by your own fire, shut out safely all the cries of distress that are ringing in the world, and you will come to the conclusion that life after all is tolerably happy and comfortable. There are men who do this. When they hear complaints, they say they are exaggerated; when their eye reluctantly alights upon the newspapers containing reports of human distress and poverty, they call such reports sensationalism, or they blame the poor for their poverty, the sorrowing for their distress, and the lonely for their helplessness. Every man, let me repeat, creates the world through which he passes. There are some of us near whom no poor man would ever come, if he could help it; he would give us room enough on the broad highway. There are others who are always surrounded by crying, distressful, sad-hearted, grief-stricken folks, so that life is spent in a kind of multitudinous hospital. You can go through life comfortably if you like, or you can acquaint yourself with the world's woe and the world's bitter grief.

What a wonderful world Jesus Christ developed! You would not have known that there were so many sick folks in the town if he had not come. The oldest inhabitant was surprised by the distress, helplessness, and sadness of life hidden in the town in which he had lived seventy full years and more. When Jesus Christ entered into the town, all its distress was in a flutter of expectancy. When the Savior came into any city, the blind heard his footfall, the deaf saw signs in the air that indicated the presence of the Beneficent One—all the sadness of the town moved itself in a new prayer, and tried with feeble trembling hand to relight its little lamp of hope.

How is it when you go into any circle, neighborhood, or town? All its fashion dresses itself, every looking-glass in the neighborhood is made to do hard duty; or all the letters or all the music of the town may be moved to expectation—but no cripple cares for your coming, no deaf man says, "Today I shall hear," no blind man gets his sight through your coming. We create, I would say again and again, our own society. The priest goes to the other side when he sees the half-murdered man, the Levite follows his chief; the Samaritan lingers in that unroofed church that he may redeem a life from destruction, and in this way sing his morning psalm and breathe his daily prayer.

You think the world is not a bad place to live in, after all. You say you have found life tolerably comfortable; you think that a great deal too much is made of the shady side of life. Who are you—what right have you to speak upon this subject? I could put my fingers in my ears and run through a crowd of people crying with pain, and say at the end of my running, "I heard nothing of it; everything was quiet when I passed through." We do not diminish the world's distress by shutting our window, brightening our fire, and drawing around us all the comforts of our own luxurious abode. The distress is still there, it is crying in the night wind, shuddering in the snow, praying to the black night.

Every preacher creates his own congregation. "Like priest, like people," is a proverb not without its application even in this sense. The congregation and the minister are one—in height, in the very shape of their heads, in the breadth of their shoulders, in the tone of their minds, in their look, in their fire—they are one. There are men we could not hear; they are not *our* shepherds. There are other men whom we could hear always, because they are our kith and kin from before the foundation of the world. As truly as a man calls around him his own companions, acquaintances and friends, as truly as a minister makes his own congregation in due time, so true is it in the deeper and more tragical sense that every heart makes the world in which it lives. If we were more sympathetic, our doorstep would be crowded with those who need sympathy, but in proportion as we are severe, misanthropic, unsympathetic, unrighteous in judgment, shall we drive away the world's distress from our neighborhood and sight, and shall come to believe in the long run that the distress we do not see therefore does not exist.

We sicken at the sight of all this sorrow which is narrated in the holy Gospels. Nearly every verse has in it something about the dumb, the demon-possessed, a man suffering from paralysis, a little child dead, a poor woman stealing a blessing from the Physician as he goes down to raise the little one from her fatal slumber, a blind man crying and saying, "Thou Son of David, have mercy on me!" a leper with his hand upon his lip, saying, "Lord, if thou wilt thou canst make me clean." O, it is heart-rending. Who would not rather read a stirring novel about something that never did occur? When the multitude became hungry, the disciples said, "Send them away." That is our short and easy cure for human malady—send it away. Jesus said, "No, never send anybody away that really needs your help." Instead of sending them away, Jesus said, "Cause them to sit down on the green grass, and bring out of your little store all that you have, and do not let a single person go away until the last crumb is eaten," and the last crumb is never eaten in the house of Christ; so long as he is at the table there is bread enough and to spare; so long as he spends your pound a week, working man, you will find in it no end of shillings; so long as he keeps your house, poor widow woman, there will be coal in the grate, there will be bread in the cupboard, and there will be oil in the cruse [see 1 Kgs. 17:11–16]. "I have been young," said the Psalmist, "and now am old, yet have I never seen the righteous forsaken, nor his seed begging bread" [37:25]. We want a change, we are tired of seeing sad and tragical sights. I, for one, am often tired of the vision; I am weary, I long to plunge my eyes into the snows of the Alps, or into the deep greens of the rich valley pastures. It would do the eyes good. Jesus Christ never tired; he went about doing good. He tired every helper; he never exhausted his own sympathy.

Let us now hear the blind men. We have considered the leper's brief prayer, "Lord, if thou wilt thou canst make me clean" [Matt. 8:2]. The blind men are quite as terse and as direct in their supplications. They cried and said, "Thou Son of David, have mercy on us!" How the right prayer rises from the heart when it is in its own proper mood. Let the *heart* grapple with the great problems of life and destiny. Snub your impertinent intellect when it undertakes to deal with the universe; let the *heart* have full swing. "With the heart man believeth unto righteousness" [Rom. 10:10]. With the intellect he may believe unto temporary conviction, but with the heart he believes unto righteousness, completeness of sympathy, and reality and joyousness of religious obedience.

Wonderful is this way of putting the case on the part of the blind men. They said, "Have *mercy* on us!" The heart never said, "Be *just* to us"; the heart has no weights, and scales, and standards, and tapes of measurement. No broken-hearted sufferer ever came to Christ and said, "Be *just* to me." That is a most remarkable circumstance in the development of human necessity and in the utterance of human need. The blind men might have said, "We have heard that you have cured a *leper*; now be impartial in your administration of the affairs of the universe; deal with an equal hand; if you have cured *one man*, you ought to cure *another*; we will charge you with *partiality* if you do not cure us as you have cured the leper, and raised the ruler's dead child, and healed the woman who touched the hem of your garment. Be *just* to us." The cry is still for mercy. We must come to Christ not with claims but with prayers.

This reference to mercy is a *religious* reference. It goes back to the roots and causes of things. Blindness is a symptom—the disease is in the heart. Lameness, deafness, paralysis—these are accidents, attendant phenomena, mere symptoms of something within, and you may as well repair your roof in order to heal your sick child as you may attend to some outward symptom to heal the life. There is but one cure; the blood of Jesus Christ, God's Son, cleanses from all sin [1 John 1:7]. You must be born again [John 3:7]. The work is inward, vital, complete. Do not fret your energy and waste your time by attempting to deal with symptoms, but get to the root and cause of the fatal malady. Blindness is the symptom, sin is the disease; there is only one disease, and its bad name is—sin. When sin is destroyed, health will be reestablished and sadness will vanish like the last night, taking with it all its blackness, and dampness, and misery.

Those men were not as blind as they looked. They were blind in the *body*, but their eyes *within* were bright as lamps, keen, piercing, far-seeing; they had the *vision of faith*. There is no other vision that will last a man's lifetime; that vision sees in the dark, sees through mountains, pierces the screen of night—it is the true vision. Those blind men had seen Christ a long time with the vision of their hearts. There is an unconscious preparation for great events; those great events seem to come to us suddenly, but in reality they are the culmination of long and subtle processes. One ought to have overheard them talking about the new man, the great Healer, the King of men. How they discussed together their manner of approach, what they would say to him, how they would bring the case under his notice, how they corrected one another as to their views and estimates of the yet unknown Healer, how Jesus Christ came suddenly—for he always comes suddenly, though he has been ten thousand ages on the way; when we hear the crush of his chariot wheel, it will startle us like thunder at midnight. They went forward, and probably did not say one word of all they had prepared. The heart must be extemporaneous in its utterances, the heart cannot have its little piece of paper or string of parchment; a thousand preparations will be made for Christ, and yet when he does come the heart will answer him spontaneously, and there is a spontaneity that is better than the most elaborate preparation.

Now let us hear Christ himself upon the subject: "Then touched he their eyes, saying, According to your faith be it unto you." We find the vessel, he finds its heavenly contents. If we have no vessel, we cannot catch the rain; if we have no goblet of faith, we cannot catch the wine of grace. We must be cooperative in this matter; there is a human side as well as a side divine in all this great mystery of human healing and human growth. Jesus Christ, as we have often had occasion to point out, gave people the impression that they had cured themselves. I have never seen Jesus Christ put the crown upon genius, beauty, power, but I have been present on a thousand coronations, when he encircled the brows of modesty with the choicest garlands of heaven.

There is a great law here, which the Church would do well to ponder. It is the law which expresses the solemn and gracious fact that *our faith is the measure of our progress in divine things*. If the healing had not been wrought in the case of these blind men, the fault would have been with the men themselves. This is the true reading of our Savior's word, namely, "According to your faith, be it unto you." If your faith is equal to the occasion, you shall have what you need; if your faith fall below the occasion, you will be as blind as ever. You may touch the right Christ, but if you touch him with a cold hand, you will receive nothing in return. Not only must we go to the right altar, we must go in the right spirit. The true spirit is shown in the conduct of the woman—"If

I may but touch his garment I shall be whole." How is it that the Church is not succeeding today? Because the Church has intelligence, but not faith. How is it that the Church is empty today, and Christ forsaken? Because his Church has taken to argument, analysis, metaphysical disquisition, controversial statement, high and dry systematic divinity, and has lost faith. Why is this the devil's carnival, why is this the saturnalia of the pit? Because we, as a Church, are clever, but not inspired. We have taken to reckoning religion, and laying a line upon it, and dividing it into fragments and sections; we have taken to a species of religious architecture, giving elevations, and side views, and sections, and detailed drawings, as if the Church were a trick in masonry instead of a glowing and living faith.

The Church will always go down in proportion as its faith declines. For God's sake do not be clever—have faith in God. Lord, increase our faith [Luke 17:5]! If ye had faith as a grain of mustard-seed, ye would say to this mountain, "Depart," and the mountain would, so to say, take to its feet and move off [see Matt. 17:3]. We now have *theories* of inspiration, *theories* of the atonement, *theories* of justification by faith. Do you mean to tell me that Christ's great work for the human family requires a volume of five hundred pages to make it clear? Then is the salvation of the world impossible. The atonement is a flash of the mind, a passion of the heart, one transient glimpse of an infinite tragedy, one touch of hot heart-blood. It is not a five-hundred-page octavo in which theology perpetrates its miserable deceiving, and creates night for the satisfaction of throwing up rockets in its face. Lord, increase our faith! Take us away from the so-called fact-world, with its misnamed realities, and lead us into the invisible temple, the hidden sanctuary, the house in the clouds, and show us there thy grace; then send us down all the mountain steep to find the epileptics and heal them, the blind and give them sight, the deaf and give them hearing. The Church will one day take its cleverness up to some Moriah, draw its glittering knife and slay the enemy, and then the Church will put on her beautiful garments, and neither be ashamed of the mystery of faith nor of the obedience of love.

"And Jesus straitly charged them, saying, See that no man know it." Mark the wisdom of this arrangement. Whatever is done to a mere individual, or to an individual merely as such, is not worth talking about. You have had your eyes opened; that is of no consequence to the universe; do not speak about that. Do not talk with a provincial accent; speak the universal language. If your heart has been blest, tell us; if your skin has been cleansed or your ears have been unstopped, keep the little news to yourself. Jesus Christ was not a mere miracle-monger, Jesus Christ was not a creator of little anecdotes, Jesus Christ was himself the gospel. Jesus Christ never said about the *beatitudes,* "See that ye tell no man." When he said, "Blessed are the poor in spirit, for theirs is the kingdom of Heaven," he did not add, "See that ye tell no man." Blessed are the pure in heart, for they shall see God—see that ye tell no man." Keep your individual romances to yourself; they are not worth talking about; if you have a *gospel,* "go ye into all the world and preach the gospel to every creature" [Mark 16:15].

Understand the difference between a miracle and a gospel, and you will understand how it was that Jesus Christ never cared about his miracles being talked about, but when he came to his gospel, the earth was too small a stage and time too mean a theater in which to declare the infinite love and bid the universe hear. The gospel is the common speech of the race. Mere eye-opening or unstopping of the ear is a case that may occur here and there; the symptom is personal and the circumstances are narrow, but the healing of the heart is a matter in which the whole race is interested. The whole head is sick and the whole heart is faint. If you can find a man who can cleanse us and make us pure and happy, tell us his name. Talk of individual cases to individual sufferers, but speak the universal language to the universal heart.

twelve

CHRIST MUST BE ACCOUNTED FOR

Matthew 9:32–35

YOU WILL find a fuller account of the same matter in the Gospel according to Mark 3:22–30:

> And the Scribes which came down from Jerusalem said, He hath Beelzebub, and by the prince of the devils casteth he out devils.
>
> And he called them unto him, and said unto them, in parables, How can Satan cast out Satan?
>
> And if a kingdom be divided against itself, that kingdom cannot stand.
>
> And if a house be divided against itself, that house cannot stand.
>
> And if Satan rise up against himself and be divided, he cannot stand, but hath an end.
>
> No man can enter into a strong man's house and spoil his goods, except he first bind the strong man, and then he will spoil his house.
>
> Verily I say unto you, All sins shall be forgiven unto the sons of men, and blasphemies wherewith soever they shall blaspheme.
>
> But he that shall blaspheme against the Holy Ghost hath never forgiveness, but is in danger of eternal damnation.
>
> Because they said, He hath an unclean spirit.

You will see from these words that Christianity has to be *accounted for.* Men must have some opinion about its origin and about its i   ration, and concerning its whole scope and purpose. Christianity in is not to be accounted for so much as is Christ himself. There is a time in the life of every considerable man when his friends begin to wonder how he came to be what he is, and that which constitutes a common theme of inquiry amongst ourselves reaches its very highest point of intensity and significance in the case of Jesus Christ, the Son of Man. Do nothing in the world, and nobody will care who you are or from where you came. You will not be a figure, you will not be a force in society, you do not start any impulses that move other men, you throw no new lights upon the path of life, there never comes into your voice a startling tone; nobody cares, therefore, who you are and where you came from, it is a point of concern to no one to account for you, simply because there is nothing to be accounted for. But challenge the thinking of the time, put truth in new phases and aspects before the intellect of the age, startle the world by challenging its ancient orthodoxies and its most accredited traditions and prejudices, then perhaps people may begin to say, "Who are you? By what authority doest thou these things?" [Matt. 21:23; cf. Mark 11:28; Luke 20:2].

These questions arose continually in connection with Jesus Christ. "Who is he? Is he not the son of Mary and of Joseph? Are not his brethren and his sisters with us? From where has this Man this wisdom and these mighty works? From where do they come?" Thus Jesus became the problem of his age. He is the problem of all time; he is the secret and the terror of human history; he is the hope and the light of human prophecy, and today men wonder who he is; they reject his claims, and they call him back to ask him further questions. It is, therefore, not so much Christianity that has to be accounted for as Christ Himself, for in very deed—Christ is Christianity, Christ is the gospel. This is a matter of personality, not of abstraction or of metaphysics.

Now there have been various accounts given of Christ, and we have one of these accounts in the text. Ask *worldliness* what it has to say about Christ and Christianity. The answer will be, "No doubt Christ is a very good man; probably a little fanatical in his methods, with very fine theories, and if they could be carried out it would be a good thing for the world, but we cannot carry them out, they are too fine-spun. No doubt he was a good man, and we have nothing to say against him"; and worldliness passes on, to add another window to its shop and another acre to its estates. Compliment is faint praise: there is no sting or viciousness in it; it is good so far as it goes.

Ask mere *intellectualism* to account for Christ. "A myth, a fable, a dream, a poem—not without fascination, often glittering in its sparks of happy suggestion, but a myth, a conception of the mind, a piece of beautiful patchwork. If we cared to go into its discrepancies we could upset the historic credibility of the whole, but we are content to say, a myth, and to pass on."

Ask *prejudice* to account for Christ and his work. The bad answer is in the text, "He casteth out devils through the prince of the devils."

Note the difference in those replies. Worldliness, engaged in its occupations, its brain in the whirl and rush of money-making and business and enterprise, says, "No doubt Jesus Christ was a very good man; we have no fault to find with him, but we have no time to go into all his claims and to settle his place in history." Cold intellectualism says, "Fable, fantasy, myth—very good in its way, nothing more." Prejudice, with low brow and muffled face, with a mien that indicates everything that can degrade human grandeur, says, "He casts out devils by the prince of the devils. He is in league with Beelzebub, and educated in Satanic tricks."

Now observe, every one of those theories has its own peculiar difficulties. The worldly man finds a character in history that stands back from his policies and programs, that says, "Labor not for the meat which perisheth. A man's life consisteth not in the abundance of the things that he possesseth. Take no thought for the morrow, for the morrow shall take thought for the things of itself. Have your treasure in heaven, where neither moth nor rust corrupteth, and where thieves do not break through nor steal" [see Matt. 6:20]; and worldliness can only say, "Very good; a fine theory, but impracticable." Still, there stands a man that said these things and that lived them: he is not put down by a compliment, neither is he shattered by an assault. Today his holy gospel lifts its sweet and serene voice amid all the tumult of conflicting teachings, and says, "Your life is *within* you: *be*, rather than merely *have*: live in God—seek first the kingdom of God and his righteousness, and all these things shall be added unto you" [Matt. 6:33]; and worldliness with its little shallow compliment, does not account for, with any adequacy of explanation, the moral grandeur of the man who kept the world under his feet and his heart in the very heaven of God.

And the cold intellect leaves the Christ just where it found him. The intellectual has to account for a man who was *dreamed* into being. Then the dreamer must himself be equal to the man he dreamed. You have to account for a man born in the imagination of some other man, and who, as a creature of imagination, has risen to the supreme place in human history, and who today rules innumerable millions of human lives and ministries and destinies. It is easy to call him and his work mythical, romantic, fabulous, but that does not account for the profound moral influence, the beneficent results, and the whole ministry that is represented by the term—Christ, or by the phrase—the Christian Church.

But what shall we say about the answer of prejudice? What *is* prejudice—who can define it? How it spoils our life, how it takes the bloom off the finest fruits that grow in the garden of human fellowship. Once let prejudice occupy your mind, and the object of that prejudice can never be good, or seem good, or do good, or think good. He may do the noblest works ever done by human energy, but you will not allow him to be crowned because he has accomplished them; yea, he may serve you and your family night and day, but you will find the devil in his prayers, selfishness in his benevolence, and his very light shall be darkness, and all his meaning shall be a piece of self-idolatry. Beware of prejudice. We can answer an argument, we can rebut a charge, but who can find out the root and the issue of irrational and vicious prejudice? There are some men who never can do right in our estimation. They may be gifted with genius, their character may be above suspicion, and all their work may be of a high type, but we hate them, and therefore, when we are called upon to explain their influence or to account for their character, we are willing to accredit the devil with the whole rather than to speak one just word about the man we detest.

Beware of prejudice: it enters the mind very subtly, and once in the mind, it is the most difficult of all its occupants and rulers to dislodge. It is irrational, you cannot get hold of it, it has no center, it acknowledges no court of appeal, it is invisible. It was from such prejudice that Jesus Christ suffered. When the Pharisees and the Scribes and the most religious men of the day heard the dumb speaking and were made aware that the deaf could hear and the lame could walk and could see all the good works done by Christ and his disciples, they were willing rather to praise the devil than to praise him.

See to what degradation prejudice may drag you; and we are all exposed to the influence of prejudice. Beware of it, it is the worst of the devils, it skulks, it sneaks, it watches in silence, it drops its poison into the cup when nobody is looking. It is the biggest of thieves, it is the most noted of liars, it is the most persistent of persecutors, and yet all the time it can cause those who are its subjects upon the largest scale to *disown* it. Have we not all heard men who were known to be all but filled with prejudice declare, with a serene innocence, that they were perfectly sure that they were not at all animated by prejudice? It is a horrible devil, it swears and breaks its oath, it will kiss any Bible, and burn the book it kissed, and put the oath into the fire, that they may both go to the same hot ashes. Are there not some men you so bitterly dislike that they can do nothing good in your sight? It was from prejudice that Christ suffered.

Now I want to turn and to consider Christ's answer to this prejudice. The answer was *argumentative*. Having heard what the Scribes which came down from Jerusalem said, he called them unto him, and said unto them in parables, "How can Satan cast out Satan? And if a kingdom be divided against itself that kingdom cannot stand, and if a house be divided against itself that house cannot stand, and if Satan rise up against himself and be divided he cannot stand, but hath an end." That was an argumentative reply. Christianity has an argumentative answer to every assault. Christianity can fight for its position with any weapons that an enemy may choose. Did you ever know a case of anything so absurd as this? The Scribes thought they had answered the whole case by referring it to a diabolic origin. Jesus said, "How can Satan cast out Satan? And if a kingdom be divided against itself that kingdom cannot stand, and if a house be divided against itself that house cannot stand."

I ask you to look at that answer in the light of argument, and tell me if it could be improved in its logical construction and force. He confounded the enemy out of his own mouth. He took the sword from the enemy and thrust it into the enemy's own heart. That is what Christianity can always do. I have heard all the arguments that can be addressed against Christianity, and I have never heard one that could not be triumphantly answered and repelled. This is a specimen of the answers that can be given: it gleams with wit, it strikes like a spear, it burns like a fire. There is no reply possible to that argument. How can Satan cast out Satan? If Satan be divided against himself he cannot stand, if a house be divided against itself it cannot stand, if a man be divided against himself he cannot stand. Division is destruction.

Consider, therefore, that Jesus Christ's answer was, in the first place, distinctly and broadly argumentative. In the next place it was *judicial*. Jesus Christ did not stop at the argumentative; having shown his adversaries how their logic limped, and how their accounting for his supremacy was not only a lie but an absurdity, he said, "Verily, assuredly, I say unto you, all sins shall be forgiven unto the sons of men, and blasphemies wherewith soever they shall blaspheme, but he that shall blaspheme against the Holy Ghost hath never forgiveness, but is in danger of eternal damnation," because they said, "He hath an unclean spirit." Christianity is something more than an argumentative contest. This is not a question of whether one point is fifty miles distant from another point, it is a question that involves moral issues, tremendous outgoings, it involves the whole question of personal and universal destiny. In the first part of his answer the tone of Christ was light, trenchant bright, as became a merely argumentative retort. Suddenly that voice, bright as all the lights of heaven, sobered and broadened into thunder as he said, "This is the kind of sin that never can be forgiven." When you come with these Christian questions you do not come into an exercise of merely intellectual gymnastics; this is not a question of one man being more clever than another in the use of mere words, it is not a clash of wooden swords, it is a question of life or death. The Scribes thought they had given an answer sufficient in its contemptuousness when they referred Christ and his miracles to the devil. They knew little about all they were doing: they were writing on heaven's own scroll their own unpardonableness.

Take care how you treat the Bible, the altar, the Church. Words of contempt may easily rise to your lips, but they may mean more than you intend them to mean. You throw a little pebble into the broad lake: you thought it would go straight down and be seen no more. So far you may be right, but the circles are on the surface, and they vibrate and widen and multiply and make the whole lake throb, and who can tell what may come out of a contemptuous criticism of Jesus Christ and his ministry? Beware of clever blasphemers, of those little agile blasphemers who make atheism an easy trick in words, and get rid of the universe and its mysteries by the nod of an empty head. There are moral issues, there are judicial penalties, there are certain ungovernable recoils. A man is not done with his words merely when he has uttered them; they go away from him and are judged and sent back again upon his life, angels that bless him, or shadows that turn his day into night. We have known this in countless instances. The men themselves have not always been able to explain the mystery, but find out men who are suffering in various ways, not always to be set forth in express words, and it is not impossible, if you trace their history sufficiently back, but that you may find that these practical bitternesses, these black harvests, are the results of early blasphemies or profanities of the heart. Understand, therefore, that the blatant atheist who sells his atheism and pronounces its first little syllable with a vicious emphasis, does not always see or feel at the moment the result of his blasphemies.

Jesus Christ is not short-coming in the matter of his forgiveness, but there is a point at which his pardons are themselves shut out. Say he has an unclean spirit, and you extinguish the sun that makes every day and creates every summer, and having put out the fountain of light, there is no more brightness possible. Consider, therefore, that Jesus Christ's answer was, in the second place, strictly and solemnly judicial. That reply was more than either argumentative or judicial—it was, in the third place, *practical*. The proof of that you will find in the thirty-fifth verse. "And Jesus went about all the cities and villages teaching in their synagogues, and preaching the gospel of the kingdom, and healing every sickness and every disease among the people." That is the way to answer your enemies: keep on with your work; any fool can resign, it requires no genius and no heroism to give up the pulpit, or to withdraw from the Church, or to throw up what is called vulgarly "the whole thing." Jesus Christ did not do that; he was sometimes driven out, but he would not be driven out till the first great thunder drops of the storm were splashing on the pavement whose dust had rejected him. Then he said, "O Jerusalem, Jerusalem, how often would I have gathered thee as a hen doth gather her brood under her wings, and ye would not, but now your house is left unto you desolate" [Luke 13:34, 35], and a great hollow wind roared through the metropolitan streets, and great blotches of black rain feel from the thunderous clouds, and the lightning looked from every point, and Jerusalem was being swallowed up. Blessed One—they told him that he was in league with the devil, and he answered them in witty argument, visited them with judicial penalty—and then went about doing good, went to all the cities and villages, teaching in their synagogues, and preaching the gospel of the kingdom, and healing every sickness and every disease among the people. Let that always be your reply to every wicked assault. They said, "He hath a devil"; he went about teaching, preaching, and healing. Beneficent in reply, sharper than wit, more intelligible than judgment. He made life, if possible more a sacrifice than ever. And who am I that I should resign, when Jesus, my Savior, might have resigned his care over me everyday since I first knew him? I have wounded his right hand and his left, and both his feet, I have thrust a spear into his side, and crushed the thorns into his temples, and I have done it everyday, and still he will not give me up. He lets the lifted thunder drop; he pursues me still. Who am I, then, that I because of some rude offense or incivility on the part of man, should run away from the altar and the work and the cross? I have not yet resisted unto blood, striving against any sin, or writhing under any insult. "Let us, then, run with patience the race set before us, looking unto Jesus, the Author and Finisher of our faith, who for the joy that was set before him endured the cross, despising the shame, scorning it with a divine heroism, and making it ashamed of itself" [see Heb. 12:1, 2].

So, then, we stand on rocky foundations. My house is not built upon a gilded cloud; I stand beside Christ, I love Christ, I know whom I have believed. He has been more insulted than any teacher; Pythagoras would have dismissed his school, Socrates would have run away from his mean pupils and vicious critics; this man never gave a lesson without having every word of it turned into a stone and thrown back into his own teeth, and still he teaches on. He was despised and rejected of men, but he shall one day be the desire of all nations. He was a root out of a dry ground, but one day he will be to the world as the Flower of Jesse and the Plant of Renown. He can wait. Falsehood is in a hurry; it may be at any moment detected and punished; truth is calm, serene, its judgment is on high, its King cometh out of the chambers of eternity.

thirteen

CHRIST'S VIEW OF
THE WORLD

Matthew 9:36–38

WHEN WE READ that he was moved with compassion, we feel that it did not require *much* to move the pity of such a heart. It was not moved now for the first time. Again and again as we come along the line of the sacred narrative we have seen his tears, we have heard the piteousness of many of his tones, and have been touched by the pathos of many of his deeds. The key-word of this divine life is—*compassion.* If you do not seize that word in its true meaning, the life of Jesus Christ will be to you little more than either a romantic surprise or a dead letter. It is not a life of genius, it is not a display of literary power, it is preeminently, yet inclusively, a life of love, a history of compassion, an exemplification of the tenderest aspects of the infinite mercy of God. Begin at that point and read the history in that light, and you will see the right proportion of things and their right color, and you will hear their sweetest and richest music. Again and again, therefore, would I repeat, the master-word of this divine life is the sweet and all-inclusive word—COMPASSION.

Observe what the word means. It means "feeling *with,*" "feeling *for,*" sympathy, a right view of human need and human distress, and a taking upon oneself all the pain, the feebleness, the poverty, and the anguish of those who suffer most. He bare our sins, he carried our iniquities, and himself took our infirmities and sustained our afflictions. You have been reading the life of Christ as if he were one of twenty men, leaders of human thought; we have lectured upon him as if he belonged to a gallery of heroes. Therein have we done him injustice, and therein, too, have we done ourselves injustice, for we have not viewed the great occasion from the right standpoint; therefore have we missed its majesty,

93

its perspective, its subtlest relations, and its deepest significance. He is not one of many, he is many in one. Therein is that singular utterance most true—he is All in All—multitudinous Man, as great a host as the throng on which he looked; they were detailed humanity, he was our totalized nature. He felt every pang, he responded to every emotion. He is not a priest that cannot be touched with the feeling of our infirmities, he knows us through and through, and he is every one of us, because he is the Son of Man.

"When he saw the multitudes." Let us lay the emphasis upon the last word for a moment, for it will enable us to seize a new meaning and occupy a novel standpoint. When he saw the multitudes he was moved with compassion; when we see the multitudes we are moved with *wonder* or with *admiration*. See if that be not so in matter as well as in humanity. When I see multitudinous matter, a mountain, I am moved with surprise, my wonder arises; I call attention to the infinite mass, and we stand before it with wide-open eyes, and the whole posture is one of amazement. We are awestruck that the rubbish should be so infinite, for it is only rubbish—the greatest mountain in Europe; no man of you would care for any spadeful of it, no man would be touched by any ten feet of it, no man would go fifty yards to see twenty feet of it; it is when it multiplies itself, foot on foot, pile on pile, mile on mile, until it cools itself in snow, high up in the rarefied air—then we run excursion trains to look at it, then we build villas near it and gaze on it with admiration, then we write about it in the public journals; it acquires fame by its *vastness*, not by intrinsic and detailed value, but by hugeness, by what we should term, in relation to human throngs, multitudinousness.

Now when Jesus saw the multitudes he was not moved with wonder, which is a partial emotion, or with admiration, which is an incomplete and babyish feeling. He was moved with *compassion*, and therein He differed from every other observer of great things. We know what it is to look at great things ourselves. If you see *one soldier*, you care but little for the sight; you may point out the intensity of the color which he displays, or the splendor of his metal, but one passing remark will suffice for that occasion. You see *an army*, and you are filled with wonder, admiration, delight; it brings to you a sense of power, grandeur, and grandeur never touches compassion, it seems rather to rebuke it. If I see a mighty throng of men, the very last feeling that would come into my heart as an observer would be a feeling of compassion. Multitudinousness means power; multitudinousness means greatness, resource, all kinds of energy, amplitude of strength. Who dare pity a multitude? It could overpower you, run you down, trample you to death — why *pity* it? Pity yourself, little creature, run away from the ever-multiplying throng that marches with the strength of an army and with the pomp of a nation.

Yet here is a man who looks upon a multitude and his heart is filled with pity. He did not say, "How great, what force, what wondrous resources of genius, and strength, and money, and power of every degree!" His heart filled with tears; he said, "It is a sad sight." If he could have taken any other view of the multitude he never would have been the Savior of the world. There you see the meaning of his life: it touches you now. This must end in fainting or in sacrifice, must terminate in shrinking from the infinite task, or in heroic conquest in the infinite tragedy.

Those tears have great meaning; those larger emotions than any we have yet seen have a remote and infinite significance. If he had been touched with wonder only he would have failed, if he had been moved with admiration he would have lost his power, but, moved with compassion, he includes every other worthy emotion, and sets himself in a right relation to his task. Nothing but *compassion* will carry you through any tragedy in life; you cannot go through it merely for its own sake. The *hireling* will fall asleep over the sick child, but the *mother* will drive sleep away from her dwelling-place till she has rescued her little one from the power of the enemy, if it be within the scope of her endurance and skill to win so great a triumph. Her compassion keeps her awake, her love makes the night as the day, her pity stops the clock, so that she takes no note of time. Every other emotion grows dumb; wonder must sometimes close its eyes, admiration falls upon itself, sates its appetite and dies of the satiety, but compassion grows by what it feeds on, and is of the very nature of the love of God. He grows in the development of his compassion; he will succeed yet. Beaten back at a hundred points, he will yet win. He shall see of the travail of his soul, which is really but another word for compassion, and shall be satisfied.

It does us good to come into contact with a teacher who sees the whole of his case. We are cursed by partial views. We elect twelve men to judge a case that we may bring twelve different minds to bear upon it and a twelve-fold power to grasp it fully. We have to multiply ourselves when we would be great; Jesus Christ always saw the end from the beginning, the entire situation, took the comprehensive view, excluded no aspect of the case with which he had to heal. As judges, we are ruined by our partial cleverness; if we could see more we should feel more and do more.

Take a view of a Christian congregation. What lovelier sight can the earth present? Many men, women, children, gathered together in one house sanctified to the highest uses, sweet hymn, noble psalm, penetrating, triumphant anthem, rich and tender prayer, reading of the divine word, exposition of the holy mysteries, exhortation, explanation poured from a loving heart and from an eloquent tongue, the spirit of peace in the house—what nobler sight is there upon the earth? I look upon it, and say, "All is well; the old earth is renewing its youth, and all is bright in prospect." Am I right? I am as far wrong as I can well be within such limits; I am deceived by appearances. I may be right as to the mere literal facts of the occasion, within the four walls of any Christian building; I have only to look outside the window, and I see that in this great metropolis today the majority of men are not in the house of God, nor do they care for its worship and service. You have only to go off the broad thoroughfare, and look down certain passages and openings on the side ways, to see festering humanity, children that were never taught to clasp their little hands in prayer, houses in which there is no word of God, men imbruted, women stripped of their divinity, and the whole human name muddied, cursed, degraded into what is practically perdition. Jesus Christ would not take the view presented by any Christian congregation only, he would see the congregation within and the multitude without; he would take in the whole situation, and seeing it, his tears would drop from our hymns, and great heart-breaking agony would mingle with our broadest and most hopeful prayers.

There are men who take partial views and come to partial and, therefore, erroneous conclusions about everything. There are those who seat themselves within some vernal enclosure or summer paradise, and say, with a foolish chuckle, that the earth is not so bad a place after all. They see a bed of blooming flowers, fiery-hued or gentle-tinted, and they hear birds in the branches twittering, trilling, singing, and making melody in their hearts, and they say the earth is a very lovely place, notwithstanding what all the naysayers say to the contrary. Now observe how they confound the partial term with the larger word. They see a *garden* and then speak of the *earth*, they see a bed of geraniums and then speak of the globe; there is no balance in their sentences, their words do not correspond with one another at both ends of their declarations. The garden is beautiful, the flowers are lovely beyond all that it is possible for the coloring of human heart fully to represent. The painter paints the *form*, but he cannot touch the *fragrance*. We admire their poetical sympathy within given limits, but go beyond the garden wall, go into the rough streets, go into the desolate places, take in the wilderness, throw the line around the entirety, bring the whole elements within your view, and then say what it is. The angel sees it, and says, "Mourning and lamentation and woe." Jesus sees it and cannot cease his prayer, Jesus looks upon it and is moved with compassion. Do not shut yourselves within your churches and say, "All is well"; do not shut the garden door and rejoice upon the verdant lawn and under the drooping tree, and say, "This is paradise regained." See every point of beauty, be thankful for every mercy given to you of the divine providence, but always endeavor to take in not a roof but a sky, not a circumference drawn by human compasses, but a horizon that required the sweep of the divine arm to form it, and when you see the entire scene you will be moved with compassion.

"But when he saw the multitudes he was moved with compassion because they fainted"—literally because they were vexed, and disturbed, and fretted, and chafed—as sheep when the wolf comes into the fold. They hear his panting, they see his eye of fire and his pitiless teeth, and they hear him as he prowls and snuffs and throbs in his cruel desire and design. Jesus not only saw the *sheep*, he saw the *wolf*; he not only sees humanity, he sees the devil and his angels, he sees how we are vexed, fretted, torn, disturbed, frightened by ten thousand black spirits that darken the day, and through whose black wings the hot sun can scarcely dart one living beam. He sees men, devils, angels, earth, heaven, and while the whole thing sums itself up before his comprehensive and penetrating vision his eyes darken with tears.

He noted that the people were as sheep having no shepherd [Matt. 9:36]. This figure of shepherdliness is most beautiful. He himself had the shepherdly heart. He is called the Good Shepherd: he knows his sheep, and many sheep he has that are not of this fold. He lays down his life for the sheep. The hireling flees because he is a hireling and cares not for the sheep. All these figures by which Jesus represents himself are figures of tenderness, sympathy, sometimes of weakness, by way of accommodation to our human infirmities. He could blow the trumpet of thunder, and stand upon the platform of the wind and roar with the tempest blowing from every point of the compass in one fierce blast, but he sees that would overpower and frighten them, so he speaks in a still small voice, thunder reduced to a whisper, and therefore not an utterance of feebleness, but a sigh of suppressed and condensed power. He is the gentle Shepherd, the good Shepherd [John 10:11, 14]. He made himself of no reputation [Phil. 2:7], he took up our forms of endearment and service and our whole nomenclature of fellowship, sympathy, and love, and he made his tabernacle in our little words, giving them infinite enlargement according to his own purpose and motive. Observe how he comes from the multitude to the shepherd, from the many to the one. It is possible to have one man who can rule and guide and bless a countless host. I am longing for that one Man; I would speak with him a long while. He would be my preacher, my teacher; he would understand me wholly, and would speak to me in great breadths of knowledge and sympathy, and if I had any bitter shameful tale to tell, I could tell him every word of it, and he would answer me in gospels and not in condemnation. Any wolf can bite, any bigot can judge and condemn, any little detestable Pharisee can sit upon the judgment-seat and pronounce upon men whose shoe-latchet he is not worthy to unloose. It takes the great Christ and the Christly heart to judge with large judgment. Show me a man that can take in the large view, who knows all the languages of the heart, all the emotions of the wondrous human spirit, and he shall teach me and shepherd me, and I will fall asleep upon his breast: I will ask no better environment on earth than his strong and tender arm. Save me from the bigot, the literalist, the sectarian, the mean soul, and if ye know where the shepherd is show me his dwelling-place, and he will make my heart bright and young with a new hope.

"Then saith he to his disciples, the harvest truly is plenteous, the laborers are few." The figure changes. He has been speaking about a shepherd, and now he speaks about laborers. He has been speaking about a fold of sheep, and now he speaks about a harvest-field, and he speaks about both in the same breath. We are punctilious about the consistency of our figures; we dare not risk our reputation by the use of a mixed metaphor; no man dare utter these words as if they were his own. He would be heard of again, he would be laughed at by the last boy that left the school, he would be left by men who may have their weaknesses if you could only find them, but who could never by any possibility perpetrate the unutterable crime of uttering a mixed metaphor.

Both the figures are right: never mind about their juxtaposition. The world is a great sheepfold and a great harvest field: it is both; it wants shepherds, wants laborers, wants compassion, wants attention. This is the great view of the great Christ; he saw the whole occasion, and saw the figures that were appropriate to it. So we can come into the text when we please. If Jesus Christ had compassion on us, ought we not to have compassion on ourselves? Is it a time for us to be flattering our heart and saying "It is all right" when Jesus Christ is crying great, bitter, hot tears? If he is uneasy for us, even to the point of agony, is it a time for us to be lying on a soft couch and to be saying "All is well"? I would rather take his view of my life than I would take my own.

And then, again, some of us are fit for bringing into the garner. I have come to seek you today as one of the laborers of God. You must not stand out there too long. Already you are golden, mellow, ripened corn, and we now want to take you into the garner—will you come? This is a harvest that cannot be cut down against its own will, and garnered against its own consent. It is a great mystery, and the mystery is larger than the figure, the figure only helping us to a very partial treatment of the mystery. You may be fifty years of age, and you have been out long enough; you may be seventy years of age, and we want to bring you into the garner this very morning. You have ripened and ripened; there is a point after which you will rot and rot. With all the love of my heart—no love at all compared with the love of Christ—I would ask those of you who are yet outside the fold to hear the shepherd's voice bidding you come in, and ask those of you who are as mellow corn bowing your heads under the blessing of the summer breeze, or the autumnal wind, to allow yourselves to be garnered in the church and heart of God.

fourteen

THE MISSIONARY CHARGE

Matthew 10:1-4

A LIGHT will be thrown upon the first verse of the tenth chapter by recalling the last verse of the ninth. "Pray ye, therefore, the Lord of the harvest, that he will send forth laborers into his harvest." Is this sentimental? Does the Lord call men only to prayer, or has he some ulterior purpose? Does he encourage them by first asking them to pray, and then when they have prayed themselves into white heat of soul, does he name the practical purpose which he had in view at the beginning? Who could bear to hear all his destiny at once? Who would like to have his destiny thrust upon him with abruptness and suddenness, like the shock of an unexpected thunderstorm? Who would not rather be gently and gradually prepared? This is the infinite statesmanship of Christ. He tells the disciples to *pray* for laborers. A lame remedy, you say, for the tremendous disease. Wait awhile: when they have *prayed* well they shall *work* well. When they have prayed for laborers it shall be revealed to them that *they themselves* are the laborers! Revelations come to men in prayer; while they are praying about others, God suddenly says, "*You* are the men—GO." That is the solution of ten thousand church difficulties. I have heard a rich man pray that God would be gracious to the poor, and when he was done I have said, "Answer your own prayer." So a man shall pray that the Church be revived, and God says, "Begin in your own heart." Others, again, are praying night and day that God would send forth laborers into his harvest, not knowing that God's plan is that when a man can pray most that laborers may be sent, he himself should herald the way and be the evangelist of heaven.

If this could be brought to bear upon us in all the compass of its meaning and in all the force of its moral purpose, we should have preachers enough, and great ones and astounding ones, and the question would run from camp to camp, "Is Saul also among the prophets?" Think of wise men, men of great capacity and considerable education, meeting together in solemn committee for the purpose of inquiring whether they cannot engage a number of all but incapable persons at eighty pounds a year! I would that some stern, strong man could break in upon their ungodly seclusion, and tell them to rise and go *themselves* and preach this kingdom.

Wondrous is the wisdom of this carpenter's son. First, he is touched with compassion when he sees the multitudes; then he calls the attention of his disciples to the destitute condition of the innumerable throngs; then he says, "The harvest truly is plenteous, but the laborers are few." He is now in his sympathetic mood; his tones have a strange melting power in them; he adds, as he only could add, "Pray ye, therefore, the Lord of the harvest, that he will send forth laborers into his harvest"; and the men prayed, and as they prayed their faces shone, and strange impulses moved their strength; and when they had marked the culmination of their prayers, he called them to him and said, "Go *ye*." He bids us add the "Amen" to our own prayers, he bids us carry out our own purposes; when we have wrestled long and strongly at heaven's gate, he says, "Now you are ready; there is fire enough in you; go ye and tell all that I have told you: freely ye have received, freely give" [see Matt. 10:8]. Thus light is cast upon the first verse of the tenth chapter by recalling the tender conclusion of the preceding chapter.

"When he had called unto him his twelve disciples." He was *always* calling these men. At first he called them and said to each, "Follow me." And then he called his twelve disciples again, and again he called unto him his twelve disciples—always calling, always creating, always shaping our manhood to new and noble uses, always enlarging the definition of our sphere and ennobling the destiny of our powers. The call of Christ is not once for all. It is a *daily* interview; the invitation to go nearer to him comes with every sunrise. We have never been so near to Jesus Christ that we cannot be nearer, and the nearer we get the softer is his voice. When we were away, far out on the barren sands, he called unto us as with the blast of a trumpet; then we became more familiar with him, got nearer and nearer to his heart, and he called us to come nearer still, and the nearer we got the less occasion was there for any vocal force on his part, till now he whispers his commands; he breathes upon us with infinitely subdued tenderness his will and purpose—so lowly, so sweetly, he seems almost to be consulting us. The great royal voice that was strong as a command is still the same, though it has dropped into a lower key, and gives us the impression that we are being *consulted!* Strange if such a leader, with such a human ancestry, be but a creature of the dust!

What does he do when they come nearer to him? He gives them *power.* Can any man amend that arrangement? Call twelve men to duty, and you may but mock their weakness and throw them back upon the humiliating consciousness of their inefficiency, but Jesus Christ, when he called the twelve disciples to him, gave them *power.* Strange let me say over and over again, until the refrain itself becomes a kind of argument, that he who was only a peasant and a peasant's son should have had this compass of mind and this marvelous sweep of statesmanlike power of getting men together, organizing them, constituting them, investing them, and giving to them, as in great handfuls, the omnipotence of God!

Not only does he give the disciples power, he gives them *consolation.* This adds a new and beauteous feature to the whole arrangement. We sometimes say, not knowing what we are saying, that if we have a duty to perform the only thing we want is power to do it. That is a narrow and foolish view. Power may be bruised, wounded, baffled, disappointed: sheer, hard, iron strength is not enough; we need encouragement, consolation; we need such reminders of human history as shall embolden us to keep our spirits up, though the wind be high and cold, and all things seem to be set in daily antagonism against us. It is poor living when we are reduced to the dry consciousness of our mere power. When a man can say, "I have power to do this," and works according to his strength, he is tempted into a tone of self-sufficiency, and it may be occasionally a tone of social defiance. But when he knows that he not only has the power to do his duty, but that when he comes back to his Lord and Master, bruised and wounded and quite tired, he will be taken up into the Almighty heart and cheered, and nourished, and encouraged, and blest with the whole baptism of omnipotence; then the tone of defiance is taken out of his voice, and he goes out—if the figure be that of a bird, with duty as its body, power and encouragement as the wings with which it flies.

"He gave them power." There are *flood times* in the progress of the mind; times when men are transported beside and beyond themselves; seasons when we feel equal to the whole occasion of life; periods when we are conscious of such an accession of strength as makes work a pleasure and danger an inspiration. We are all conscious of such times in our life. We say, "Would that these hours would continue, and we should break the mountains in pieces with a threshing instrument of iron having teeth, and should scatter the broken dust upon the mocking wind." Grand hours these of inauguration and coronation, almost of apotheosis. We are lifted up into our deific state, and we set our feet upon all lower things and triumph over them with power not to be measured by human terms. Then we vehemently desire the battle, and are impatient because the trumpet blast that calls us to it is long delayed.

Sometimes God seems to dwell in us as in a tabernacle, which he has specially chosen, and his light gleams out of us to the destruction of all darkness. It is perhaps well that we have not the incessant consciousness of this power, for we might then come to think it was our own. The intermissions of such consciousness may be as much a blessing as is the consciousness itself. It does a man no harm to be speared in the side and to have blood and water let out, or to have the thorn-points crushed into his temples until the blood starts and his life becomes a great agony. These things have deep meanings; their significance is not in the little letter; these are not little rills that run upon the surface—they are waters that come up from the hidden rocks. Our weakness has its lesson as well as our strength—indeed, sometimes we can say, "When I am weak, then am I strong" [2 Cor. 12:10].

"He gave them power." Yet he did not weaken himself. This is the test of original strength. If we have only the oil we have bought we may run short at an unlucky time, and the upshot may be that we are barred out when the bridegroom comes and constitutes his household. "The water that I shall give him," said Christ, "shall be in him a well of living, springing water, and he shall not know when the sun scorches up the streams of the earth. His shall be a perennial flow of divine water" [see John 4:14]. If you have your sermon committed to your memory, and are repeating it like a parrot, and are afraid that you will forget the next paragraph, you are no preacher. If Christ has given you power, the word shall be in you a living, springing water, and it shall flow forth for the refreshment and the cleansing of those who attend your ministry. Take no thought how or what ye shall say. Christianity is not a literary argument, a literary essay, or a forensic success according to human standards and canons;

it is a voice that surprises the speaker himself as much as it ever can surprise the hearer, and the accents are taught for the moment and for the moment's uses.

To give power and yet to retain all you give is the mystery of *originality*. The only natural suggestions that we have of such power, and they, of course, fall infinitely short of the reality, are the sun and the sea. The sun is the same old light that shone upon Eden and warmed its flowers into color and beauty, and today he shines, unshorn of a beam, always giving, never the less luminous. And the great sea takes into it all the rain clouds, and is not conscious of any accession of water, and allows the evaporation to go on continuously; and yet who can say that the sea has shrunk one hair's breadth? These poor emblems help us to understand what is meant by the ever-giving God, never impoverishing himself by what he bestows. Ask, and it shall be given you; bring with you great petitions; do not stint your prayer, for the word is, "Open thy mouth wide, and I will fill it" [Ps. 81:10]. "Ye have not because ye ask not, or because ye ask amiss" [James 4:2, 3].

What has become of the Church's power? I cannot tell. It is partially, almost wholly, lost. The Church is now prudent, self-regarding, self-admiring, self-protecting, trimming her hedges, locking her gates, repairing her walls, talking much within her borders. Where is the old world-shaking power? So far gone down that men mockingly say, "Soon there will be no Church, or there will be a Church without an altar." O for a lamp enkindled by other than human hands! The harvest truly is plenteous, but the laborers are few; the opportunities were never so broad and so grand as they are today; pray, therefore, the Lord of the harvest that he will send forth laborers into his harvest, and while you are praying the revelation may be flashed upon your own mind that *you* have to conclude your prayer by going forth.

Observe *the kind of power* that Jesus Christ gave his disciples. He gave them power against unclean spirits to cast them out, and to heal all manner of sickness and all manner of disease. It was, then, *a power to do good*. When did Jesus Christ send forth any man with a rod, and with a judgment fire, and with destructive force, concerning anything that had in it the least hopefulness of ever being rescued and saved? The Son of man is not come to destroy men's lives, but to save them; the bruised reed he will not break, the smoking flax he will not quench, the little child he will not reject, the creeping, crawling sinner, that waits till the dusk that he may grope his way in the darkness, shall not be turned aside as a coward, but shall be *looked* into a new man. If this was Christ's own purpose, it follows as a matter of consequence that the purpose of the Church must be akin to it. It was a beneficent power. Jesus Christ gave his disciples power to relieve human burdens, human distresses, and to heal all manner of sickness and all manner of disease. He detests their presence; that there should be disease in the creatures he named, that his machinery should have gone wrong, that the joints and valves which he fashioned and connected should have gotten out of gear, that any creature which he made should say, "My head, my head," or "I am weak," or "I am in pain," or "I am in sorrow," — it came not out of the compass of his counsel; an enemy has done this. It is his wish that we should all be well, without headache, or heartache, or broken joint, or poisoned blood, or reeling brain; we should be strong, grand, massive, royal, and if we are otherwise an enemy has done it, and he must be found and slain.

It was power, too, that could be *easily appreciated.* Everybody could test that kind of influence, and the Church must engage itself to this kind of work more and more. The Church should be a hospital, the Church should be a nursery, the Church should be a home of the destitute and a shelter for those who are cast out, the Church should have both hands filled with bread to deal to the hungry; when the Church ceases her more or less impotent and inconclusive *speculations,* and engages herself to this beneficent ministry, the world will soon know that the Son of God has come in deed and in power.

Yet the ability which Jesus Christ gave to the twelve men was strictly *limited.* Men do not understand the whole of their ministry at once. We grow into conceptions of our power and our duty; we begin feebly, externally, we take upon ourselves in the strength of divine grace to fulfill the very smallest occasion, and being faithful in few things, we are afterwards made rulers of many things [Matt. 25:21, 23]. Having kept one city well, we have ten cities handed over to our charge.

The twelve men were not sent forth with any great psychological purpose, to analyze the minds and souls of men and hold high discourse on things recondite and afar from their daily thinking. They were sent forth to do practical work, physical work, work that could be instantly appreciated even by the least enlightened minds. Let us begin where we can: if we cannot preach we can give, if we cannot give we may be able to instruct, if we cannot say much it may be given to our hand to express, in masonry unknown to other men, the sympathy of a fellow feeling.

"The twelve apostles are these." Now look at their names — names that do not stand out in history: with one or two exceptions the most of the men named here were obscure. We cannot all have pedestals; we may be apostles though we may not be famous. The whole twelve are named — but only two or three have any fame that fills the world; the last has an infamy that fills earth and hell; he is always named *last*. There are some names we are *reluctant* to breathe, they are only forced out of us that we may make a literal completeness of a statement. And they were men who had no *other* power. Jesus Christ does not clothe with additional influence men who have already attained a certain height of celebrity and power. It is all his gift: they bring nothing to him, he gives them all. Shall I take my little lamp and say to him, "Lord, this is a lamp of my lighting, if you can add anything to it I shall be pleased"? He will not hear me; he must find the lamp, he must find the fire, he must renew the light; I must live, and move, and have my being in him. He does not *supplement* me, he creates me.

Perhaps a misconception of this law may have something to do with our spiritual poverty and feebleness. We may have thought that God would eke out our respectability. It may have occurred to us that we may bring fine culture to heaven, and heaven may be only too glad to accept it. O cursed profanity! Yet I dare not say that some of us have not brought our scholarship, or culture, or outward polish, and have expected the Church to be only too thankful to accept such astounding respectability. We must be *creations*, not improvements; we contribute nothing. "By the grace of God I am what I am" must be the humbling yet ennobling consciousness of every man who would do any real and lasting good in the world.

Thus we have spoken of the gift of power. To what intent the power was given will appear in our next reading. The gift was directly given by the Son of God. Can he be but a *man* who has such gifts to give? He is more than a man to me; he is my Lord and my God. He invokes no sacred name, he utters no incantation, he mutters from behind no veil of mystery. Seated there, in absolute littleness of simplicity, he conducts the investiture of twelve men with the almightiness of God, within the circle which he describes for their mission. From his own heart as from a quiver he draws the arrows which these men are to shoot. Who was he?

Why did they not give him power? How came he to be the origin and fountain of this might? How was it that he always *gave* and never received?

How this power will be wielded we shall see by-and-by. Perhaps under its exercise the wilderness may blossom as the rose, and the sandy places may be green as the fertile meadow.

fifteen

THE USES OF INSPIRED POWER

Matthew 10:5-23

WE ARE NOW studying the charge which Jesus Christ gave to his twelve disciples, when he sent them upon their first missionary tour. In the charge we found three things—Power, Service, and Consolation. "Jesus Christ called unto him his twelve disciples and gave them—*power*." Today we have to look at the *uses* to which that power was to be put. Power is another name for duty; the measure of power is the measure of obligation. It was never God's intention that you should take the power which he gave you and enfold it and lay it aside, to be merely kept in its first state—which indeed is impossible, for power that is not used declines and dies. This we know in our intellectual education, in all the exercises of life—the power which falls into disuse soon becomes powerless. Whatever power we have, therefore, is meant to be used for the good of others. If we cannot work miracles, we have the power of eloquence, the power of money, the power of sympathy—we are clothed not with *less* power than that with which the early disciples were invested—it has *another aspect*, and in some sense it may be turned to other methods and uses, but essentially it is divine power, and it is meant to be expended for the good of the race. It is not a personal possession or a personal luxury only, it is meant for expenditure, for spreading over the largest possible surface, and for accomplishing the largest usefulness.

What is your power? You can speak a kind word, you can illuminate a dark mystery, you can soothingly touch some bitter distress of the heart, you can utter a hopeful word to the man who is in despair, you can sit down and listen sympathetically to the heart that has a long tale of wonder or of woe or of bitterness to tell. Find out what your particular personal power is, and understand that wherever power is given, duty is implied.

Jesus Christ always used his power beneficially. When all power was given to him in heaven and on earth, how did he employ it? I know of no words more sublime in their moral pathos than the words which he used when he declared that all power was given unto him. He mentioned nothing about destruction. He made no reference to retaliation, he did not say, "All power is given unto me in heaven and on earth, therefore gather mine enemies together that I may consume them with sudden fire." Pause and hear what he has to say, and tell me if ever logic was surprised into such sequences as in the case of his great speech. "All power is given unto me in heaven and on earth—go ye *therefore*" [Matt. 28:18, 19]. You call the word *therefore* a logical word, you say it indicates a sequence, and unites what is coming with what is gone. Observe into what wondrous breadths this *therefore* expands itself. "Go ye therefore and teach." That is the true use of power—to *educate*, to *teach*, to communicate ideas, to build up a spiritual kingdom, to deliver men from darkness and error and narrowness, and to lift them up into a larger self-hood. Such is the purpose of Christianity, and while the Church holds her faith to that intent, whosoever speaks against it but wastes his own breath.

Let us now hear what Jesus Christ says to his twelve disciples when he sends them forth. He says in verses nine and ten—"Provide neither gold nor silver, nor brass in your purses, nor scrip for your journey, neither two coats, neither shoes, nor yet staves." That is the way to evangelize the world. He never amended that method, he never said a single word about outfits and guarantees and supports and home refuges in the case of foreign disappointments. It is the method that must be adopted *today* if Christian men are in earnest. Go to foreign lands with nothing—nothing but yourself and God. Do you want to be a missionary to barbarous lands—to savage people? Then go at once and tell no one about it. "But I cannot pay my passage." Then *work* it. Pull ropes, carry chains, keep fires—work it, or you do not mean to go. "But I must have time to buy an outfit." On what compulsion must you? You are not a missionary. If you had the fire of God burning in you and wanted to go to reclaim the moral wastes of the world, you would be off! You would not need to go and converse with your minister about it, and consult a number of elderly persons concerning it, and to go around certain circumlocutionary paths to come to it—we would ask "Where is he?" And by-and-by the answer would come, that

Christ had sent you forth, without purse, or shoes, or coats, or staves. The Church now goes respectably, well equipped—the Church now goes to taste the ill-smelling dish of heathenism, and if its nostril be offended by the flavor, it comes home.

That kind of energy, if energy it may be termed, will never conquer the world. If Christ has called you very closely to himself, and has told you to go and be a missionary, then go. The Norwegians are following in this matter the counsel and will of Christ. They went into India and said to the people with whom they came in contact:

"We have come to teach you Christianity."

"Who sent you?"

"Nobody."

"What have you to live upon?"

"Nothing."

"How do you mean to live?"

"We mean to do you all the good we can, and we are sure you will not let us starve."

"But what if we have nothing?"

"Then we will have nothing along with you."

There was no answer to that argument. The Norwegians meant it, sat down and did it. Now, my young friend, you who are talking about going to be a missionary, why do you not start off on your beneficent journey at once? You may be killed if you touch mechanism; the machinery of the Church is now so complicated that if you do not take care some crank or wheel will catch you, and in you will go, and you will never come out again.

This is exactly how Christ himself came. "Who, being in the form of God, thought it not robbery to be equal with God, but made himself of no reputation and took upon him the form of a servant" [Phil. 2:6, 7]. Just what I told you now to do—take upon you the form of a sailor, work your passage out to the land you want to go to, and Christ will go along with you, and you shall not have gone much over the land till the Son of man be come. He comes in strange ways, in great broad lines, in swiftly expanding consciousness of his presence, by filling the mind with new brightness and the soul with new emotion, and lifting up the life to higher and diviner energies. It is not the case of sending men into Christian cities to speak to the Christian intelligence and the Christian luxury of the age. We are talking to the intelligence, and culture, and wealth, and social influence of the metropolis. That is not the case described in the text. We are men who profess to know the truth and to love it, and we have established amongst ourselves constituted and permanent ministries of the truth. We must, therefore, not apply to ourselves passages, directions, methods, and schemes which were suggested in reference to nations that knew not that Jesus Christ had come.

Jesus Christ, therefore, appears before us as a man who undertakes a great work, upon conditions which cannot be disappointed. He wants only *meat*, and there is something in human nature that will not let the earnest man starve. The workman is worthy of his meat. Go where you will, earnest man, you shall have bread enough and to spare. Not, perhaps, today, but tomorrow you will have more than sufficient, and that you can keep for the day that is to follow, or give it away as you please. But you cannot show disinterestedness, the passion of enthusiasm, the divinity of absolute consecration, and be left to starve. There are always kind hearts, open houses, thoughtful minds, liberal hands; God has his elect everywhere — out of hell. Our care must be about the truth; God will take care of your need for food. If Jesus Christ had set up a missionary scheme with most intricate, and complex, and expensive mechanism it would have come to nothing, but its conditions are so simple, so heroic, so grand and so perfectly exemplified in his own person, that they apply to all times, lands, climates, and social conditions, and national and world-wide necessities.

In sending men forth to their duty, Jesus Christ shows them clearly what they will certainly have to bear. He does not promise them a downy pillow, he does not promise them genteel society, he does not offer to them any social bribe; he says:

> You will be like sheep in the midst of wolves, they will fall upon you, break your bones, suck your blood; ye shall be brought before governors and kings for my sake. The brother shall deliver up the brother to death, and the father the child, and children shall rise up against their parents and cause them to be put to death, and ye shall be hated of all men for my name's sake.

There is no mistaking the lot of the true Christian evangelist. He has a hard time of it. Goodness is always hateful to evil; the beasts that gather together in the nighttime hate the light — you torment them if you turn a sudden blaze upon them, for they hasten and fly, and gnash their teeth, and display animosity and resentment. Goodness can never establish itself anywhere without a battle. Do not suppose that you can lull the enemy to sleep and put up your house, and when you have roofed it, and completed it, and furnished it, can then tell him that it is beyond his strength. The establishment of goodness is a daily battle. You cannot take upon you a new habit without having to fight for every inch of ground you make; you cannot exert yourself to throw off slothfulness or any self-indulgence without having to fight for the end.

What is true in discipline is true in the education and moral conquest of the world. In proportion as you are free and easy in your methods of going into any company, and taking its similitude and speaking its language, will you have an easy time of it, but if you have a grand program, a rousing and elevating purpose, you will go as sheep among wolves. Do not imagine that goodness is peaceful. Goodness is controversial. They who "make a desert and call it peace" may never intermeddle with anything that affects the integrity and nobleness of society, and then say that they are living quiet and peaceable lives. Quiet lives they may be, but not peaceful. Peaceful—that is a resultant word, it combines many elements and many considerations, and reconciles into one sweet harmony forces which, taken separately, are among the most combatant energies of the universe. Goodness always sends a sword upon the earth, and kindles a fire, and divides families; sets the father against the child and the child against the father, and the brother against the brother, and kindles a great fire upon the earth. We have succeeded now in putting the fire out, and have come to the age of courteous civilities and tender regard for one another's evil habits. The old goodness, heaven's own angel, the Christ-goodness, fought everyday, not with a blade of steel but with that keener blade of conviction, enthusiasm, sacrifice, that counted not its life dear unto itself that it might win the battle against evil, and darkness, and corruption.

One would have thought that in sending forth goodness the angel would have been recognized at once and welcomed with broad and generous hospitality. This historical reception of goodness enables us to answer and destroy a fallacy which is common in modern reasoning. People say, "Show a beautiful example, a beautiful God, a beautiful gospel, and there will be an answer of devotion and homage in every human heart." That has been proven to be false. The example is not enough; men are not saved by spectacles: we need something higher than a spectacular gospel. Men get used to beauty, and theirs is a familiarity which is followed by contempt. There are men amongst us who care nothing for the sunrise; there are men who could gabble in a sunset; there are persons who could chaffer and joke upon the great sea. Understand that surprising miracles of beauty are like surprising miracles of truth — men may become so accustomed to them as to let them pass by without recognition or homage.

Goodness has always had a hard time of it. In proportion as the Church becomes luxurious will the Church become feeble. In proportion as the Church says to the world, "Let us compromise this business and say nothing unpleasant to one another, but sit down and enjoy ourselves as far as we can," the Church has disestablished itself in the confidence and esteem of men, and has broken the trust and vow paid before God's heaven. A little persecution and difficulty would do the Church good. We have heard of some preachers who would be mighty speakers if they could only be contradicted in the middle of their discourse, but left to themselves they are inclined to maunder, and stammer, and become feeble, and monotonous, and pointless. If an antagonist could arise in the congregation and say, "That is not true," such preachers would become different men, every energy a flame, and the whole voice a thunder sent down from heaven.

It is even so with the Church: we have it so much our own way now, the lines of demarcation are broken up, and the old points indicated by Christ of antagonism, and assault, and aggression are, if not utterly obliterated, so treated as to have lost their accent and their force. Only this morning I was reading the old story of Hannibal — one winter in Capua brought about a ruin which the snows of the Alps, the suns of Italy, the treachery of the Gauls, and the prowess of the Romans failed to accomplish. So long as he was a soldier only, stern in discipline, rigorous in his habits, devoted with indivisible strength to his duty, he feared nothing — the setting down of his foot was as a battle half won, but the blandishments and enfeeblements of luxurious Capua sucked the strength out of the giant and left him a common man. The Church has gone to Capua, the Church is wintering in luxurious places — the grand old Church that wrote human names high up above all other human scrolls, martyrs, heroes, leaders — she can now hardly write her name in common ink.

Jesus Christ told his disciples how to treat the cities and towns that rejected the message which they had to convey to them. "Whosoever shall not receive you nor hear your words, when ye depart out of that house or city shake off the dust of your feet." They mistake Christ who suppose that he is soft, indifferent, easily imposed upon, and who can be treated contemptuously without feeling it. We read of the wrath of the Lamb, the fire of love, the indignation of grace—God's heart burning like an oven. Jesus Christ here bases his directions upon the grand and indestructible principle which lies at the very base, and forms the very strength, of all high educational purposes. What is that principle? It is that no man has the right to *reject* truth. He has the *power* to do it, but not the *right*. We have liberty to go to perdition, but not the right. You have no right to refuse a just idea, you have no right to shut yourself up in solitude and say, "I will not listen to the ministries of civilization that are going on around me." It shall be more tolerable for the land of Sodom and Gomorrah in any day of judgment than for you if you adopt so unrighteous and ignoble a policy. No man has any right to refuse to read a book that will open his eyes and give him wider light than he has yet enjoyed. He may decline a *privilege,* he cannot thrust from him a *right* without incurring loss in himself and divine punishment from without. This is not arbitrary doctrine, this is no conception of any individual thinker; all the history of our education and civil progress testifies to the same thing.

What new responsibility this throws upon us! We have not the right to reject truth; we have the right to examine our ministers; we have the right to examine every spirit that comes to us and challenges our attention, we have a right to examine personal credentials and personal authorities, but where any *truth* is established no man has a right to reject it, and if any man reject a truth, even unwittingly or unintentionally, he shall suffer loss; he himself shall be saved, but very narrowly. If I keep out any part of the sun that can really do my life good, I suffer loss in proportion to the sunlight which I exclude.

Jesus Christ, then, defined the service which his disciples are to perform. In our last address he clothed them with power; today he indicates the field of service, he will next come to us with his sweet consolations and encouragements; he will lower his voice into another key, and speak sweetly to the heart. We saw that it is not enough for a man to have power to do his duty; sheer, dry, hard strength is not enough. The man will come home disappointed; he will not see the result of his labors, and he may cry bitterly for his failure, and it is in that hour of darkness that Jesus Christ will draw him nearer than ever to his hospitable heart, and speak to him in tones of ineffable sweetness the infinite consolations which sustained his own strength when he trod the winepress alone.

One remark occurs to me which might have been made under our last discourse, but which might be made appropriately in any connection when speaking of Jesus Christ. In the last verse of the ninth chapter Jesus said, "Pray ye the Lord of the harvest that he will send forth laborers into his harvest." In the first verse of the tenth chapter we read that Jesus Christ gave his disciples power, and that he sent them forth with his gracious commands. The Lord of the harvest is to be prayed to that he would send forth laborers; Jesus Christ himself sends forth laborers—was *he* Lord of the harvest?

sixteen

CHRIST'S CONSOLATION
FOR WORKERS

Matthew 10:24–42

LET ME call your attention to an instructive fact. All these tender consolations were given *beforehand*. Jesus Christ did not wait until the disciples returned, bruised and shattered, and then gather them into his heart and heal them, as it were, with his sympathy and blood. Jesus Christ once said, "I will give the multitudes bread, *lest* they faint by the way" [see Mark 8:3]. That text gave us a discourse upon the *preventive* ministry of Christ. He did not wait until the people had actually fainted, and then give them bread: he gave them bread to *prevent* the fainting. He has prevented me with his loving kindness—that is to say, he has run before me to get ready for my weakness and hunger, and before the blow has been struck the healing has been made ready.

I hold it to be a noteworthy fact that this comfort formed part of the *inspiration* of the disciples. The comfort was, so to say, part of the capital on which they had to live. If Jesus Christ had been sending forth men to add to the leprosy of the world, to strike thousands more of its inhabitants blind, and to deafen as many as possible, he could not have forewarned his disciples of greater dangers and distresses. "Ye shall be hated of all men for my name's sake." How are we to account for this issue? He gave them power against unclean spirits, and he sent the disciples forth to cast them out, and to heal all manner of sickness, and all manner of disease, and to preach, saying, "The kingdom of heaven is at hand," and then he added, with an abruptness which must receive some profound explanation, "Ye shall be hated of all men for my name's sake." Where is the balance between the men and the fate? I repeat, had he sent forth his disciples to break up the world, to diminish its joys, to add to

117

its distresses, he could hardly have painted a more tragic issue. He sent them forth on a beneficent errand, and told them that they should be brought before governors and kings, be cast into prison, be called Beelzebub, and be forsaken and hated of all men for his name's sake. Herein once more is the statesmanship of that wondrous Peasant, and herein do I find his Godhead. Not in the small grammatical cleverness of the Biblical exegete, but in these disclosures of his shrewdness, of his insight, the penetration that pierced everything, and saw essences and realities, and the vital parts and secrets of all things. Who but himself could have seen that the casting out of devils, the cleansing of lepers, the giving sight to the blind and hearing to the deaf, and the preaching of the nearness of a new kingdom could have ended in scourgings and contempt, and hatred and death? But this forecast has been abundantly established by facts.

Jesus Christ knew that there are men who will never allow good to be done, if they can help it, by any method but their *own*. There are men who would rather see you damned than see you saved by irregular means. They would rather have you lost in what they would term an orthodox manner, than see you saved by a method which to them would seem to be unorthodox or heretical. They would like their own little prophecies confirmed; they do not want their conceptions, low as a ceiling, heightened into a sky; they do not want their little conceptions of fellowship, narrow as the walls of a man-built house, widened out until they touch God's horizon.

This was the principle which Jesus Christ proceeded on in delivering his charge. He told his disciples they would everywhere meet the diabolical spirit of sectarianism; they were irregular, they were nomadic, they were persons who had not upon them the usual seal, they did not bear upon their arms the accustomed badge, and though they might have good in their heads, good in their hearts, good in every tone of their speech, they would be hated of all men. Let us beware of the sectarian spirit; it blinds us to the excellences that are beyond our little boundaries; let us say with Paul, "Some preach Christ in one way, some preach him in another; whether in pretense or in truth, Christ is preached. Therein," said the grand old prisoner, "do I rejoice; yea, and will rejoice" [see Phil. 1:15–18]. Is the Pauline spirit dead?

As we have read this chapter you must have been struck with the number of times the word *therefore* recurs. It would seem as if nearly every other verse was a statement of some logical sequence. There is a deep logical sequence in the fact, that as the *warning* was given beforehand, so the *consolation* was laid up in store. Jesus Christ set forth the whole case; he told his disciples what to expect alike from man and from God. And this is precisely what he tells everyone of his followers today. Jesus Christ—regarding him now as nothing more than the greatest of statesmen—said to himself:

> These poor little children (for they were little better) must be delivered from the peril of *surprise*. Things must not happen *suddenly* to immature minds. I must go before them, and give them the outline of the whole course. They must not come back when they have accomplished their journey, expressing any surprise at the greatness of the difficulty. When they do come back it must be with the surprise of joy.

To *that* surprise he sets no period. It is his plan that no man shall ever come back to Christ and say, "Thou didst not tell me half the peril, and thy description of the burning, cutting pain was understated." No; he said, "Ye shall be brought up in the synagogues and scourged there, and the scourge shall cut your flesh and find the bone, and ye shall be brought before governors and kings for my name's sake, and ye shall be hated of all men." This was not a Man who tempted a few disciples by vivid pictures highly colored, and glowing promises. He told them they were going into a black tunnel, and at every step an enemy would endeavor to seize them, but he also said, "In the midst of that dark and terrible valley God's revelations will flame upon you and many an angel will surprise you into sudden and ecstatic joy." We know the future perfectly well. All its great broad lines are drawn in a manner which cannot be misunderstood—trouble and joy, tears and delights, the grave and the bright heaven are all before us—not in detail, indeed, for no man knows the hour of his death: it is enough for me that I know I must die; the day and the hour has no man known—they are hidden in heaven.

Jesus Christ gives his disciples the infinite consolation of knowing that when they suffer, the Master suffers along with them. "The disciple is not above his master, nor the servant above his Lord. It is enough for the disciple that he be as his Master, and the servant as his Lord. If they have called the Master of the house Beelzebub, how much more shall they call them of his household?" No blow falls upon you that does not also fall upon your Lord and Master. Your tears flow through his eyes. We have not a High Priest that cannot be touched with a feeling of our infirmities: he knows what the force of temptation is, for he has felt its entire strain upon his own beating heart. It is something for the private soldier to know that he is fighting side by side with his General; there is something in such companionship that amounts almost to an inspiration. I suffer less when I suffer in certain society. The very pain that would distress me if I were in society that I hold in contempt lifts me up into a new strength when I endure it in association with men whose names are the inspiration of history and the hope of the world. What more could he have said than that:

> Whoever undervalues you undervalues me: the insult is not meant for you; it is meant for your Master. When they spit upon your face they mean to spit upon mine. They could despise you from a social point of view; from the point of view of rabbinical learning and culture they could hold you in ineffable contempt, but it is through you that they see me: when they scourge you it is upon my flesh that the thong falls?

If the men heard these words right they must have been ennobled for the occasion. In proportion to their love for their Master would be their joy in thinking that they should suffer anything in his name, and afterwards men went out of the presence of the council rejoicing that they were counted worthy to suffer shame for his name. That was the *heroic* age of the Church, when men lived in God, and represented the very sun of the divine image.

When we suffer *alone* we get no advantage out of the suffering—we must offend CHRIST; when we think we are suffering alone we go contrary to his whole teaching, for he says, "Whoso receiveth him I send receiveth me: whoso believeth on me, believeth not on me but on him that sent me. As my Father hath sent me even so I send you" [John 20:21]. "He that despiseth, despiseth not man, but God." This is the root out of which all consolation comes. We do not suffer alone; we have a fellow-sufferer. Whenever you are laughed at because of your Christianity, if it be real, simple, true, noble, honest, and healthy, the laugh is at the *cross*. Whenever you suffer, which few men now do, for your faith's sake, it is not you that suffer—the Son of God is crucified afresh and put to an open shame. Let us take care lest we mistake this matter of suffering in Christ's stead. Sometimes we suffer for our errors and not for our truth, for our impertinence and not for our fidelity, for our selfishness and not for the divine breadth of our character-building. If, therefore, we suffer on our own account, I wonder not that the pain should be sharp and intolerable, but insofar as our character and spirit and action are right, and we suffer, it is not we that suffer only; it is the Son of God whose face is smitten and whose heart is bruised.

Jesus Christ goes even further than this, for he connects the whole mission of the Church expressly with the Father. It is *God* himself that suffers, and it is God that identifies himself with the whole purpose and issue of the Christian economy. When the disciples were speaking in their own defense, Jesus Christ told them, "It is not ye that speak, but the spirit of your Father which speaketh in you." "A sparrow," said Christ, "cannot fall to the ground without your Father." So the universe is one: no man can touch the truth without touching the whole kingdom of heaven; no man can injure a single truth without injuring the whole quantity called truth, for the truth is not a question of single filaments and threads, particles and details: the truth is one, indissoluble, and to touch it to the injury of any part of it is to touch it to the pain of its very heart.

The universe is one: some of us worship in one place and some in another: but to God there is no space that can be mapped out in separate localities. He fills all in all. If you are not against him you are on his side. Therein have I sometimes endeavored to teach men that though they be not nominally in Christ they may be under the inspiration of his Spirit. Men know not what they do even when they put the Son of God to shame. There is a forgiveness that may follow their blasphemy; there is in heaven a consideration for human ignorance, though that ignorance culminate in the tragedy of Gethsemane and Golgotha. Truth, let me say again and again, is one as the universe is one. There is nothing despicable or contemptible; the fall of the sparrow is watched, and the very hairs of your head are all numbered. God puts our tears in his bottle, and he writes our names in his book of life. Sacred universe, sensitive universe; if I lift a hand I send a shudder to the stars.

So my whole thought and wish and purpose and prayer—what are these but so many vibrations that tell upon lines that do not come within my view, and that stir influences which I can neither understand nor control? So Jesus Christ identifies himself with his disciples, and identifies himself and his disciples with the Father that is in heaven. It is one Church, one life, one temple, and to touch it at any point is to cause an influence to be felt throughout the whole living faculty. These are not tiny solaces, these are not little plasters for little wounds: these great solaces are redemptions; they enter the very secret place of the life; they do not evaporate in the sun—they feed the very soul.

Another consolation you find in the words, "He that endureth to the end shall be saved." There is where so many of us may fail: we endure a little while; the seed springs up speedily, and because there is no deepness of earth soon withers away. This is not a question of enduring for a little time; it is a question of enduring to the end. The end—who can tell when that shall come? Life is full of endings—life is full of beginnings. Knowing how distressed we are by monotony, God has taken care in the economy of the universe that there shall be little or none of it. So he has broken up our life into day and night, the beginning of the week and the end of the same, the day of birth, the day of marriage, the day of peculiar joy—so many beginnings are there to tempt us into new views and lure us into deeper resolutions and give us fresh chances in life, and yet all these beginnings and endings culminate in one supreme finality—no man can tell when it may be: my end may be this day. It is well we do not know when the final point comes into the literature of life.

"He that endureth to the end." Paul did. He said, "I have fought a good fight, I have finished my course" [2 Tim. 4:7]. "Weary not in well doing, for in due season we shall reap if we faint not" [see Gal. 6:9]. Jesus Christ himself said, "I have finished the work which thou gavest me to do" [John 17:4]. And again he said, "It is finished" [John 19:30]. Take care lest you come almost to land, take care lest you be almost saved. The old Puritan divine, the Shakespeare of the pulpit of his day, wound up one of his grandest appeals to his people by saying, "To be almost saved is to be altogether damned." Take care lest you be almost in possession, and yet fail of clasping within your glad hand that after which you have been aspiring. Let us endeavor to the last hour. To fail within sight of the prize, to perish within sight of land, to be able to hear the welcomes that ring from the shore, and yet not to land there—Oh, that is painful beyond realization.

I shall never forget how, recently, we approached the city of our desire. The day before the rain had been continuous, and the mists afterwards very thick, and there was a sudden fear in the minds of men. Then came out the evening sun, and touched up all the sullen clouds into a very apocalypse of glory and beauty. I never saw such a sign in all the heavens, that are full of pictures to the eye that searches for them. We moved on through the water, and the day of landing came, and when persons saw their friends in the near distance, there was much signal giving and signal exchanging. One young boy came to me with his eyes alight and, to explain his joy, he said, "I see my father." I heard a lady say, "I see my brown-eyes." I heard another say, "I see my sister." Was it possible to fail just *then*—to fail within a few minutes of the landing-place—to be lost before hands were grasped in the reunion of grateful affection?

Take care: we are going towards the end, but we may not accomplish it; God give us strength to fulfill every mile of the road, and to fight the last battle, and to pluck the sting from the last enemy. It is the *end* that determines everything. The greatest ship may go down in sight of port. Oh, may we—many of whose ships are not good, much tried, storm-beaten, creaking because of weakness—may we all be brought in, and so at last—

> O'er life's rough ocean driven,
> > May we rejoice, no wanderer lost,
> Whole families in heaven!

Ye did run well; who did hinder you? Are you going to give up now? Say, "By the grace of God we will continue in patient well-doing till we have accomplished our days upon the earth."

seventeen

A REVIEW OF MATTHEW 10

Matthew 10

A GREAT MISSIONARY campaign was proposed: Jesus Christ himself proposed it. Now what was his idea of such a novel campaign? This is the largest thing he has yet attempted, we may therefore naturally expect to gather from it some hint of his intellectual quality. How does he address himself to great undertakings? What was his intellectual energy, what his moral tone, what his propagandist audacity? How will he grip a great occasion? In studying the Temptation we thought we could discover from his answers the quality of his character, as from the devil's questions we formed a deduction as to the devil's nature. Now from this great and luminous Charge, addressed to twelve men in view of a missionary campaign, it is possible we may be able to gather something further concerning the intellectual and moral purpose of the Son of God. To this study I now invite you. First of all, Jesus Christ sent forth his disciples *two and two.* That was a shrewd and gracious arrangement. He might have covered double the ground if he had sent them out one by one. It was not his purpose in the outset to cover much ground; he was more careful at the beginning about the men and the strength and utility of their service than about the mere acreage of surface which he was to cover. In due time he will lay his hand upon the whole world, but it is early morning now, the dawn is just beginning to make the eastern sky a little gray, and at the outset he says, "You must go out two and two. The lonely heart is soon discouraged; two are better than one, for if they fall one will lift up his fellow, but woe to him who is alone when he falleth." That was an ancient proverb: it was within the pen of Solomon to write that wise word, and it comes within the range of Jesus Christ's purpose to take up our little common proverbs and to give their religious applications and religious securities.

Not only did Jesus Christ send forth his disciples two and two, but each two made up something like one whole. It was as if he had put together hemispheres, and thus made a complete globe of character and service. Look at the names. Peter and Andrew. Peter, full of fire, daring, passion, enthusiasm, an impetuous man with a strange faculty of leaping and making beginnings of things without any certainty that he would ever continue them to their completion. Andrew—his very name is a character, his very name is a certificate. If he be other than a *man* he will be a living irony, for his name means—*man*, and he was manly in all his conceptions and movements. He was as one who broke up the way with a strong hammer. They will do well together, these two—probably they will not fall out by the way.

The next couple—James and John. James is elsewhere called a "son of thunder"—a great rousing, violent voice that came in shocks and claps and bursts, and John was idealistic, contemplative; his eyes often settled into a calm, dreamy wonder, and his whole face looking as if his eyes were fastened on God's great eternity. There will be no occasion of difference between two such men; they are well mated. This also comes forth from the Lord of hosts, who is wonderful in counsel and excellent in working.

The next couple—Simon Zelotes, Simon the zealot, Simon the hot coal, Simon the fervent man, all fire, clothed with zeal as with garment, and Judas Iscariot, cold, calculating, shrewd, representing the secular, administrative, executive side of things. If any man could go with Judas, Simon is the man to accompany him; if Judas can be trusted in any company, it was well to bind him to the fire. If there is purification and disinfection to be had anywhere it is in the red flame—so potent is fire.

What think ye of Christ? He did not allow the men to go out two and two just as *they* pleased, but two and two as *he* pleased. He sets the stars in their places; he fixes the bounds of our habitation; there is a balance in his hand, and he goes into the detail of every economy he administers. The very hairs of your head are all numbered, and he who watches the night lamps of the heavens watches the small birds that fall upon the earth. We may repeat, therefore, that in this arrangement there was at once great shrewdness and great grace. Is it not a fact well attested amongst ourselves that some men ought never to be thrown into association with one another? Each of the men is good, but they ought never to have come into nominal *union*. They do not understand one another, they are out of sympathy and *rapport*, they cannot comprehend one another's purposes and impulses, they are, perhaps, too much alike to be agreeable the one to the other, or there may be something about their dissimilarity which does not admit of immediate reconciliation; there is a lack of adaptation between the two, and yet the character of each may be excellent. Matches are made in heaven in the widest sense. God knows all about the law of harmony and companionship, and he is the wise man who waits till the colleague is found in heaven. I ask you, therefore, in the beginning of this study, to estimate this arrangement as affording some illustration of the compass of mind which proposed this great missionary campaign.

The next point which is illustrative of the character of Christ is in the fact that he impoverished the disciples materially, and enriched them to infinitude of redundance spiritually. Never was master so severe with servant as to all material possessions and equipment. Christ's charge was a process of stripping in the first instance. No man was to have two coats or two staves; he was to take neither gold, nor silver, nor brass in his purse; everything that could be taken from a man was stripped from him by the very hand that sent him forth. There was no encouragement on the material side; no bribe, allurement, inducement, or promise was given on the side that was purely secular and worldly. And yet, on the other hand, as to the enrichment of the men, why, all heaven was placed at their disposal spiritually. They were to have inspiration, speech, comfort, at every point; nothing was withheld from them that could give them solace and ennoblement and quietude and the positive triumph of security. He was a statesman, he took a view that was bounded only by horizons, his plan was a firmament. Our little plans are broken arcs of his great circle. We are indebted even for the little arcs we draw to the great circle which he described. Remember there was no missionary society when Jesus Christ uttered this charge; there was nothing to go by; there was no hint in any human mind of such a scheme as this. We must therefore divest ourselves of all the conceptions and prejudices which they have gathered throughout nineteen centuries, and set ourselves at the chronological point of Christ's planning and thinking, if we would rightly estimate his method of spreading a Christian gospel.

In the case of Christ, poverty was to become a kind of holiness. To have two coats was to break a vow, to have two staves was to be suspected of disloyalty, to have a look of having anything of your own was to be brought under the suspicion of distrust in God. Outward grandeur would have clashed with spiritual nobleness and aspiration. To make the case clearer upon that side, Jesus Christ not only stripped the disciples of everything in the form of an encumbrance, but he further depressed the materialistic side by telling them that they would have blows, taunts, insults, scourgings, hatred of all men for his name's sake. This was a tremendous depression of the material side, an infinite discouragement to Judas Iscariot. It is the same today.

What think ye of this Man? We move by making great promises, we inspire by bribing, we encourage by *enriching,* in a material and physical sense. But Jesus Christ stripped every man of the twelve of everything that looked like encumbrance, or ornament, or personal security, and sent him forth with nothing but—God. His kingdom was not of this world, his masonry was not a building up with stone, his purpose was a great spiritual one, and evidently, from this very inception of his plan, he means the spirituality of his kingdom to be distinctly revealed to every eye. The kingdom of God cometh not with observation, the kingdom of God is not a material success, the kingdom of heaven is within.

Then look, in the third place, at the kind of homage which he claimed. It was preposterous, if not divine. There was no other name for it than the name that describes its ridiculousness, if it was not a divine claim. Father and mother must go, sister and brother must be surrendered, houses and land must be abandoned, the world reduced to one pair of sandals and one stout staff. "He that loveth father or mother more than me is not worthy of me. He that loveth sister or brother more than me is not worthy of me. Except a man hate his father and his mother in comparison with me, he is not worthy of me. He that taketh not up his cross daily is not worthy of me." He himself was the one inspiration of the disciples, his name the only name they knew or were called upon to breathe; this was the homage he demanded—no oath in mere words, no vow spoken into the vacant air, to be lost in its ample spaces, but direct, positive, complete surrender. I do not ask you to form any opinion of the homage itself at this moment, but to form your estimate of a man who, in ordering twelve men to do a work, says that if he is not supreme beyond father, mother, sister, brother, houses, land, any man who professes to do his work does it with hireling fingers, with a mercenary and dishonorable soul.

It was a bold claim, and it was most graphically expressed. This was not the way in which an *impostor* would have moved; he would have sought by guile, and promise, and bribe, by all the tricks known to imposture, to have endeared these men to the cause he wished to propagate. But the impostor has no cause which he wishes to propagate except the cause of *himself*. Jesus Christ had this great cause to propagate—the kingdom of heaven, as first seen in the cleansing of the lepers, the healing of the sick, the blessing of the unblest, and the sending of a plentiful rain upon lives that were perishing with thirst.

There was another point in his charge that must reckon in the great argument, and that was the command to avoid all religious mystery, and monasticism, and jugglery, in founding the new kingdom. "What I tell you in darkness or in secrecy, face to face, in this private interview, that speak ye in light, and what ye hear in the ear, that preach ye upon the housetops." There are no little corners and monastic enclosures and priestly confessional boxes in this great kingdom of Christ. This is no branch of the black art, this is not a question of attainment in priestly mummery and symbolic representation, and things that can be only penetrated and expounded by the initiated and the learned. This is our conception of the kingdom of heaven, and we believe it to be Christ's own, that the Book revealing it is open to everybody, that the Book can now be read in our mother tongue, and that every man is responsible to God directly for the use which he makes of that Book. Herein I rejoice to believe that we have the truth of God. You may know about it as much as I do, if you will attend to it with your whole soul, and study it with your whole affection. I do not believe in any ministerial *class*; there is no minister that knows more or needs know more than the plainest man in society, except it be by some specialty of intellectual gift, or by some opportunity of closer literal study, but as to all that is essential, substantial, vital, in the gospel, I would just as soon have you consult the man who sweeps the floor of the church than have you consult me in my purely so-called "professional" capacity. I have no profession; if I have not a *vocation* then am I nothing in life. We are *all* ministers; some are speaking ministers, some giving ministers, some sick-visiting ministers, some quiet sympathetic ministers, but all the Lord's people are prophets, and we are only in the apostolic succession so long as we succeed to the apostolic *spirit* and to the apostolic *doctrine*.

The ministerial class must be put down and discouraged by the true spirit of Christian Protestantism. The ministerial class spirit may become the curse of Christendom. I would have everything done in the light; I would have what is called a "layman" preside at the Lord's Supper as certainly as I would have any minister that ever was garbed in the official clothing of the Church. Go directly to your Bible and to every honest man you can meet, and get light from all quarters, and know ye that the Church does not represent some little secret trick, some art of spiritual conjuring, but is an infinite gospel of love, welcome, hospitality, to those that are lost.

He was no mean man who delivered this great Charge which we have thus from time to time read and studied. He was a grand man. There is no paltry idea within the whole compass of his Charge. There is no heel that can be wounded in this Achillean address; every word is sublime, and the whole purpose is beneficent. I ask you to call this Man Savior, Lord, King, Priest, and from this day to say you fall within the inspiration of his charge, and will be the soldiers of his cross. The Church is nothing today if she be not inspired. I will not listen to any toothless old Church that does but mumble a literal creed. The Church must lay her claim upon my attention by her *inspiration*, by her power to touch my heart's disease, my life's sharpest pain, my soul's bitterest accusation. Do not let us go forth with symbols and signs and fine traditions, and grandly outlined and highly elaborated faiths and creeds and professions, but let the world feel that we have an answer to all its charges, a reply to all its inquiries—

> A sovereign balm for every wound,
> A cordial for its fears.

Do not let us secrete ourselves in a corner, huddled together like sheep, afraid of a rolling thunderstorm, but let us be out everywhere inquiring, looking, testing, and offering our gospel. Let us translate it into every language; let us take it into every society, some speaking it as a high philosophy, others breathing it as a gentle blessing, others loving it as a high promise and tender solace, and all displaying it with a chivalrous and useful consistency. Then shall the Church, though nearly twenty centuries old [nearly twenty-one centuries old at the time of this printing], be fair as the sun, clear as the moon, and terrible as an army with banners.

eighteen

CHRIST'S ESTIMATE OF JOHN THE BAPTIST

Matthew 11:1–10

"AND IT CAME to pass when Jesus had made an end of commanding his twelve disciples, he departed thence to teach and to preach in their cities." He sent out his disciples two and two. He himself goes out alone. Who could have gone with him? The two and two went out on terms of equality: there can be no equality with God! He gave the commandment, but he did not receive it: he delivered the charge, it was not delivered to him. He is always fountain and origin, source, beginning and spring—he was always alone; he longed that others might have been one with him, but it took his own prayer to bridge over the infinite discrepancy between himself and every other man.

He went forth to preach and to teach, and did not sit at home for the purpose of receiving *reports* from those whom he had sent out himself. He did not say, "I have delegated the kingdom of heaven to twelve men, and I will take my ease until they return to tell me with what success it meets in the world." He had been the Master giving commandment and charge, and now he was himself the slave of slaves. He made himself of no reputation, he took upon him the form of a servant, and he went out to preach the gospel which he himself had been putting in charge of others. I would rather have heard the Master than the servant, I would have rather had one glance of him than have spent a lifetime in the sight of the twelve.

But this is not his way: he was with us visibly for a little while, and as a cloud received him out of our sight he said, "Lo, I am with you alway, even unto the end of the world." The Almighty did not allow himself long incarnation amongst us: this was his infinite wisdom; it would never

131

have done to have looked upon the fleshly form longer than men were permitted to do. These revelations are timed: God turns over the pages lovingly, not arbitrarily—he knows precisely when to take us out of one school and send us to another, and he who gives himself up lovingly to the guidance of God will remain in one Church until he is fit for the revelations and exhortations of some broader and nobler teacher. Yield yourselves to divine inspiration: keep down your impatience as you would keep down a wild beast, and rest peacefully, waitingly, patiently upon God.

There was a servant in prison: he had been in prison all the winter, he had heard the revels of the not distant court, and as the weary months dragged themselves over his life he began to wonder. The devil always takes advantage of us in our lower circumstances. He gets a man into a wilderness and tries to stab him, he drags him into a prison and tries to impoverish him of his faith. There is a good deal in *places,* there is a subtle mystery about atmospheric influences, there are points in space at which we can receive no temptation, and there are other points that seem to be fitted as the very battlefield of hell.

When John heard in the prison the works of Christ, he began to wonder. Consider John's position. He had actually pointed out the Messiah, he had said, "Behold the Lamb of God, that taketh away the sin of the world" [John 1:29]. Now he had been month after month in prison. Who can see far in a prison light—who can see much with dungeon walls for a horizon? What poetry is there in Herod's pit? What wonder if the dungeon were diapered with strange cross-lights and shadows, and if the place itself were vocal with unholy suggestion? Some persons want to make out that the doubting wonder began in the disciples of John, and not in John himself. I cannot read the text with that meaning. Possibly they may all have doubted, but the message was sent from John, the answer was returned to John, and the after discourse about John has a wondrous suggestiveness of love and tender shielding and ample defense which we must presently study.

Observe that John sent *directly* to Christ. He might have sent to the Scribes and Pharisees, he might have discussed the question at large with such disciples as were about him. It is in this way that we repeat our most mischievous errors. Men will not go to Christ himself and have out their doubts, suspicions, and wonders, as it were, face to face with him. That is where you have been going wrong. It may be that you have been reading commentaries and annotations and dissertations about Christ—go to him immediately without interposition or mediatory influence of any kind, shut yourselves up with the four Gospels, and with an honest heart study the Man. That is what you have to do. You have not done your duty when you have read a few verses or an occasional incident—you have done nothing until you have read the four Gospels clear through, and have wrought their narrative and precepts into the very tissue of your mind. I never knew a man do that honestly, and reverently, who did not come out at the other end with a great love in his heart, with great tears in his eyes; and if he did not fall down and worship, he stood still and wondered, religiously. History records the case of men who sat down to disprove the Scriptures, and who, in order to qualify themselves for their disproof, honestly read them through, and then dipped their pens to write a vindication of the holy records. Go then immediately to Christ, make yourselves perfectly familiar with every word and title in the four Gospels: do not dimly and vaguely refer to portions, parts, and aspects of those Gospels, but have them in you as a living word, easy of allusion, literal in your quotations, perfect in your recollections, and then say what you think of this Man. Come back with your answer, and let us know the sum total of your reasoning.

See how Jesus Christ treated this inquirer. He called attention to his works. "Go," said he, "and show John again those things which ye do hear and see. The blind receive their sight and the lame walk, the lepers are cleansed and the deaf hear, the dead are raised and the poor are evangelized." That was Christ's graphic answer; not metaphysical, not doctrinal, not a matter of opinion elaborately stated and eloquently discussed, but *facts*, palpable results, active and noble beneficence. A man's work should praise him; a man's life should be his vindication. You may be ruined by complimentary testimonials; you must be your own testimonial if you would vindicate your claim to any degree of authority and sacred influence in society. It is not what men say *about* you, but what you *do* yourselves, that must speak for you. Many men have come to me with testimonials which have nearly blinded me: they have been such great men that I could do nothing for them, and yet there they stood in the form of paupers, seeking for something to be done. But the testimonials said they were so educated and so eloquent and so capable and so excellent, that I have thought they must have been testimonials meant to be presented at heaven's gate for admission into some higher sphere than this. Do not be overweighted with the complimentary testimonials of your flattering friends, but by your own energy, force, wisdom, love, sanctified and inspired from heaven, make such a mark that the doubter himself shall be asked to consider it and decide as to its value.

This is what the Church must do. The Church cannot live in its books of mere divinity. The Church can make no impression upon the age so long as it indulges in merely wordy controversy. What is the Church doing? Are the lepers being cleansed and the blind receiving their sight, are the deaf hearing, are the dumb speaking? This is the only proof the Church need supply for its divine inspiration and its divine authority. All this can be done today. We narrow Christ's meaning and evacuate it of all high significance when we imagine that to open the eyes of the blind is a merely physical operation, or to cleanse the leper a ministry that begins and ends in the flesh. Those miracles were introductory, symbolic, wholly preparatory and suggestive. Christ says, "I am looking for greater works than these, which ye shall be called upon to do," and which he promised they should do when he went to the Father. The bad man is a leper, the man who is in intellectual error is the blind man, the one whose mouth is open to utter forbidden words is practically the dumb man in God's high sense of speech and music. When the Church works these miracles she need not defend her credentials, and write a great deal about her ancestry and her literature. Her answer is not in the *library* only, it is on the public thoroughfares, it is in the homes, lives, and businesses of men.

Why will you not bear witness for your Master in these matters? Why will you receive blessings in Church and be speechless about them? It is not so in any other church than Christ's. If I go for a moment amongst those who are studying music, I hear no other subject referred to from the time of opening the conversation to the time of closing it. It is delightful to witness the enthusiasm of the student and the devotee. Is there any shame about them? Not a particle. They speak of their difficulties and their intricacies, their pleasures, their high enjoyments, their disappointments, their raptures, the time they spend over it, with delight—the Christian professor, a dumb dog that dare not name his Master. Christ is wounded in the house of his friends.

If I go into the company of painters, they talk all the time about painting: where they have been, what they have seen, what they have on hand, what interaction they have had with fellow artists, and they glow over the subject, their hearts warm, their eyes dilate, their cheeks flush with noble pride. Whoever hears Jesus Christ referred to? I seldom do, and the answer is that it is too sacred a subject to be talked about. O, but the devil is cunning: he says, "Do not mention God, the subject is *too sacred:* do not refer to Christian experience and Christian service, because the subject is *too holy.*" You have only to make a subject *grand* enough to have it utterly ignored! I love to hear you young people talk about your artistic studies, your musical studies, your literary studies, and to speak of your teachers and masters and helpers: it is inspiring, it is like breathing a sea-breeze to hear you talk; I wish the Christian professors could learn something from you! If their Master were *less,* they would say more about him—so they seem to suggest. Two musical people will not be five minutes together before they are in the very midst of their subject; we shall all disperse after public worship and probably not a soul refer to the exercises in which we have been engaged.

How will Christ treat the doubter or the inquirer? Will he be harsh with him? I never knew him harsh except with the persons who claimed infallibility, ancestral righteousness, and authority in things of which they knew nothing. Will he rebuke John? I never knew him send a rebuke to a prison in which lay any poor soul suffering for Christ's sake. Will he send a blessing? Yes, that would be like him, wholly, so he says, "And blessed is he whosoever shall not be offended in me." He might have said, "Cursed is he who doubts about me, blamable is he who asks a question that suggests a wonder or a difficulty." Christ knew what we call the art of putting things. You may send a cruel message or a kind one, all by turning the sentence and setting it in its right relation—"And blessed is he whosoever shall not be offended in me, who shall wait for the revelation, who shall submit himself to the training and discipline of God, who shall accept God's way of doing things, however mysterious it be; for that man there is reserved a whole summer of benediction and affluence redundant, after the pattern of God's love in all his universe." Sometimes we must show our Christian confidence by patiently waiting, and at all times we must show our Christian confidence in trusting a man where we cannot explain the process of his action.

Jesus proceeds to speak about John. One wonders how so great a Speaker as Jesus will speak about any human creature. He speaks about John in noble terms, his eulogy seems to fill the sky, there is no word too good to be spent upon the character of this modern Elijah. First of all he proceeds to correct the notions of his time concerning John. "What went ye out for to see? A reed shaken with the wind, a man clothed in soft raiment, a prophet?" This is the transition through which every honest man passes when he comes into new social conditions. No minister can arise today who should be enabled by the Lord to do anything, who would not pass through precisely these three periods of criticism, unless he died under one of the first two, and never came to his due recognition. Thus, a reed shaken with the wind, a nine days' wonder, a little fluttering thing in the air, here and gone—that is the first criticism that is passed on any great reformer or noble teacher or self-sacrificing soul. A man clothed in softs, literally, that is the next criticism; he is working for himself, he is doing it all with a purpose, he is trying to make his bed soft, his house rich, his position strong: he has an aim in all this. Time rolls on, and they begin reluctantly to say, "He is a prophet." They can turn around as completely as that. The newspapers can—the French newspapers did so about Napoleon: he was a thief, he was a Corsican, he was a pretender—and the next day he was the emperor. That is a very small miracle in the way of a newspaper, for men sometimes grow rapidly under journalistic influences. Walk on, persevere, hold the plowhandle with all thy force; keep at it, John the Baptist, and you will pass the period of being a reed, a man clothed in soft clothing—you shall be a prophet, and a voice shall say, "Yea, and more than a prophet, a flower with a fragrance, a sun with a halo, a prophet *plus*." That is so with everyone of you, great and small, speakers and hearers, public men and private men; in proportion as you are honest and true, real and reformative in your spirit, you must be a reed, a self-seeker, a prophet.

Dr. Arnold, of Rugby, is, happily for himself, dead. In his day he was a heretic and a latitudinarian and a dangerous person. He speaks bitterly in his letters and in his sermons, and today he is worshiped and loved and honored, and men call their firstborn sons Arnold, after the king of Rugby. A prophet? Yea, I say unto you and more than a prophet. It is a long tunnel, but at the other end of it is the warm, genial, hospitable summer. God give thee strength, patience, and courage!

Jesus Christ, in indicating the greatness of John the Baptist, shows that the revelation with which he was entrusted culminated and died in his personal ministry. "Notwithstanding," Christ adds, "he that is least in the kingdom of heaven is greater than he." Life is a series of kingdoms; in my Father's house are many mansions; all things move in circles, there are no straight lines except within given and compassable points—even straight lines themselves are running on into circles; if we could project the vision far enough, we should see where the straight line begins to take the form of the globe whereon it is drawn. So John completes his revelation, and those who are in the kingdom of heaven in the higher revelation are, even the very least of them, greater than he. A little blade is greater than the seed out of which it came, the tiniest child born yesterday is greater than the grandest sculpture ever chiseled by Phidias or his successors, the smallest flower that blows is greater than the finest artificial plant that ever was fashioned by the most cunning fingers. He that is least in the kingdom of heaven is greater than he that is greatest in the kingdom below. So we grow. If we are greater than John the Baptist, let us prove our greatness by our beneficence, our nobleness, our heroic self-sacrifice, our splendid service, our uncomplaining industry.

Then Jesus Christ takes an opportunity of discoursing upon himself and upon John. He said, "John came neither eating nor drinking, and the people say, He hath a devil. The Son of Man came eating and drinking, and they say, Behold a man gluttonous and a winebibber, a friend of publicans and sinners." Every ministry has been rejected, the ascetic ministry, the genial ministry—each has in turn been despised and rejected of men. You cannot please men who are determined not to be pleased. Men will not look over the fogwall of their prejudices. Here is a minister who will please you; he neither eats nor drinks—what is your judgment? "He hath a devil." Here is a genial man, he comes eating and drinking—what say you? "A gluttonous man and a winebibber." The truth is, you do not *want* the minister. I speak now to those whose hearts are of stone, whose will is marked by invincible obduracy. Will they stick at anything in their road? Not they. He has a devil—take away his character. He is a gluttonous man and a winebibber—take away his character. There is nothing too bad for the bad man to do. He would uncrown the monarch and set fire to the throne, he would assault the reputation of angels rather than fail of his malignant purpose.

Blessed Savior, this is Thy defense of Thy servant. O what shielding! O what gentle protection, what ample security, what noble eulogy! He is the same yesterday, today, and forever. If we try to serve him, though our dispensation be brief and small, he will recognize our efforts, and no eulogy shall be so sweet and so full of satisfaction as his will be. Is he your Master, is he mine? Do I love his name? Do I abide by his cross? Do I imbibe his spirit? Do I display his love? Then, though some may say we have a devil and are mad, he will come with the explanation, he will vindicate every servant of his, and their enemies will he clothe with shame, and upon themselves shall the crown of his favor flourish.

To this Master I call you. You are not ashamed of any other Master you have, why be ashamed of this King? You speak of those who taught you to paint, to sing, to draw, to speak, to write — do you ever mention his name, who loved you and gave himself for you?

nineteen

SEEKING FRUIT AND FINDING NONE

Matthew 11:20–24

THIS IS a new tone in the voice of Jesus Christ. All that has yet come out of him has been an utterance of love and hope and hospitality, great offers of healing and peace and joy. Now comes the tone of reproach. It must come sooner or later in all human training. Every man who is deeply interested in the race has had occasion to utter a keen voice of reproach at some period of his generous toil. It is important to observe that in this instance the reproach is founded upon absolute reasonableness. It is not petulance; it is the result of labor not misapplied, but unworthily received. And we are accustomed amongst ourselves to utter reproach under precisely the same circumstances. Sometimes there is a whining and unreasonable reproach among men, but, as a general rule, in the deeper experience of life our upbraidings and reproaches are founded upon reason.

How do you address the boy upon whom you have lavished all your care; upon whom you have spent a fortune, little or great; whose well-being has been the one object of your desire; for whom you would gladly have suffered the loss of all things that he might be wise and good and useful; and who, when everything has been done for him human love could devise and human sacrifice provide, has turned out ungrateful, unfilial, a disappointment, a wreck? Is it possible for you to look on with complacency? Do you feel no pang of the heart as you look upon the result of all your prayer and toil and care? What if there break from the tongue of the most patient some bitter cry of regret, some tone of parental disappointment—would it be unreasonable? Its pathos would be in its reasonableness.

You speak of the land you toil upon, and on which you bestow money and labor and care, and which does not reward your industry, in almost anger and contempt. You look for results; you have a right to do so; you have labored, and you say where is the produce? Yet the land will drink up all you pour upon it, eat it, and be as lean as ever; and if you visit that land with a judgment of condemnation you are acting reasonably in so doing.

These illustrations may help us to understand in some degree the pathos of this reproach, the bitterness of this cry, and the more so because the object of Jesus Christ in all his labor is distinctly laid down here. The reason given is, because they repented not. It was not petulance on the part of Christ; there was no tone of merely personal disappointment; it seemed as if he had made the cities worse rather than better; it seemed as if they would have been better if they had never seen him, for having seen him, they rejected him with despite and contempt. Surely it would have been better for some of us if we had never heard of Christ. No man can hear of Christ and be just the same after hearing concerning him and his gospel as before hearing the revelation of his person and ministry. The gospel makes a man better or it makes him worse; it is a savor of life unto life or of death unto death. No man is the same after church as he was before church; the prayer is an event in his history; any offer of divine mercy, any display of divine love, is a crisis in the man's personal history, and if he accept not the offer that was made, it were better for him that the offer had never been presented to his attention.

We may no longer then doubt the one purpose of Christ in working his miracles. The object which Christ had in view in working miracles was to bring men to repentance. He upbraided the cities that had seen his mighty works because they repented not, the argument being that the miracles were performed for the purpose of bringing the people to repentance, and that object having failed, the whole purpose of Christ came to nothing. They were not performed to startle, to please, to amuse, or to gratify curiosity, but to bring the heart to contrition; they were assaults upon unbelief, they were appeals to obduracy, they were so many forms and methods of gospel preaching.

The miracles will be a continual stumbling-block to us if we do not seize this view of them. Regarded by themselves, they stun the mind and excite many eager questions, but placed in their right atmosphere and read in the high light of their generous purpose, the miracles are but the emphasis with which divine messages were delivered. No miracle is to be torn out of its setting, wrenched away from its proper atmosphere, and judged as a thing complete in itself. Every miracle belongs to something else, and if you do not bring that something else within your view, and add that in the consummation of your argument, you will miss the whole purpose and meaning of Christ's miracles. Yet this is how the miracles have been treated. They have been taken out one by one, brought away from their natural atmosphere and proper surroundings, and each has been judged as a thing that had no relation to anything else. Now Jesus Christ adds, in one utterance of reproach, the miracles to a grand moral purpose. He upbraided the cities and cried in terms of bitter reproach because the miracles had not produced *repentance*. They might have excited the cities to applause, roused the cities to admiration and delight, as mere feats of power; Christ would not have found, in such external enthusiasm, the result of his purpose.

Understand therefore, in reading the miracles, that every one of them has a *moral issue* in view in the scheme and providence of God, and we must not detach the miracle from the moral and beneficent purpose which God had in view in working that wonder in the sight of Man. Take the Incarnation of our Lord himself. As a mere incident in human history, it is incredible. But the Incarnation of our Lord is never set before us as a mere incident in human history. It is not an anecdote complete in itself, it brings up the ages with it, it sums infinite processes into one grand manifestation. As a divine method of coming into the race, it was from the point of reason the only method of approaching the solemn work which was to be done. Given, God's purpose to manifest himself unto the world in visible form, and the gospel method of incarnation was not only the best possible, but the only possible method. I wish we had the opportunity of working out that theorem to its fullest issues. It needs to be stated over and over again until men become perfectly familiar with its terms. Not only was the Incarnation of our Lord the best possible method of coming into the human race, but the only method of doing so. And this I undertake to show on the ground of natural reason itself.

God could not come into any common man as he came into Christ without first destroying that man's identity, altering the center and the weight of that man's responsibility, and placing that man in a totally false relation to every other member of the human race. The Incarnation of God in Christ exactly as it is stated in the gospel alone fills my imagination and satisfies my reason in its sternest mood. It would have amounted, had God come into any common man as he came into Christ, to an invidiousness which would have insulted every intelligent creature, and would have set up a perpetual irritation in every process of moral reasoning. He chose one of ourselves, and out of the lips of that elect man he rebuked everyone of us. Why did he not choose everyone of us, why did he not come a million strong, why not incarnate himself in *every* creature that bore his image? He incarnated himself in one common man, picked up one of ourselves, dwelt in all the fullness of his deity in him bodily. Why did he not repeat the miracle according to the number of millions of human creatures upon the earth, and then the whole work would have been done? But to tell me that he incarnated himself in a creature precisely of my own kind and standing precisely on a level with myself, and then left me out and spoke to me through the man whom he had thus made his own tabernacle, insults my reason, annoys my sense of justice, fills me with contempt. But take the gospel method, coming as Christ came into the world, begotten by the Holy Ghost, conceived of the Virgin Mary, made like unto us yet without sin [Heb. 4:15], and it becomes a mystery indeed, but a mystery before which our reason uncovers its head and bows down in lowly wonder and worship. As it is, I can say, "Great is the *mystery* of godliness," God manifest in the flesh, but upon any other theory I should say, "Great is the *injustice* of godliness"; a common man is chosen and purified as a vessel of God, while other men are left to be touched and moved by his inferior ministry.

Do not detach the miracles from their atmosphere, above all things do not create any space between the miracle and its *moral purpose*; the moral purpose of every miracle was to bring men to consideration, to spiritual softening, to individual repentance, and it is through that moral purpose that the whole scheme of the miracles must be viewed and estimated.

Jesus Christ tells us that judgment is to be in proportion to opportunities. Tyre and Sidon will not have to answer for more than their own advantages. But this law, so simple and so just, adds to the gravity of living now. If we grow in responsibility as we grow in age, what arithmetician in all this house shall add up the sum of our obligation? He that despised Moses' law died without mercy under two or three witnesses; of how much more sore of a punishment do you suppose he shall be thought worthy who has trodden under foot the Son of God and has counted the blood of the covenant wherewith he was sanctified an unholy thing, and has done despite unto the spirit of grace? It is an awful thing to live now. We live longer than Methuselah lived; we are astounded by patriarchal statistics as to human age, but there is not a child living who has not lived longer than Methuselah lived. We live longer in a week than Methuselah lived in a century; his age was but a span to ours; everything is made ready to our hands, the whole world is now a grand machine for the instantaneous doing of things; there is nothing more possible in our case. If I were called upon to say what more could be done, I should be at an utter loss to reply.

What more could be done in your case? Let me for a moment ask, individualizing any one of you. Tell me wherein you have been neglected. Have you heard every variety of human voice, have you heard the son of thunder and the son of consolation, do you have the open Scripture in your house, written in your mother-tongue, is not the air full of sacred ministry, in every street is there not a sanctuary throwing open its hospitable doors and inviting you to its hospitable refreshment? Haven't you been reared in a Christian home, taught the prayers that Jesus breathed, have you not been prayed over, cared for, watched, written to in many a tender motherly epistle, spoken to, and had the advantage of much fatherly counsel? Have your friends not gathered around you and welcomed you to some higher life and nobler purpose—what more can be done? What if the next voice shall rend the air and a bitter wail of reproach shall fall upon your ear, God's own upbraiding, because you have returned to him the prophets and minstrels, the holy books, the cross, his son, the Holy Ghost, as unequal to the breaking up of the obduracy of your selfishness and the fortification of your selfish will. If you were to ask me what more could be done I should be, I repeat, at a loss to reply; you have heard the thunder, seen the light, listened to the music, had an opportunity of entering the open door of hope—a thousand new chances have come to you and offered you new light, to every one of these appeals and opportunities you have returned a sullen "No," a selfish denial, and God has nothing else. He said, "I will send my Son, they will reverence my Son, they will see me in my Son," and we have taken his Son and stoned him and slain him and have bound our oaths with his sacred name. O the tragedy, O the awfulness beyond all human speech! It shall be more tolerable for Tyre and Sidon in the day of judgment than for us, if we have refused the gracious offers of God.

To me there is a glowing and final proof of the eternal truthfulness of Christ in the fact that he never concealed his own failures. No impostor can afford to make the worst of his case. Impostors magnify their successes; through one success impostors try to force their way to others. Impostors live in grand reports, they publish their statistics to an admiring world—they never tell you of their failures. Truth alone loves truth. Jesus Christ never gave us a colored picture of the successes of his ministry. He did not hide his disappointment, he did not tell the disciples around him that Chorazin, Bethsaida, and Capernaum were much better than they looked, and there were instances of encouragement and germs of promise, and he did not tell three of the disciples that they themselves came out of the very Bethsaida on which they were looking. No, he was true, he spoke the truth, he confessed the terrific tragedy of his soul's disappointment. "And when he came near the city he wept over it, and said, O Jerusalem, Jerusalem, how often would I have gathered thee as a hen doth gather her brood under her wings, and ye would not" [Luke 13:34]. Ye will not come unto me that ye might have life" [John 5:40]. "We will not have this man to reign over us" [Luke 19:14], you say. He upbraided the cities wherein most of his mighty works were done, because they repented not.

You will always find Christ consistent with his own truthfulness. He has nothing to color, pervert, distort, tinge with glowing tints, in order that he may win further support. He says, "I have labored and I have reaped nothing. I have toiled and my labor has been my only reward. I came unto my own, and my own received me not." There is a ring of solemn truthfulness in all these declarations. Impostors would have seen the glitter and called it gold. Christ saw the failure, and upbraided those who had caused his ministry to return to himself as a bitter disappointment.

But this question arises: Is it possible for Jesus Christ to have come into any city and to have preached the gospel, and to have shown his mighty works, and yet for that city not to repent? Let me tell you that we have too many analogies in our own common life to allow us to doubt that possibility for one moment. Some of us have sinned away the very highest advantages of secular life. Here is a man of the highest education; he was passed through a university career and brought out after him all the prizes the university could offer. He is adorned at every point, the very ripest specimen of the most modern culture, so far as his intelligence is concerned. It would be impossible for that man to do the dishonorable deed, to speak the dishonorable word, to play falsely, to be guilty of malfeasance; he will be true, upright, noble, pure, beautiful as a beam of light. Not *necessarily* so. We have known such men use their intelligence as an increased facility for doing mischief.

Here is a man surrounded by all that art can do for the adornment and the enlivenment of his home, every panel a picture, every window a hint of beauty, the whole surrounding a triumph of the highest art. As the man sits there, his thoughts will correspond with his surroundings. He will say, "It will be impossible in this sanctuary of beauty to be other than beautiful myself; my souls sings in this place of color, and my heart is at ease amid all this harmony of architectural and artistic relationships. There can be no unrest here; all the lines fall into one another; all the colors hold sweet fellowship; the whole house is all but alive; it will be a sacred place." Not necessarily. In that palace of beauty plots of iniquity may be hatched; under that fair ceiling sin may perpetrate its most cunning victory; amid all that beauty there may be a moral hideousness which may make the angels weep. The life of that man may be a daily insult to every soft color, to all the blended lights and shadows, and to the very genius of the sanctuary of art and loveliness. In many a humble cot, in many a lowly home, with hardly a little engraving in it, you will find a moral loveliness which would turn that debased palace into a scene of a most ghastly hideousness.

Yes, it is possible to sin away music, beauty, love, life, light; possible to sin away all the ministry of wife, child, friend, picture, and all that makes life deep, solemn, lovely. If it be so, then it is but a step to the other possibility of sinning Christ out of the life, urging him away, rebuking him and bidding him depart out of the region of our thought and love. My friend, I know of no ghastlier sight than grand external exaltation associated with moral perversity and putridity. Men would be shocked if they found under royal purple and regalia a skeleton propped up at the feast, with a foaming glass fastened in its bony and icy fingers. That would drive them mad; that would be intolerable irony; yet this is commonplace in the moral world. If you could go into the banquet house, and sit down next to the royal purple, and feel your face flushing with pride because of the association, and could then turn around and see that under the purple there was a dead carcass, you would never forget the sight, and you would refer to it as the most tragic of your experiences. You would shudder in horror every time you recalled the instance. My friends, 'tis nothing—a gibe, a joke, a thing to laugh at, compared with the *moral* skeletons that are around the table of the world everyday. Fine coats do not make fine characters; fine houses do not always mean splendid tenants; the basest metal may have a covering of gold. I wonder not that Jesus Christ, looking upon some men, said, "Whited sepulchers, full of dead men's bones, and men walk over them, and are not aware of them" [Matt. 23:27]. It required his eye, the eye in which is the light that shall make the glory of the resurrection morning, to see those whited sepulchers, and count those dead men's bones.

He sees us as we are; he conceals nothing of the ghastly reality; he prophesies no smooth things to sinners that are living lies. Thank God for the truthfulness of Christ. If you want to know what you are, go to him; he makes no false reading of character; he makes no miscalculation of human force and value; he is the one character that tests every other living man. O that upbraiding face, may we never see it! O that upbraiding voice, may we never hear it! Every eye shall see him, and they also that pierced him shall look upon him and mourn, and shall call to the rocks and to the mountains, saying, "Fall on us and hide us from the face and the wrath of the Lamb" [Rev. 6:16].

I have seen faces so laden with sorrow that to look upon them was to feel an intolerable burden of self-accusation resting upon and distressing the soul, without a word spoken, just as your mother looked when, after a thousand prayers, you came home—a wreck. She said, "Speech is useless; I have spoken, and my throat is sore." But O the look, the reddened eyes, the wet eyelids, the swollen face, the trembling lips, the whole look! It said, "How sharper than a serpent's tooth it is, to have a thankless child." And the old man, as he looked up off his book, and saw you, said nothing, but his eyes were judgment, his glance was hell.

O that upbraiding face, O that upbraiding voice—may they never come within our experience!

twenty

CHRIST'S JOY

Matthew 11:25–30

IN LUKE we read, tenth chapter and twenty-first verse, "In that hour Jesus rejoiced in spirit." There is no mention of the joy in the Gospel of Matthew. A great gladness filled his heart and while the fire burned he spake with his tongue. Why did he rejoice? Had riches been left him? Had he escaped the cross? Had great men fawned upon him? Did his age understand and appreciate him? Nothing of the kind. The scope of divine revelation had been indicated. He saw where the light was always to fall first; and when he saw babes become chosen angels of God, his soul was lifted up in holy rapture. There is no movement worth anything that does not begin with the babes; no solid and permanent kingdom can be set up in the ages that does not begin upon the babe-line. From that line you move upward through all classes, and take them all as you move in your comprehensive ascension and progress. Jesus Christ saw this, and when he saw it he rejoiced and thanked God.

We see how clearly he estimated the intellectual character of those who were called his disciples. He never supposed them to be great men intellectually; he knew what was in men; he did not suppose himself to be surrounded by the philosophy and the culture of his age. When he called twelve fishermen and men of other business around him to occupy the name and discharge the functions of disciples, he knew how humble were their intellectual capacities, how small and contemptible their mental culture. To his eyes they were little children, babes that knew nothing, persons whose eyes were filled with wonder and mystery and expectation, and who could give no full reply to any question that was put to them, but could turn their eyes of expectancy to their Master and Lord.

147

Jesus Christ was consistent in his appreciation of the child-mind. "Except ye be converted and become as little children, ye cannot enter into the kingdom of heaven" [Matt. 18:3]. He took a child and set him in the midst of them, and said:

> He that is most like this little child is greatest in the divine house. Take heed that ye despise not one of these little ones, for I say unto you, their angels do always behold the face of my Father which is in heaven. Suffer little children to come unto me, and forbid them not, for of such is the kingdom of heaven.

Was there ever a great nature in this world that did not go out towards the children redeemingly and gladly, with all hopefulness and most religious admiration, and find in every child a germ of something that had not entered into the imagination of man to conceive, as to its possibility of grandeur and magnificence of destiny? Was there ever a great nature that was not more than half womanly? O ye who have been making foolish calculations upon your slates as to greatness and grandeur and nobleness, know ye that the child is the best hope of the angel, and the woman nearer God than the man.

What is this child-heart? I would have it; tell me what it is. You must take the ideality of the case and not torment yourselves with accidental incidents. You must not point to this child as petulant and to that child as stubborn; you must—putting away all the incidences of the case—look at the ideal child-spirit. It is teachable; it does not come with propositions, suggestions, plans of its own. Assuming the unconscious dignity and attitude of teachability and expectation, it says in its religious silence, "Lord, teach me; show me what thou wouldst have me to do. Command me, do not consult me, but teach me what is right, good, true, wise, beautiful. Explain it all with that explanation which itself is the surest guarantee of its practical fulfillment in life."

Have we that spirit? Then God hides nothing from us of all his light. There is no secret which we could bear to know that he would keep from us if we were thus docile. Our prudence he disappoints; our wisdom he blinds with light; he rebukes it with darts of fire, but our childlikeness, littleness, nothingness, humbleness, why there is nothing which his great hands can hold, and which we could possibly receive, that he would keep back from us.

What is this child-spirit? It is *obedient*. To know is to do. To receive the word is to go out and carry it into practice—joyfully. Many of us know and fail to do; hence that sharp and fatal judgment, "To him that knoweth to do good and doeth it not, to him it is sin" [James 4:17]. But who can obey? We get the instructions in the inner sanctuary, and the devil always meets us at the threshold and says:

> Are you quite sure you heard the right voice? Are you
> perfectly clear that you understand what you have to do?
> Do you really appreciate all the complications and diffi-
> culties of the case? Do you fully realize to your own mind
> the fact that conditions change with ages, and that what
> might be suitable centuries ago is no longer suitable
> today? May there not have been some mistake in the in-
> terpretation?

And we who had gotten the staff in the hand and the sandals on the feet, and were going right out not knowing where we went, begin to hesitate and wonder and calculate and consult a thousand interests. Then the devil leaves us, and owns that his side of the battle is won. Hesitation is the ruin of obedience. To falter is to perish; to read over again the instructions is to lose the very vision which first beheld them, and the insight which first penetrated their sacred beauty.

The child's spirit is *trustful*: it nestles, it hugs, it clings to, it depends upon, it is wholly simple in its confidence. How then is it with our hearts— are we wise and prudent, or are we babes? God's best things are hidden from our mere cleverness: revelation is not the result of an intellectual process, it is the reward of a moral condition. We must be so far humbled as to accept the doctrine that we never conquer spiritual truth by intellectual cleverness. It is the lowly heart that reaps the harvest of this sunny field. "With the heart man believeth unto righteousness" [Rom. 10:10]. "Thou shalt love the Lord thy God with all thine heart" [Matt. 22:37]. Cleverness troubles itself with definitions, controversies, verbal consistencies, and subtle distinctions—the heart knows nothing of all this mischief. We are not saved by the head, we are saved by the heart; the heart waits upon God, the heart waits for God, the heart asks only vital questions, the heart utters only vital prayers. God will spare no revelation from love. "If any man love me," said Christ, "I will manifest myself to him. If any man love me, God will love him" [John 14:21].

Love is answered by love, cleverness is confounded by omniscience. If we will be clever in God's sight, he blinds us with the wisdom we would foolishly imitate. "To this man will I look, even to him that is poor and of a contrite spirit, and trembleth at my word" [Is. 66:2].

Why then are we not further advanced in the divine life? Simply because we are not further advanced in the *divine spirit of love.* We are orthodox in the *head,* we are unorthodox in the *heart.* We speak the right word, but we always speak it in the wrong tone. We are unimpeachable in verbal statement, and the whole heavens of God impeach us in every emotion and outgoing of the spirit. That is the lesson which needs to be forced upon every man in every age. What he has written upon paper may be right, may be beyond just impeachment on biblical or ecclesiastical grounds, and yet it is possible to read the Bible in an *unbiblical tone,* possible to say, "God is love" in a tone which spoils the beauty of the revelation. Are you orthodox in voice, orthodox in spirit, orthodox in temper, orthodox in desire? Then is there a happy and lasting harmony between the music of the heart and the music of the intelligence.

These reflections lead me to say that you must never look to any order of men who, by virtue of intellectual capacity and by culture *alone,* are authenticated as the teachers of Christ's religion. Get rid of the deadly sophism that there is a class of clever men called ministers or priests to whom *alone* God has committed his revelation. That, I repeat, is a deadly sophism, an utter, blank, black falsehood. Many a poor suffering woman knows more about the inner meaning of the Bible than any of its learned annotators have ever been able to reveal. No great preacher ever lived that was not great because of his littleness, modesty, teachability, trustfulness of heart before the Cross. There is no great preaching in the letter. The letter has its place, and a place that must be gratefully recognized and justly honored, but if ever I would penetrate into the inner and hidden meaning of any passage, I must shut myself up with God, and look towards his holy habitation through my blinding tears, and listen as if for life to the still small voice. Only the afflicted man can expound the promises of God, only the man who has been torn down, the roof pulled off that sheltered him, the fire put out that warmed him, the bread snatched out of his hand that fed him, and who has been scourged into the wilderness for forty days together and more, can expound to me the deep, rich things of God's heart.

There are great messages to declare which young persons inexperienced may well speak, for in the delivery of all the messages of this kingdom we want young voices, silver trumpets, grand outbursts, jubilant cries, herald-like clearness and precision of delivery, but when we come to ask our deeper questions, and confront the more solemn problems of life, we must go near to the bent old man whose once thunder voice is now shriveled into a croaking whisper, and learn from him what the deep messages of God to the human heart really and forever mean.

Thus we all come upon one level. There are no ministers that are classified and set in rows, and specially authenticated with the keys and with the authority of heaven except those ministers—men, women, and children, rich and poor—who have the child-heart, the child-eye, the child-life, and who utter music, and do not know themselves to be more than instruments of God. The greatest revealers of the divine message are men who hardly know that they are revealing it. They speak light, and they wonder that everybody else does not speak in the same way. The man of the keenest insight into Biblical revelation that has lived in this age, so far as I am aware—the man of the eagle eye, the eagle-visioned heart—is Frederick William Robertson, of Brighton. He seemed to know all God's heart. When people wrote to him with puzzles and mysteries of a religious kind, he sat down like a little child on the roadside, and said, "I will tell you how that is," as if he wondered that they did not already know; and his sentences are lights, his pages are luminous. When we have read him, we say, "What fools we were not to have seen it before." Yet was he persecuted unto the death, utterly killed and slain by men who have yet to face the judgment of God on his account.

Read your Bibles for yourselves; read them in your mother tongue. It is possible not to know in what language the Bible was originally written, and yet to know all its deeper meanings through the translation that is in our hands today. Say, "Open Thou mine eyes, and I shall behold wondrous things out of thy law; open my understanding that I may understand the Scriptures. Make me a little child in thy school, Thou gentle Christ, and let every word come to my heart in its simplest and most direct meaning and force." Then shall we be all Bible scholars, learned men in the school of Christ. Come with your grammars, your dictionaries, your culture, your cleverness, your controversial powers, your faculties all awake, questioning and cross-questioning and examining point by point, and consistency with consistency; and the Bible can make itself very haughty; like its central figure, it can draw itself up into fatal silence, and look at you as if it heard not a word uttered by your clamorous tongue. I will hasten to my Master, knowing nothing, and asking for knowledge from him, and I will take with me no part of my schooling and cleverness, and sharpness, and shrewdness, and sagacity. I will leave all these things right away behind me, and I will say, "Lord, what wouldst thou have me to do? What is thy will? Show me the meaning of this. If Thou canst not say it in letters on an example board, show it in life, though it come to tears and all the agony of life-long tragedy—yet in me magnify thyself. Whether by life or by death, show me thy meaning, and let my heart be the first to see it."

Jesus Christ sets himself up as an example of the child-mind in verse 27. "All things are delivered unto me of my Father, and no man knoweth the Son but the Father, neither knoweth any man the Father save the Son, and he to whomsoever the Son will reveal him." Observe how the words are paternal and filial—the Father, the Son, the Father knowing the Son, the Son knowing the Father, and the Son revealing the Father to other sons, for to "as many as received him, to them gave he power to become the sons of God" [John 1:12]. It is therefore to the child's spirit always that the revelation is made. Have we the child's spirit? We must be born again.

There is another indication of the spirit which Christ will bless—the new-born spirit desiring the sincere milk of the word [1 Pet. 2:2]—little children knowing nothing, but laying their ear on their father's heart to catch the music of its beating. Let us from this moment renounce ourselves, our cleverness, our ability, our so-called genius and talent, and let us know that the only genius that has any power in the sanctuary is the genius of love. Sorrow hears more than strength and fullness can ever hear, and when we are weakest then are we strongest; when we are most like little children then are we most like the angels of God.

The next words do not break the thread of sacred discourse; they rather give it a practical and beneficent aspect. "Come unto me, all ye that labor and are heavy laden, and I will give you rest. Take my yoke upon you and learn of me, for I am meek and lowly in heart, and ye shall find rest unto your souls. For my yoke is easy and my burden is light." How sweet can be his tone, how near the heart he can come, with what delicate expressions he can indicate the bitterest experiences of the world. How he knows us, in and out, through and through altogether.

"Come unto me, all ye that labor and are heavy laden with your controversies, misunderstandings, ceremonial observances, burden-bearing of every kind. It is a mistake, it is needless—come unto me and I will give you rest." This message I deliver in the name of Christ, to you who have been vexing your intelligence with a thousand questions and problems which you can never answer. My message thus takes upon itself great breadth of application, for I question whether there are many here who have not at times troubled themselves with a thousand outside inquiries which do not relate to the vital essence of this faith, and have nothing to do with the secret of this sanctuary. I question whether there are many here who have not tried to wash their hands when they ought to have known that it was their heart that needed cleansing. Today bring to me your diaries, your vow-books, your plans, your programs, your habits, your beginnings and your endings, your fire-lightings, your bullock-offerings—bring them to me and we will burn them in one common blaze and begin again by being nothing at all but little children in God's house. You want rest, and you can never secure that prize by your own effort. There is not a soul here that does not sigh for rest. There is no rest to be had except through Jesus Christ. The restful alone can give rest, peace alone can give peace. He will self-poise us, set our nature in its proper balance, bring all our faculties into harmonious relation and interplay, and thus he will establish us in the comfort and quietness of his own peace. We have seen this done in countless cases: in every instance we have seen apathy, deadness, surly reluctance sometimes mistaken for resignation, but only in the Christian sanctuary have we seen death accepted as life and the uttermost sorrow drunk as a sacrament of blood.

I have just perused the memorials of Catharine and Crawford Tait, the wife and the son of the Lord Archbishop of Canterbury. I will risk any argument upon the divinity of Christianity upon the experiences recorded in that volume. Your child died: but have you had two children dying, and as soon as the second died the third sickening for death, and as soon as the third died the fourth getting ready for heaven, and no sooner the fourth taken up than the fifth withers and dies—week after week till the whole five go, and all the little graves are green together, and the stranger unable to tell which of the five was cut first? And then have you been able to say, "Even so, Father, for so it seemed good in thy sight"? Then truly have you found rest unto your soul! Have you for years watched over your only son, and just when he was coming into the full fruition of his power and beginning life, buried him when he was but nine-and-twenty—the only son, the son that was to bear on the family name, the great and honored patronymic—and have you in the midst of all this yourself fallen down once and again all but dead on the floor, and lain in the sick-chamber for six and eight and ten weeks at a time, hardly able to breathe, much less to speak; and have you at the end of it all said, "Even so, Father, for so it seemed good in thy sight"? Then truly have you found rest unto your souls!

These are the triumphs which no hand can spoil, *these* the miracles that have an everlasting force in the calculations and reasoning of the soul. Jesus Christ is therefore not without witness in the families of the earth of his power to give quietness and rest and expectancy of a high kind in the time of flood and fire and sore distress.

Little children, let me tell you something before I sit down, bearing upon this same subject. A gentle man visited a deaf and dumb asylum, and having looked upon all the silent inmates, he was requested to ask some of them a question by writing it on the blackboard. He did not know what question to ask, but at last he ventured to write this inquiry in chalk upon the board, "Why did God make you deaf and dumb, and make me so that I could hear and speak?" The eyes of the silent ones were filled with tears: it was a great mystery. Their cleverness had no answer, but their piety made eloquent reply. One of the little fellows went up to the board, and, taking the chalk, wrote under the question this answer—"Even so, Father, for so it seemed good in thy sight." That lily we cannot paint!

twenty-one

THE SABBATH

Matthew 12:1–13

JESUS CHRIST treated the Jewish Sabbath in what the Pharisees thought was a rough manner. In their sense of the term he never kept the Sabbath at all. This was a continual subject of controversy between them: perhaps no subject of a special kind occupies in its treatment so large a space as this subject of Sabbath observance, as between the Pharisees and Jesus Christ. The fact was that Jesus Christ was going to establish a Sabbath of his own, and he began to indicate its character by putting the new wine into the old Sabbath bottle and thus breaking it. In due time he would prepare a new bottle for the new wine, and thus both would be preserved.

We learn from the incidents reported in this chapter how Jesus Christ wished to have the Sabbath regarded. In the first place, that which was necessary was to override that which was ceremonial. This was shown in the case of David. Hunger has no ceremonial law: where life is in danger, ceremony must go away. There was a kind of bread, as we have just seen, which the priests only got to eat. It was called the shewbread. The law distinctly said that it was for the priests alone. Yet when David and his followers were seized with the pains of hunger he broke the law in the letter, and yet kept the law in the spirit. Always be sure what law it is you are talking about: whether it is the little law, the incidental and temporary law, the law ceremonial, or the all-including law of which these are but parts or transient phases. In the case of David and the people who followed him, you have a necessity of a severe kind.

In the next place there was a necessity of a ceremonial sort by which the priests in the Temple profaned the Sabbath and were blameless. Fires were to be lighted, sacrifices were to be slain, the whole Temple service was to be set in order and carried out. Without such labor the service would have been impossible, yet the priests performed the labor and were blameless. They broke the Sabbath in the letter, they kept it in the spirit: they did that which was forbidden to be done, and yet, because it was necessary to be accomplished, there was no blameworthiness in their profanation of the day.

Thus, again, you must distinguish between laws. Always remember that one law belongs to another, and the highest law of life known amongst us is the law that man must be preserved. Man's highest interests must be consulted and secured. The law of necessity is above all laws of ceremony: the law of life determines the law of arrangement. Well, this simplifies the whole Sabbath question, if rightly accepted and applied. There are certain necessities which settle everything: what these necessities are must be left to the individual conscience to settle: do not attempt to draw time bills and regulation rules and schedules of observance—all that is mechanical, and possibly all that is nothing but silly childishness. Life cannot be codified, inspiration is better than regulation; if we have the right spirit, we can easily decide the right action. You will never determine a question of this kind by approaching it mechanically, with weights and scales and tapes and standards and measures of various kinds. It is a question which belongs to the spirit, to the inner sanctuary, to the noblest consciousness of humanity.

This is the whole essence and burden of Christ's meaning. The Pharisees broke the Sabbath in the very act of keeping it, so others may keep the Sabbath in the very act of breaking it. Again and again I would say, do not attempt to settle this question by little rules; you can only settle it insofar as you have the spirit of the Lord. I want to know how Christ treated the day; I will draw the whole of my inferences from his spirit, words, and conduct. As a Christian preacher and student I have not to consider whether I will have a Sabbath or not, I am bound in this, as in all other things, to study Christ, and by that study I will abide.

Jesus Christ lays down the sovereign law, "I will have mercy and not sacrifice; I will have the substance, not the shadow; I will have the heart's love, and not the hands' reluctant service." This spirit would settle everything in the broadest and most divine manner, and would so operate as to commend itself to both master and servant, to both leader and follower. In this spirit we should never have to see how much would be done on the Sabbath day, but how little. Some things definitely need to be done; David's hunger falls upon us, and the priest's necessities follow the Temple throughout the whole history of time. All work cannot be suspended: God suspends none of his own operations on Sunday; the sun shines, the river flows, the bird sings, the fruit ripens on Sunday as on Saturday, and yet he rested on the seventh day and blessed it. This is not a reading of the letter, but a reading of the spirit: the rest is in the soul; I can do all my labor of the week in one sense, where necessity compels it, and yet I can do it as if I were not doing it. It is another work when I do it under different conditions. I have to pursue much of my daily home-life just on Sunday as on Saturday, and yet I do it in no Saturday spirit, but with a new inspiration, broader meaning, tenderer love, and I lift up the action into a new atmosphere, and upon all the breadth of its face there shines the light of a new intent. The work done is not labor, it is done in the spirit of the day, and therefore the work itself becomes real and sacred rest.

Do not consult the mechanic as to how the Sabbath is to be kept, nor the precisian, nor the purist, nor the man who lives in the mere letter, and within the space, four square, of an arithmetical table. On the Sabbath day the blind must be lifted, the bed must be made, the table must be spread, the fire must be lighted, as on every other day, and yet quite differently. When I open my shutter on the Sunday I open it to take in a stranger with a known face, a visitor from heaven, a messenger with gospels on his lips. When I light my Sunday fire it does not crackle and smoke like a Saturday flame; it preaches to me—there is a sacred glow upon my face as I light it, and my heart is full of a new ardor, and I forget the toil in the sacrifice.

You cannot keep the Sabbath by precise rules. If I am ill I must have the doctor; if he is in church he must come out. Life rules your little laws. One far greater than the Temple is in it; the Temple is but the shadow, robe, type, symbol, and he represents all the higher laws that gather up within their operation all human necessities and conditions, and determine everything. The ships must go on Sundays; and yet there is Sunday on the sea, the spirit of rest gets hold of the great ship in the middle of the waves; and it is possible, with the splash of the waters around you, and the throb of the great fire-power stunning your ear, to be in church, nearly in heaven—a little speck upon the foam, and yet throwing out some little tendrils or fingers, to lay hold of the upper and better side of things.

The city must be kept on Sunday, it must be watched; the law must be abroad, all your institutions that are to be healthy and lasting must be based upon broad foundations, and not upon a point here and an incident yonder.

What this means you will know better in your heart than can ever be explained in words. The kitchen must be opened on the Sunday as well as the parlor, and all necessary things must be done by horse and dog and man, and yet they may be so done as to have in them all the divine music. This is not to be set forth in sentences that cannot be taken to pieces by critics, but those sentences may help to teach the deeper meanings which lie far down in the honest heart. When men combine to secularize the Sabbath and to make it of set purpose as common as any other day in the week, they become as great ceremonialists as the old Pharisees were; they are secular Pharisees, and they meet their old brethren at the other end of the line. There is a ceremonialism of destruction as well as a ceremonialism of preservation. In both cases the divine meaning may be lost. In pretending to do good the anti-Sabbatarians really do harm: they operate upon a one-sided view of the case, and all infidelity and non-Christianity does the same thing. I never met a non-Christian argument that did not treat life as if it were a straight line; it failed in perspective, in comprehensiveness, in that wholeness, that entirety of grasp and view, which alone can deal with the comic-tragedy and the tragic-comedy of this mixed and self-colliding life.

Our human education does not lie upon any one side of our nature: it is a complex process, and I have met with no religion that goes round and round the whole case with amplitude of seizure and sympathy but the religion of Jesus Christ. Those who would secularize the Sunday degrade the day as a certainty from a religious point of view, but there is no certainty that having degraded it at one end they can elevate it at the other, namely, on the side of the people for whom they have degraded the institution. There is a certain degradation at the one end, and not a certain elevation at the other; therefore the ways of the secularists in this matter are not equal. In my opinion they should begin at the other end by elevating the people and enlarging and purifying their conceptions of sacred and noble institutions. The Sabbath is an older institution than any picture-gallery or museum that I know anything about, and if any men are anxious that the working classes should have an opportunity of seeing pictures, monuments, and curiosities, let them cut a day out of their own time, and not steal a day which has another seal upon it. If you are in awful agonies of desire that your working-men should see pictures, shut up your warehouse half-a-day, and let them see them at your expense. If it really takes away your sleep that somebody cannot see a museum, then do you arrange for their seeing it without any loss on their part. There is a cheap generosity: the generosity of those who would secularize the day on these grounds degrades the day without certainly elevating the people. It is as if men should say: "Let us put an end to poverty by altering the law of property. That is a short and easy method of dealing with the pauperism and the whole necessity of the country. Here we have certain people called merchants, capitalists, millionaires, and here are certain other people without possessions of any kind: let us abolish the law of property, and raise the pauper and thriftless class by dividing the money of the wealthy, and thus making all men equal." One wonders that such an idea never struck anybody before, it is so clear, so simple, and so admirable—for those who have nothing. Let us make everyday alike, you know. Why are you not faithful to your own logic? Why are you not consistent with your own principles?

Now God, who gave us all our time, has laid his hand upon one day and called it his. On that day we are asked to think of him, commune with him, and rest in him. We must not steal the day; we ought not to deface it. Works of necessity must be done, and, so done, are blameless; if we want to give men more time for recreation or sightseeing let us give them some of our own time, and do not let us rob God. I believe that great improvements are possible in the way of rearrangement of our times of labor; I believe that all men who labor should have equal rest and recreation and enjoyment. I am not addressing myself to that side of the question now; I am only seeking to point out that even things desirable in themselves may sometimes be secured at too great a cost, and may sometimes be sought in a wrong light and under the inspiration of a false principle.

But Christ says the Sabbath was made for man. Precisely; and therefore man should take care of it. A false argument is often set up on this expression, as if man could do what he pleased with the Sabbath. The Sabbath was made for man, but was not made for man to destroy. The earth was made for man, but not for him to neglect or desecrate. The very expression itself is a proof of the sacredness of the day. It is not said that Monday was made for man. A special meaning attaches to this gift of time;

it is holy, it is a piece cut out, it is a sanctuary, it is a resting-place on the journey of life, it was made for man, it was set apart for man, it is God's gift to man, it is a hint and type of heaven. I should therefore be very careful how I touched its sacredness.

There may be special cases in which the Sabbath may be profaned and the profaners may be blameless. If any man should stand up here and say, "I can get nearer heaven when I muse alone in the field or in the forest than when I attend any Church," I am not going to call that man of necessity a Sabbath-breaker or a profane person: I do not believe in his reasoning purely as logic, I do not believe in the facts of the case as entitling me to generalize so as to include the whole population of the land: I would make special arrangements for such special cases, I would judge individual cases with the largest charity, but my own feeling is this, that no man who uses the Church as the Church ought to be used can find anywhere an influence that ought to admit of a competitive position for one moment, when the Church services are rightly conducted, in their music, in their devotion, in their pulpit instruction: when the revelation of God is treated in all its firmamental breadth and all its solar lustrousness there will be no place on all the green earth so attractive and so grand as the house of God.

We may have to begin by enlarging our definitions of that very name. It is possible that we may have to rearrange our whole method of observing the Sabbath within the sacred walls. I am not set upon any form of observing it in any Church: I hold myself open to inspiration from heaven, to guidance and suggestion from good men and experience: and it does appear to me perfectly possible that we may have to enlarge our conception of the divine service in the divine house. But if there is any meaning in the words "Day of God, House of God, service Divine," the Church ought to be able to look down upon all competition with a dignity that need not be contemptuous because of its superlative and unquestionable grandeur.

I do not wonder at people running away from certain kinds of service; I do not wonder at any patch of green being a more favorite spot than the places where certain methods prevail of conducting the service in the sanctuary. I have attended services which have done me great harm, and if the service was limited to what this or that man has done or said I would never enter the place again with any hope of being edified or blessed. I have had to exclude the external and shut myself up with God himself, or I should have been lowered and narrowed and de-based by things pronounced without the spirit of the Sabbath animating their utterance or lifting them up into the region of music.

On both sides of the subject there are great difficulties, and great differences, and when it is said the Sabbath was made for man it was meant for man to keep and not for man to throw away. Professor Tyndall says, in a really beautiful document, written in the most tuneful English, that he would like to see tramways from slums and back places of the city out into the green fields on Sundays. Very good, Professor Tyndall, we will lay tramways, and you shall drive the cars. So many persons propose these grand arrangements who also propose to be passengers themselves. I have never known any article-writers propose to be *drivers*.

The Professor says that a rigid Sabbatarianism has been tested and has resulted in ghastly failure. I do not propose a rigid Sabbatarianism: I know nothing of mechanical rigidities in God's house and God's service. When a man talks about a rigid Sabbatarianism he changes the ground of controversy and changes the issue of the argument. I am speaking of a day of rest, a day of joy, a day of fellowship with God. But the Professor must be just, and allow us to say, on the other hand, that we have seen a lax Sabbatarianism tested, and the results have appeared to us to be hideous failures. I know of no sight abroad that has distressed me more than a week without a Sabbath. I would avoid narrow-mindedness as I would avoid offense against God and against man, but speaking with my present information and under the influence of what I believe to be a good feeling, I would pray God that England might be saved from what is known as a Continental Sunday.

The people who quote the expression "The Sabbath was made for man" forget the further expression, "The Son of man is Lord even of the Sabbath day." The servant, then, should consult the Lord if he would know how the Lord's gifts are to be enjoyed. What would Christ have us do on this day? What value does Christ set upon the day? When it is called the Lord's Day, what is the meaning of the expression? If any man find it hard to spend one day with Christ let him eke out his day with green fields and silvery streams, and tuneful woodlands, and all the other enjoyments of nature. To me the day is too short: I would the sanctuary could be opened with the dawn and closed with the midnight bell. What is the day meant to be? A day of joy. "This is the day the Lord hath made; we will rejoice and be glad in it"[see Ps. 118:24]. It is resurrection day; its morning opens with visions of angels, with empty tombs, with risen lives and sweet comforting of peace. It is the day on which the seed brings forth sixty and a hundred fold; the heart sees widening heavens, and hears supernal music, and responds to new calls of duty, and hears a voice ruling the tumult of time and hushing the wild uproar of all passion. Today the heart drinks wine with Christ, today the banquet hall is open and the hungry are called to great feasting. Never was this intended to be a day of gloom, of long faces, of dejected aspect and afflictive memories. Yes, some so-called Sabbatarians have injured the day, have degraded its meaning; they have narrowed its benevolent purpose, they have assumed a solemnity they did not feel, and they have lost the naturalness of their voice in a whining piousness as offensive to God as it is objectionable to man. To me the day is full of joy, a great golden day, lacking only in one thing, and that is in duration—so short, a flash and gone. If ever we may be glad even to passionateness of joy it is on this day, with its resurrection light and its triumphant Lord.

We are sometimes asked if it is not better to go to a picture-gallery than to a public-house. There is no meaning or essence in the question; we are not shut up to *that* alternative. The question does not narrow itself into picture-gallery or public-house; if it did so we could settle it in a moment. Certainly to the picture-gallery and remain there all day. Beware of the sophisticated inquiry whether it is not better to do this than to do that; no greater argument rests upon such narrow alternatives. It is better to steal wheat than to steal nettles, it is better to steal oil paintings than to steal photographs, it is better to tell lies for a thousand a year than to tell lies for a hundred a year—but this is not the question, this is a sophist's inquiry. The question is, What is *right*? What is *good*? What is God's law? What is best for the human family at large? The question can have no difficulty as to the true value and purpose of the Sabbath. Christ gave the Church his laws, and I should wish to keep my Sabbath just as Jesus kept his. My distinct view is that instead of having too much time for religious service and instruction we have too little. Rather than destroy one Sabbath I would create two. The rest is always profitable. You do not rest half enough, you men of business. Napoleon truly said that no man could long work for seven days in the week. Religious rest is indispensable. He is the true benefactor of England who holds to the sanctity of the Sabbath, and makes that sanctity not a miserable gloom, but a radiant and grateful joy.

twenty-two

MIGHTY WORDS AND MIGHTY JUDGMENTS

Matthew 12:14–37

"THEN THE PHARISEES went out and held a council against him, how they might destroy him," because he had broken the Sabbath day. The penalty would seem too much, but it is the way with passionate men that they should overleap themselves, and show by the severity of their penalties some sign of the errors of their own supposed piety. You will generally find that a man's condemnation of other people is meant to be a recommendation of himself. Study this law of social penalties, and you will be amazed, I think, to find how constantly it operates in this direction. A man severely condemns this or that offense on the part of his fellow-creatures. Is it a really honest judgment upon the offense or the sin? Is it not oftentimes a backhanded compliment to himself, as who should say, "What a virtuous man I am: how my indignation burns like an oven against such offenses. Trust me, I am judge and purist and honorable man"?

The Pharisees sought to destroy Christ because he had broken the Sabbath day. This was the exaggeration of piety—a piety that, by its own exaggeration, broke itself, and became impiety, so that extremes met. But what could you expect from men who actually wrote in plain letters this doctrine, that to eat with unwashed hands was more criminal than homicide? That to eat with unwashed hands, let me explain to the children, was worse than to kill a man. It is thus that good doing falls into Pharisaical impiety when it is left without a divine and living center; this is what we come to in the absence of a legitimate and adequate authority: our morality becomes offensive; we rearrange it: we put it in new lights, and place it at new angles, and we make experiments of it, and we run it through all the gamut of our own imagination, until at last it becomes the wildest farce, the most consummate and intolerable nuisance. We want a standard authority, a court of appeal, a law that says, "Thou shalt and thou shalt not," and a spirit which interprets that law with all the breadth of poetry, and yet with all the clearness and narrowness of the highest rectitude. This law and this spirit we find in him only who is the Son of man.

"But when Jesus knew it, he withdrew himself from thence." This was the true courage; it was no use opposing physical force to physical force. The man whose life is founded upon a great plan does not live by mere surprises, nor does he trust to what is called the fool's Bible, namely, the chapter of accidents. He removes the occasion; he will not even lead his enemies into temptation; he can always get out of the way. No man could hide himself so impenetrably as Jesus Christ, no man could look so speechless. He looked at Herod until Herod was glad to call in a score of servants to keep him company. No man could be so silent as Christ, could withdraw himself to such infinite distances as Christ, even while he stayed and looked at you. He frightened Pilate like a ghost leering out of the darkness.

This was part of the wisdom of Christ, that he should not bring his enemies into temptation to kill him. He kept back force by that subtlest and mightiest of all forces, true prudence. Force, you fool, is not in your fist; that is the simplest of weapons; it is in wisdom, compassion, abstention from violence, in the negativeness that simply withdraws and calmly awaits.

Yet Jesus Christ could not withdraw alone under such circumstances. "Great multitudes followed him." The multitudinous heart knew Christ, the sectarian heart hated him. Which is yours—which is mine—the heart that would slay him because of his violation of a rule, or the heart that would trust him because of the pain of a great necessity?

"But Jesus Christ was so distressed with his official reception, or reception by the official mind, that he paid no heed to the multitudes, fell into a great gloom—his lips were shut up in stubborn silence, and his hand, that had never been put out but to bless, fell in paralysis at his side." The story might well have read so, but it reads wholly different. "He healed them all." But there was a council whispering away yonder in the city, and the meaning of the whisper was the death of this healing Man. He nevertheless kept on with his healing. Let that be your policy and mine; if men hate us, let us heal all who come lovingly within our influence.

Beware of the evil influences of mere disgust. Never be disgusted. Look at the work, and not at the difficulties of the way; look at the Master, and not at the provocations given you by many of his servants—have the *end* in view. Jesus Christ endured the cross, despising the shame, looking onward to the glory that was to come. This is the secret of steady, continuous, and divine work. Little natures fly off on little excuses. Little natures gather up all the provocations that have been launched against them until they become one great agony which the mind can no longer bear. Jesus Christ kept on healing the multitudes, though councils gathered against him, and officers of the Church made it their one business to shed his blood. "Let this mind be in you that was also in Christ Jesus, who, being in the form of God, thought it not robbery to be the fellow of God, but emptied himself and became a servant and obedient— obedient unto the death of the cross" [see Phil. 2:6–8].

"And charged them that they should not make him known," that a great prophecy might be fulfilled. Jesus Christ did not want to be made known through his miracles only; it was a poor thing to be known as the chief of magicians, which he might have been mistaken for by those who had not the true reading of the signs and wonders which he came to perform. He knew that they would take the narrow view, they would read the lines upon the surface, they would not hear the inner music nor see the inner light, nor feel the inner pathos; they would talk about miracles and wonders and startling signs, and thus would feed their curiosity, and pay no attention to the deeper hunger of the heart.

Jesus Christ never made much of his miracles, except in an introductory and illuminative sense. He never wished to be known through his miracles. You cannot point to an instance in which he said, "This miracle is enough to astound the world and bring it to a spiritual conviction regarding my Messiahship." If ever he referred to them it was to satisfy vulgar curiosity, and not to satisfy a deep spiritual instinct. Now and again he had to point to his miracles, but it cost him something to stoop to such condescension as to indicate the mere issues of his power. His friends were always tempting him in this direction. They took the low, vulgar, and narrow view, which we are all inclined to take of great souls. We wonder how they do not do more; we could show them how to come more boldly out, and to take the age so as to incite in it a more profound amazement and a keener surprise. We know what to do, though these great souls know it not themselves. So Jesus Christ's friends came around him once and said, "If thou do these things show thyself to the world." That is the vulgar Christianity of this day, not seeing its spiritual aspect, not feeling its tender unction, not knowing the meaning of the compulsion of pure love. Tell me if the world or the Church has got one inch beyond this program of the friends and relatives of Jesus Christ, namely, "If thou do these things show thyself to the world. Make a show of the miracles, publish a list of them, take the greatest place that is at liberty, and repeat these miracles night by night to thronging multitudes. Take thy position at the front." That is the program which makes a splutter at the first, but that dies like a spark in the river. There is no solidity in it, nothing lasting. The true program is—Be true, love the truth, move in God, be silent because of the very majesty of thy faith. Less faith would mean noise and crying and great demonstration; completeness means quietness.

Herein are so many mistakes that are made about men and things. I have observed as men grow in education and in wisdom, and in all moral and spiritual refinement, they grow in composure. The last result of education is peace, quietness, rest. The vulgar man looks at the man of deep thought and great learning, and says, "Not very happy looking, is he? His eyes were nearly shut, his mouth was firmly set, and he seemed to be looking at nothing." The man was beyond the appearance of looking, he was absorbing everything all the while, and, as he added feeling to feeling and line to line in the upper progress of his soul, he lost the fuss, the noise, the love of demonstration which belonged to the earlier period of progress than the one which he had attained. Jesus would influence the world on permanent lines and from permanent centers; he was not an acrobat that would fling himself into fantastic attitudes in the air to cause a moment's laugh or shout, and then die away—he takes the ages to grow in, he takes all time for his summer and his harvest, and he reveals himself not to our surprise or curiosity or haste, but to the ages, in all the vastness of their compass and all the profoundness of their solemnity.

By a very beautiful figure is the peacefulness of his disposition indicated. "A bruised reed shall he not break, and smoking flax shall he not quench, till he send forth judgment unto victory." What is this bruised reed? Is it as a bulrush, crushed by some great beast as he moves towards the river? Jesus Christ takes it up and rejoints it, or spares it, or makes nature pitiful to it with extra nursing and love—for nature is a great mother, healing every scar and hiding every wound and working a great wizardry of concealment around all the great gashes and bruises of the world. Or is the reed the musical instrument of the primitive kind, on which the shepherd played upon the hills and in the valleys, and had it gotten out of order so that the tune would no longer come out of it? Jesus Christ says, "Give it to me, and I will repair it, and that bruised reed shall be as musical as ever." He did not come to destroy but to save, and the exquisiteness and the perfectness of his saving purpose are indicated in this analogy, that even the bruised reed, not worthy of saving, is one of the fragments that he will gather up that nothing be lost.

"The smoking flax he will not quench." Is it some poor man's one candle just going out, an inch of wick and no more, and will he take it and shield it, or wave it gently in the air so as to renew its life? Is it the one mean spark on which everything depends, and will he put his arms all around it like a great defense, or will he breathe upon it so as to save its flickering flame till it burst out and seize the entire substance and consummate the purpose for which it was lighted? Take it in any way, it means this—that the Son of man is not come to destroy but to save [see Luke 9:56]. He is mighty to save: he came into the world to save sinners [see 1 Tim. 1:15]. "Thou shalt call his name Jesus, for he shall save" [Matt. 1:21]. This being the purpose of his life, the whole meaning of his incarnation, you will find that everything falls into its proper place in relation to the sovereignty of this aim. Do not read the life of Jesus Christ as if it were a series of unrelated anecdotes; find the central purpose of it, and see how everything sets itself in happy crystallization around that purpose, and helps to explain and commend it.

Having been engaged with great multitudes and healing them all, the Savior is next engaged with an individual instance. "Then was brought unto him one possessed with a devil, blind, and dumb." Sometimes the one case is the multitudinous instance, sometimes you find in one case the adding up of a host of cases. Devil, blind, dumb, pronounced incurable, written down amongst the hopeless—it seemed to be a single instance. In reality it was a multitude of cases all in one. Everyone of us is a multitude in this sense. Life is not all in little drops of ink or blood, which can be indicated by brief names and summed up in an *etcetera*. In my heart, in your heart there is a legion of devils, and yet the plural and the singular come together in most suggestive conjunction in the delivery of that fact. "What is thy name?" said Christ.

The answer was, "My name is legion" [Mark 5:9]. Not *our* name is legion—*my*. "I am many in one, I am one in many. I am not broken up into a multitude of incoherences, but I am one." Study human history and get from it what hints you can of the diabolic administration, and they will all help you to understand that the crowning characteristic of the diabolic monarchy is persistent and indestructible unity. You never find Satan divided against himself.

Now the Pharisees come again upon him. They heard of this instance, and they said, "This fellow doth not cast out devils but by Beelzebub the prince of the devils." They have been unable to *kill* him, but it is still within the compass of their malignity to *denigrate* him. Once your Savior was called "this fellow," once a reed was taken and with it he was smitten on the head, once that face was spat upon, once that unwrinkled cheek was smitten, and the work was never given up for a moment. He endured the cross, despising the shame, because of the glory that was set before him [Heb. 12:2]. Poor hasteful man, you want to be a king all at once, not knowing that any kingdom that is worth having is entered by a straight gate and approached by a narrow path. "Enter ye in at the straight gate . . . for straight is the gate and narrow is the road that leadeth unto life" [Matt. 7:13, 14].

This instance, however, gives us a new view of the ministry of Jesus. He seldom condescended merely to argue with his opponents, he simply pursued his work and allowed his work to be his witness. In this case, however, he turns around upon those who malign him and answers them argumentatively. Let us be present when he answers his enemies—there is always a treat in store then. There was no such replicant as Christ: his answers admitted of no retort; no man, according to this history, ever ventured to reply to his answers. Collect the answers of Christ to his enemies, and tell me if anything can exceed the polish of their wit or the pathos of their feeling. Here is a case in point. Having read the thoughts of the Pharisees and understood the case, he answered them logically. "Every kingdom divided against itself is brought to desolation, and every city or house divided against itself shall not stand. But if Satan cast out Satan, he is divided against himself—how then shall his kingdom stand?" As if he had said, "See the absurdity of your position from a merely logical point of view. If Satan were to cast out Satan, his kingdom would be overthrown by his own hand, and if I by Beelzebub cast out devils, by whom do your children, or your countrymen, cast them out?

You are making a fool of the very devil you seek to credit with this mystery of wonder."

Thus he reduces to absurdity the thought or suggestion of the Pharisees. The devil is one, and he works with all the strength of unity. Do you know what the supreme prayer of the Turk is? You may be surprised to hear it, but it is a clever prayer from the Turk's altar. He prays to his God that the discords of the Christians may never be settled. Clever Turk, cunning Turk, he prays that we as Christians may never settle our controversies, for while we are fighting he is safe. It is the devil's prayer, if ever he turn his eyes of smoke and flame to the blue heavens, that the Churches may never settle their grievances, and never bring to a happy harmonious reconciliation the differences which trouble and vex them. He thrives upon our discord; there is joy in the presence of the demons of hell over every fight that divides and disables the Church.

Having answered his assailants logically, he proceeds to answer them judicially. Standing and looking at them as a scourging fire, he says, "Wherefore I say unto you, all manner of sin and blasphemy shall be forgiven unto men, but the blasphemy against the Holy Ghost shall not be forgiven unto men." So then Christianity is more than an argument; an argument it certainly is, having command of all the forces of logic and wit, swift repartee and complete reply, but Christianity is not a battle of words, it is a judgment upon the spirit, it is an anathema or it is a benediction, it is the savor of life unto life or the savor of death unto death. When you touch this Christianity, you touch something more than a mere competitor for your intellectual appreciation and your intellectual confidence: it is as a stone which, if a man fall upon, he shall be broken to pieces—happy breaking—or if it fall upon the man it will grind him to powder, and there are no hands with skill and strength enough to reconstitute that powder into the solid stone.

Beware of this unpardonable sin: not one of us has yet committed it: it lies within the power of the lowest of us *now* to do it. Take care how you lie unto the Holy Spirit or deny his ministry or insult his beneficent majesty; take care how you cut yourself off from the currents of life. If a tree could seize itself and drag every fiber of its root out of the earth, what would become of the tree? All nature would fight against it and kill it, its juices would be sucked out, its veins would be dried up with an everlasting drought, and never more would the birds of the air tenant themselves in its leafy boughs; it has cut itself out of the grooves along which nature sends her life-currents.

Take care how you uproot yourself and seek isolation; take care how you say you will not have the light, and you will not have the dew, and you will not be dependent upon the earth. If a man could so cut himself out of the ministry of nature, what would become of him? Rottenness and putridity would be his lot, and because of his very noisomeness men would hide them away. It is even so spiritually. A man can put the knife through every filament that binds him to the universe, he can cut down his veneration, his imagination, his impulses towards the morning, and all its blue and tender light, he can snatch himself away from the altar and never pray another prayer, he can thrust his face into his chest and look downward to the dust to find what he can in the simple stones beneath his feet, he can separate himself from all social charities and all happy fellowships, he can rebuke the child that would kiss him and run away from all the influences that would redeem him, and having done so, what has become of him? He is twice dead, plucked up by the roots, he is a cloud without water, he has offended the spirit of the universe, he has sought to live alone, and that is the impossibility of human life.

Hear the gospel then this day, men of business, men of toil, women, children, whole families, masters, servants — here is a man who heals on the Sabbath day, and today is the Sabbath: here are those who object to him and still he proceeds with his gracious work: here are those who carry their objection to black blasphemy, and they are told that one step further and they go into a new gravitation and never can arise again.

twenty-three

CHRIST'S DENIALS

Matthew 12:38–50

IT WAS ALWAYS difficult for Christ to say *No*. Surely he was not born to say that cold word to any human heart that asked a question of him. The negative did not come easily to those beneficent lips—they were shaped rather to say with all tunefulness and sympathy of love, "Yes," to every human desire, to every yearning, loving spirit. Yet in this case Jesus Christ says "No," and no man can say "No" with so severe a firmness. In his lips, under such circumstances as are detailed in the text, his No was final. He had an intermediate No, which he never meant to stand as such—the No which he said to the Syro-Phoenician woman—it was an experimental No, there was no hollowness of final, negative purpose in it, it was one of the trials or temptations addressed to the human heart by him who intends to fill that heart with larger blessing in consequence of its temporary denial. When did Jesus Christ say "No" to the sick, to the weary, to the broken-hearted, the bruised, the helpless, the wounded spirit? When did he say it to any little child that asked the favor of his smile? Yet in this case, standing up in front of an evil and adulterous generation, he said "No." 'Twas unlike him and yet very like him: he would rather have said "Yes" to human prayer, but it is sometimes quite as merciful to say "No" as to say "Yes."

What was it the Scribes and Pharisees wanted from Jesus Christ? They sought a merely intellectual gratification, they wanted a sign, something to estimate, something to speculate upon, another link in a chain of argumentative evidence. Jesus Christ never came to satisfy the mere intellect of man. Therein have all the doctors and sages and leaders of the Church made many a mischievous mistake. They have written evidences, and built up proofs, and conducted a high intellectual argument. The gospel has nothing to say to the intellect merely as such; to the intellect, stiff and blind in its godless conceit, the gospel has nothing to utter but a plain disappointing "No." The wisdom of this world is not the wisdom of God. What are called proofs, in the lower schools of men, are not to be taken as proofs in the higher reasoning and in the more divine culture. "With the *heart* man believeth unto righteousness" [Rom. 10:10]. "Blessed are the pure in *heart*, for they shall see God" [Matt. 5:8]. "To this man will I look, to him that is of a broken and contrite *heart*, who trembleth at my word" [see Is. 66:2]. "The secret of the Lord is with them that fear him" [Ps. 25:14]. In the sixty-first chapter of Isaiah, in which the mission of Christ is stated in many particulars, I find no reference to the intellect. "The spirit of the Lord God is upon me, because he hath sent me"—what to do? To give signs and wonders, to satisfy mere intelligence and carnal curiosity and intellectual ambition? No such line can be found in this loving and beneficent specification of duty and vocation. The meek, the captive, the bound, the tired, the helpless, the mourning, the tearful, the sad—all these are gathered within the enclosure of Christ's purpose, but the merely intellectual and literalistic and argumentative, where are they? Outside, of no consequence in this great strife—they will be brought in by other processes, yea, they shall be found on bent knee, worshiping him who is the King. Meanwhile Jesus Christ keeps his great answers and his great promises and benedictions for the meek, the brokenhearted, the sincere, the child-like, the docile, and those who have no self-confidence.

What does Jesus Christ teach in this broad answer? Jesus Christ teaches that there is already enough in human history to satisfy every healthy and earnest mind if right use be made of it. The great questions of the heart were answered at the beginning; the gospel is in Genesis; God planted every tree from the very first, and the after ages have but developed the roots set in the human heart by the divine hand, or planted in heaven by him who plants only the trees of righteousness. All great answers have been given. Jonah and the queen of the south have their counterparts in all histories and in all cultivated and developed human lives. If you have not lived the story of Jonah the dictionary can never explain it to you. The whale and its mouth, and a thousand mysteries that gather around it—you will never be able to understand it, but if you have been Jonah, and have been in the whale and in the deep, and have been cast out, and have passed through all the tragedy, you will know the meaning of the spirit, without being able to give any satisfaction to those who live in the universe of a zoological garden, and who never penetrate the inward poetry and apocalyptic meaning of the things that are happening around them everyday. The earth is full of signs, the heavens shine with tokens, all life is a witness and confirmation. We need no more proof; what we do need is to make better use of the proof we already have.

Let me, therefore, speak with all moral incisiveness and positiveness of meaning, to those who are yet among the Scribes and the Pharisees, saying, with vulgar or ill-concealed conceit of intellect, "Master, we would see a sign from heaven." There shall no more signs be given; what we now have to do is not to add to the evidences but to utilize them. You do not need a new Bible, you need to read the Bible you already have in your hands. There is not a man in a thousand who knows anything about the Bible vitally and really, in all its grasp and meaning. There is no book of such momentous purpose and significance so little read and so little understood. We are outside, and we see only the edges and surfaces of things written in the inner book. We do not want more evidences, evidences have often misled the thinker or have only been food to the pride of his intellect, or have only established him in the confidence of his own conceit, for wherein he has mastered them, he has said, if not in words yet in effect, "See how able I am, and how clever and how masterly is my grasp of things." That man has not come into the kingdom of heaven at all. I will not say he has not come in by the right gate, he has come in by no gate, he is as one who walks around it and takes observations and makes measurements, but has never been caught in the whirlwind of its music, in the fire and sacrifice of its ineffable passion. You do not need more evidence, you need the understanding heart, the clean heart, the right spirit, the child-like disposition, all prayers in one, "Lord, teach me what thou wouldst have me do."

What do you think? Here is a man who is filling his grate with all kinds of fuel, and a beautiful grate it is, not lacking in capacity. And still he rearranges the material, again he redistributes the fuel, he takes it all out and puts other fuel in, and calls the attention of men to the size of his grate and to the purpose of his life, and he challenges men to find any better fuel than he has yet secured. What should he be doing? Not playing himself at grate-filling, but setting fire to the material already in his possession, and thus kindling a friendly influence in the house, the fire, that household apocalypse, that household revelation, that chamber of the picture-gallery, the fire—wherein battles are fought and victories won, and temples built and sacrifices offered, and great motions continually are proceeding which are to be caught by the imagination and transformed into all kinds of utility in the life. O, fool, light the fuel you have; other fuel will be needed and will be ready to come, not for ornament but for use.

Jesus Christ gave a broad answer, we have just said, to this inquiry for a sign. "When the unclean spirit is gone out of a man, he walketh through dry places, seeking rest and finding none: then he saith, I will return." That unclean spirit is *curiosity*, idle, vain, self-seeking curiosity, and when once it has been satisfied by the great replies of history, and still needs a further satisfaction, and goes out to find it, it will return and become sevenfold greater than it once was. Beware how you keep your curiosity chained. Strengthen the chain everyday. Once you get into the spirit of sign-seeking and question-asking, and vital piety becomes an impossibility in your case. Never let question-asking get the upper hand of you. In this solemn department of life keep curiosity in its right place, which is outside, mile on mile away from the letter. Consider how easy it is to ask for signs, how poor and feeble an intellectual condition it is merely to be able to ask questions, to propound difficulties, to suggest troubles, and to bewilder and puzzle those who are endeavoring to do great good in the world. Do not mistake question-asking or sign-seeking for intellectual greatness.

The doctrine is not only true intellectually, it is true *morally*. If once you get over a bad habit you must do something more, or that bad habit will come back to you, and finding the house empty, swept, and garnished, will bring with it seven other habits worse than itself, and the last state of your heart shall be sadder than the first. What is that other thing a man has to do after he has rid himself of a bad habit? He has to cultivate a good one. It is not enough to cease to curse, you must learn to pray; it is not enough to throw away from you the evil-spirited book and to say, "I will never read another line of you"; you must replace it by a wise and good book, otherwise the old appetite will wake, and will urge you to its cruel satisfaction.

Herein it is very important that all merely negative reformers should be followed up in their noble and beneficent course by those who have something distinctive and positive to offer to such as have been re-claimed from open and scandalous vices. You have been converted from the sin of drunkenness; it is not enough that you be a mere abstainer from intoxicating drinks, you must be surrounded by the noblest influences, you must be intellectually enlightened and trained, you must link your-self to some grand moral purpose, you must become deeply interested in some philanthropic and beneficent scheme, and thus must complete in positiveness what has been so happily begun in the region that is merely destructive or negative.

The unclean spirit will come back. No man can remain in the same state from time to time—getting no better, getting no worse—it is not in human nature to be thus stationary. "The last state of that man is worse than the first," said Christ concerning those who had not filled up the house of the heart with good and heavenly spirits. We become worse and worse everyday if we are not pursuing the right course; we do not stand still. Nor is the decadence and corruption of our nature a rapid and vis-ible one; the process is silent, subtle, often invisible, and not seldom un-felt in its detailed action. The sapping goes on quietly, the strength is sucked out of a man little by little, so that he shakes himself and says, "I am as strong as ever," but there comes a time when in shaking himself he re-veals himself to himself, and feels that he is no longer the young, blithe, strong, clear-headed man which he was in his earlier life. Sometimes the collapse is sudden; there is nothing in the outward circumstances to show what has been proceeding within, but at one critical touch the whole outline gives in and the collapse is complete. I may have illustrated this to you before by the action of the white ant. The white ant will enter into a door and will eat it up; every fiber of the wood will be consumed by the little creature, and the paint will be left untouched. You would say, "The door is there, open it." If you touch it it falls; the whole of the wood-work has been consumed by the little mischief-maker. It is also the same in our life. We appear to be the same; to all outward seeming we are just as we were twenty years ago, but if we have not been growing in the right direction, there will come upon us a touch, and we shall sink and per-ish, and the tremendous reality will be revealed.

"While he yet talked to the people." We must not forget the circum-stances under which the next event occurred. Jesus Christ was in the ex-citement of speech; when he spoke, everything in him spoke; the whole life was an utterance; in no cold blood did this mighty publisher of eternal truths declare his testimony; his quietness was power suppressed, his whisper was a thunder-burst in the azure, when he spoke he trembled, thrilled, vibrated through and through to some influence within and above. "While he talked to the people, behold his mother and his brethren stood without, desiring to speak with him. Then one said, Behold, thy mother and thy brethren stand without, desiring to speak with thee." His mind was moving forward with the sweep and wholeness of a great river; a man in the crowd sought to turn the urgent river from its channel; Jesus answered out of the inspiration of his human enthusiasm, "Who is my mother, and who are my brethren?" You cannot understand these words in cold blood; there are fingers so icy that they ought never to touch this Book; there are eyes so cold they ought never to look into these immortal pages. You cannot understand the prophets and the apostles in cold critical mood; you can vivisect their words, etymologize them, searching into remote meanings and earlier definitions, and when you have done all that—as I shall endeavor to do in a few instances this evening in this church—there remains a broader interpretation which can only be exercised by those who are blazing aflame with the very fire of God.

We all know what it is to speak out of a holy and sublime excitement. There are sacred hours, when we see the broadest and grandest bearings of the lines of life, and in which we seize the innermost meaning of common or tender terms. Our little self is lifted up into a heroic personality, in which no local relation is destroyed, but rather ennobled and sublimed. You must therefore look at Jesus Christ's words in the light of the fact that they were uttered while he yet talked to the people, his soul aglow, his eye alight, his blood fevered with the fire of God, and his whole individuality lifted up into a broader self-hood than was measurable by the merely human eye even in its keenest observation.

Look at this wonderful speech of Jesus; it recalls his earliest recorded words. Said his mother: "Thy father and I have sought thee, sorrowing." Said he: "Wist ye not that I must be about my Father's business?" [Luke 2:48, 49]. Already, at twelve years of age, he was more than just the son of Mary and the reputed son of the carpenter. Already he had seized the key-word of the universe and realized that relation which makes all other relations fall into their right perspective and assume their proper proportion and color. We are too local, we are too small, we build ourselves up into families and we enclose ourselves within square huts, and we have terminal points—we begin here and we end there, and so far we know nothing about the spirit of Jesus Christ, the great humanity, the world-feeling—we do not realize our ancestry and our posterity and our whole bearing in the universe; we detach ourselves: we belong to this sect, or to yonder clan, or to the other fraternity; we are English, or American, or Italian, or Chinese; we have these little narrowing dwarfing terms always clinging to us and impoverishing our speech. Use them as mere conveniences and they may be of some utility, but there ought to be times in the consciousness of every Christian heart in which every land is home and every man a brother.

This answer explains Christ's true relation to the human family. "Whosoever shall do the will of my Father which is in heaven, the same is my brother and sister and mother." It is not a question of local pedigree, it is not a claim that can be set up on partial lines. This *whosoever* is as broad as any *whosoever* uttered in all the great and inclusive language of the Bible. "Whosoever shall do the will of my Father which is in heaven." He keeps to the key-word, he involves the center, he stands on vital terms. Not "whosoever shall be born in my day and age, whosoever shall be born in my country, whosoever shall speak my language with my accent"; not "whosoever shall be great or noble, or rich, or mighty"—but "whosoever shall do the will of my Father which is in heaven." Then that gives me my chance. I may be a relation of Jesus Christ—poor, obscure, unknown, helpless; even I may enter the household of faith and be permitted to touch at least the hem of his garment. I may be one of his family; I may be a kinsman of the Son of God; I need no longer be a stranger and a foreigner, but may enter into the household and commonwealth of heaven.

I have thus to offer you a grand ancestry; to offer all men new vitalities, new surroundings, new kinsfolk. This shows the uniting power of Christianity. The Christian religion never divides men, never splits up a human family and belittles our human relations. The Christian religion would have us all brought into a common sympathy, united by a common spirit of loyalty to the same Savior, and would give each of us the same badge, the old, grim, black, accursed cross, which may be turned into the very symbol of the heart of God himself, the greatest Sufferer, the one Sufferer, the only Heart that knows the meaning of infinite woe.

Here, then, is our standing; this very day we are members one of another. Whether one member suffers, all the members suffer with it; whether one member rejoices, all the members should rejoice with it, and have common dance and song and high delight in the holy place. "Bear ye one another's burdens, and so fulfil the law of Christ" [Gal. 6:2]. Be no longer strangers and foreigners, but of the household of God. We are not isolated individuals; we grasp hands with the ages, the glorious company of the apostles, the holy band of the prophets before them, the noble army of martyrs uniting them both, the holy Church throughout all the world—this is the household of God. Beautiful picture! Tender relationship! It cannot be realized in all its ideal perfection here and now, but we ought always to cling to the inner and vital truth which it typifies, that the Church is one—indivisible as the heart that bought it with blood.

twenty-four

THE PICTURE GALLERY OF THE CHURCH

Matthew 13:1–23

JESUS CHRIST shows us how to deal with a great *multitude* in preaching the gospel of the kingdom. "The same day went Jesus out of the house and sat by the sea side, and great multitudes were gathered together unto him, so that he went into a ship and sat, and the whole multitude stood on the shore. And he spake many things unto them in parables." Do not expect great multitudes to follow connected discourses. Crowds must be caught by *points* rather than by *arguments*. In speaking to the crowd, I find that the Master spoke *many* things—many things to many hearers. That is the great law of successful speech to multitudes. Yet the many things were about one thing—the subject never changed. The one thing was the kingdom of heaven, the many things were the many parables. There was unity in variety, and there was variety in unity. The subject was the kingdom of heaven, and the illustrations were brought from every quarter of life and nature.

We enter then upon a new phase of the divine preaching. Hitherto it has been doctrinal and advisory, now it is imaginative and pictorial. These marvelous parables are the picture-gallery of the Church: the parable shows what is usually called the ideal side of the kingdom. This is the painter's art. The painter is not a copyist or a literalist: he does not transfer a tree to his paper or his canvas, he puts meanings into his work which grow upon the mind and hold it in new fascinations evermore. The amateur daubs flat paint upon flat canvas, and the canvas is but the heavier for the lifeless load. The true painter makes the paint throb, and fills the canvas with the electricity which burns in his own hand.

We never get all the meaning of the parables: we never get all the meaning of any truth. The parables bear inspection forever: they have revelations suited to the morning light and to the noontide glory and to the mystery of the solemn gloaming. To all the ages of the fathers they have been uttering their music, yet their music comes today with swells of power and cadences of persuasive pathos which our fathers never heard. Do not suppose that you have read all the parables and have gone through them. There may be men who have littleness of mind sufficient to enable them to get done with the parables once for all; on some of us they grow, and they are bigger and brighter and more tender everyday. The parables sent from heaven are always new, so is the preacher sent from God—he is always new, fresh, dewy, original, vital. His words may be the same, but there is a new color in them; his is not a monotony of artistic iteration—the actor's perishable art—it is the marvelous boom and emphasis, or equally marvelous whisper and suppression of vitality.

Never man spake like this man. He never uttered the same word twice in the same tone, therefore he was no actor. The actor repeats, the preacher sent from God *creates*. His echo is as original as his voice: the fragments fill more baskets than the loaves filled. This is not to be explained in words: it has no other self in the dictionary; it is *felt*, and the heart, glowing with wordless delight, grips and loves the tender meaning. Herein the sanctuary must always be the first of all places upon the earth for permanence, for durability, for abidingness, for the unwearable substance of truth. Other men come and go like spasms that cannot be reckoned, but the preacher, the parabolist, sent from heaven abides always. The more he is needed, the more he is. This is the secret of living in God.

These words are to be taken as introductory to all that may be given me to say upon these wondrous parables. In the parable before us we have a great advantage over many others, for we have not only the parable but the explanation. Jesus gives both the text and the sermon. We have the same thing put from the inside and from the outside. It will be my business to show that we have here the *key* of all the parables—in other words, this comment upon one will give a hint as to the right method of commenting upon all others.

This, then, is a solemn moment in the spiritual education of some of us who really care for these matters; it is the day on which the key is handed out. If I can master this parable of the sower, all the parables are mine.

Let me show you how all the parables firmly base themselves on *great human facts and social parallels,* and how true they are to all that is known to be true among ourselves. Let me strip these parables of all ghostliness and other worldliness so far as it might frighten the soul, and show you how these parables are all great *human truths,* lifted up into heavenly lights and bearing upon them interpretations of divine things. You can never get to the top of any ladder the foot of which is not upon earth. Let me show you that these parables are ladders, well fixed upon the earth at the one end, and rising up into all the mystery of heaven upon the other. Can I succeed in this? If so, I shall give you rich gifts, gold and gems, treasures more precious than rubies, and today will be a birthday in the soul of every man. Holy Spirit, writer of all the parables, in light, in color, in the forest, on the sea, in the heavens, on the green earth, come and rewrite them everyone, as to their spiritual meaning and force, upon every honest heart!

This representation of the kingdom of heaven is true of *all kingdoms that are themselves true.* The proof is easy—you need not the divine, technically so-called, to explain and establish this gracious doctrine. The marvelous fact connected with the kingdom of heaven is this, that it takes up all other kingdoms into itself and shows that insofar as they are true, they do but illustrate on incomplete lines what itself would do upon the whole lines of universal thinking and acting. Do not get into the notion of imagining that religion is something separate from life. Avoid the priestly superstition, the soul-damning fanaticism that religion is something separate and isolated from all the courses of thinking and loving and service familiar to us as men. It is the last expression of all that is best and dearest in our own consciousness, experience, and aspiration, like as a father, like as a shepherd, like as a nurse, like as a mother, by such analogues does the kingdom of heaven shine forth its tenderest glowing and meaning upon the eyes that want to see the gracious revelation.

This parable of the sower and the seed belongs to every kingdom that is true. It belongs to the kingdom of *knowledge.* No man ever yet went forth to teach mankind letters, philosophy, science of any sort, but came home a living exemplification of this very parable. This is not a priest's conundrum, this is not an ecclesiastical enigma to be answered only by ecclesiastical genius—this is the world's experience in all its teachers, schools, wise propagation, and healthy progress. Therefore it is true at the other end, because it is true at the end with which we ourselves are minutely and practically familiar.

Is there any man here who ever undertook to conduct in his country a great reform? Any man who has been interested in the education of the people, in the conversion of the people from great vices, in the enlightenment and general progress of society—call himself atheist, or secular humanist, or agnostic, or non-theist, or what he pleases? I will give him his report in the very words of this parable, and he will say, reading the parable as a report, "This exactly represents my own experience as a propagandist of wise ideas, and as an educator of the people." There is nothing therefore magical here: the kingdom of Heaven claims no more than any other kingdom, except insofar as itself is more. All the boats go on the same sea, but some draw more water than others. Herein no ghostly claim is set up, there is no mystery, or magic, or curious wand-waving in this strong human teaching. The fate of the upper kingdom is the fate of every kingdom that is good. It goes forth with risks and experiments and comes back with disappointments and satisfactions.

Read your Bibles in the light of this suggestion, and the old Book will flame with a new glory. The mischief for which I blame the priests of every age is that the Book has been separated from all the literature of the world, and locked up with a death's head in a closet of its own. Read in the right way, it expresses the experience of the world in the language of Heaven; taken from the right point of view, it combines all that is most precious, tragic, contradictory, noble in human souls and human experience.

This view of human society is true to fact in every age of human history. This classification is universal; the men of this parable are the men of today and the men of everyday. These are not waxen figures made eighteen centuries ago, and which have melted in the process of the suns—these are living figures, breathing men and women, sitting in these pews today, and who will sit in the pews of every church till the bell of time announces the day of doom. We have in all ages those who hear the Word and understand it not, those who joyfully receive the Word, and having no root in themselves, endure only for a little while; those who hear the Word, but are overmastered by the world and by the deceitfulness of riches: those who hear the Word and understand it, and grow in great plentifulness of precious fruit. Is this a priestly thing, an ecclesiastical picture, to be seen only on Sundays, when the church door is open? These are the men that are encountered by everyone who attempts to instruct his fellow-creatures. Here, for example, is the lecturer upon some department of *science*. What have you to say, sir? You have fifty pupils or students attending your lectures from time to time—what account do you give of them? These are not religious curiosities, these are not Christian fossils, these are the men that are living and breathing around us all the day. Teacher of manufactures—how is it with you in your great place? What about your apprentices and workmen—do they all take the word with equal ease? Do they instantaneously see your points and receive your instructions? Are not there men in your warehouse, your factory, the dull of mind, those who see a thing for a moment, and say they see it, and go out and forget it in an hour; and those who receive your instructions and are led away the moment they get fifty yards from the premises, and are found with the time-spender and with the drunkard, and with the gambler, or with the lounging idler; and are there not those in your place of business who are honest of heart and quick of mind, and who take up your instructions and reproduce them in honest labor?

This parable is true about the kingdom of heaven because it is true about your school of lecturing and about your place of business. The foot of this ladder is upon the earth; therefore its head may be in heaven. See how by one outstretching of his hand Jesus Christ grasps all sorts and conditions of men; not one is missed; they are all here; he lays hold of the whole occasion; there is nothing magical here, nothing ghostly or terrifying—this Man grasps and expresses the reality of things. Never man spake like this Man; therefore he stands today crowned above all others, mightiest in power, tenderest in gentleness—a Shepherd, a King, a Father, a Brother, a Root out of a dry ground, the Flower of Jesse and the Plant of renown. Read his words in the light of these human analogies and parallels, and you will begin a course of proving and testing which will satisfy the most common or the most cultured mind of the soundness of the foundations upon which the Christian kingdom rests.

What is true of the kingdom and what is true of human society as represented in this parable is true of the *results* which are here indicated. The results can be tested in every section of the human family. The proof of this is not to be found in the Church only. Why, I find it in your families, as you yourselves do. The family is one, the teaching is one, the seed is the same, the care taken of all the little creatures is the same care—

none is esteemed above another, but the same patience and love and light, anxiety, solicitude are expended upon the whole six. Now let me look at them. Would it be possible to find six souls more diverse? One of your sons seems to have had no instruction at all—has he had any? You say, "Certainly, he had precisely the same instruction that the others received." "Well," I say "but look at him—careless, thoughtless, all but mindless." You say, "That is true, and it is a mystery to me, for I take as much care of him as I take of the others." Take another: you gave him instruction along with the others, and he has forgotten every word you ever said to him. You say, "Because he no sooner gets out of the house than somebody lures him away from the path upon which he started. If this boy were promised a coin of silver—indeed, when he was younger, if anyone had tempted him with three marbles—he would have forgotten every instruction his mother gave him as to the day's duty." And this pride of the family, gem of all, thoughtful, loving, wise, industrious, his mother's other self, his father's all but idol—the seed was sown in this case in good ground, and has brought forth an hundredfold.

This is the parable over again, certainly, and there is no other parable! This is the one report; it was read over eighteen hundred years ago [now nearly 2,000 years ago. *Ed.*], or rather spoken, from the ship; it has been read in all the missionary halls in Christendom year after year ever since, and the last report that will be read in those halls will be this parable modernized. The tone, the music will be the same, the figures only will be changed; there will be no change in the inner and vital substance until, indeed, the time shall come when Christ shall have the heathen for his inheritance and the uttermost parts of the earth for a possession—when there will be but one sentence in the report; that sentence, "Hallelujah, the Lord God omnipotent reigneth." But until that report be rendered, this parable will continue to be the basis upon which every secretary of every society, the head of every school, the lecturer of every college, the leader of every reform will base his annual report.

I see this, of course, most plainly in the matter of *Churches*. The sermons are the same, the labor of a lifetime is the same—what is my report about you? Precisely what I find in this parable: I cannot get away from the lines of this parabolical representation of you all. I have uttered common prayer, I have spoken to the congregation, as a whole, year after year, I have done my best to arrest attention and satisfy pious expectation—what is the result today? This parable, and nothing but this. Some seed has fallen by the wayside, and has been picked up; some in the stony places, a joy for a moment or two, great delight while the service lasted, but there was no deepness of earth, and it soon withered away. Some has fallen among thorns, and some of the seeds have fallen upon good ground. I need not any learned and ingenious mind to expound this parable to me or prove its underlying truth. It is the picture of every ministry, philanthropic, educational, and religious.

The explanation given in verse 15 is somber, yet satisfactory. "For this people's heart is waxed gross, and their ears are dull of hearing, and their eyes they have closed, lest at any time they should see with their eyes and hear with their ears and should understand with their hearts, and should be converted, and I should heal them." They suffer the consequences of their own acts. Observe the expression, "Their eyes have *they* closed." It is not "Their eyes have *I* closed": the action was their own, and they suffer the results of their own perversity. "Be not deceived: God is not mocked: whatsoever a man soweth, that shall he also reap" [Gal. 6:7].

The twelfth verse is fulfilled in every man's history. "For whosoever hath to him shall be given, and he that hath not from him shall be taken away even that he hath." We lose what we do not use, we forfeit what we do not employ, what we put away falls into disuse, and is cankered and is lost. To him that hath exercised his muscle more muscle shall be given; from him who hath not exercised his muscle shall be taken away even the muscle which he began to have. We cannot keep things at a standstill: it is always gaining or always losing: a man is not the same at the end of twenty years as he was at the beginning. No man is the same at the end of a sermon as he was at the beginning of the discourse: new responsibility has entered into his life, a new chance has operated in his thinking, a grand opportunity has been presented to him which he has either accepted or neglected.

These laws and principles have been regarded as great mysteries, whereas they are among the common facts of human history. This is the sovereignty of unchangeable law, this is the law of the garden and of the field, it is the law of study, it is the law of action and of prayer. Wherever you find any operation you find this law, wherever you find any capacity you find the reason of it in the man himself, wherever you find stupidity you find it in the action of the man himself. The light would stream over the whole house if we would open the windows: Heaven's angels would sing to us if we would but listen. But if we close our eyes and stop our ears and fill our hearts with vanities and lies, we cannot wonder that the holiest revelations fall upon us like rains upon the wilderness, or pass unrecognized in the stupor of our sleep or in the absorption of our worldliness.

twenty-five

THE TARES AND
THE WHEAT

Matthew 13:24–43

WE FOUND that the parable of the sower has its proofs in human history, and being true in human society, we had no difficulty in understanding its application to the kingdom of heaven. Our test inquiry regarding all these parables, is—How do they fit *the circumstances which are now around us?* Are they little pieces of ancient history, graphic enough as bearing upon the time to which they specifically refer, or are they parts of all history, running contemporaneously with human development from age to age, always new, always just written, the ink never dry? The first parable which we have just studied fits the circumstances of today perfectly: let us see whether the second fits them equally well. It should be pointed out that in adopting this method of criticism we are keeping strictly within the limits of the parables themselves, because Christ does actually liken the kingdom of heaven to earthly persons and earthly things. We study the parables at the earthly end. The kingdom of heaven is like unto a sower, like unto a merchantman, like unto leaven, like unto a net, like unto a treasure hid in a field—so he gives us the earthly end as well as the heavenly end, and we can thoroughly examine the one and thus enable ourselves wisely to judge the other. Let us follow these same lines of inquiry with regard to the parable of the wheat and the tares.

This parable is an exact picture of *all endeavors to do good in the world.* We have not gone one inch beyond this parable today, with all our improvements and amplifications of service and readjustment of methods. The account which could be given of all educational, philanthropic, patriotic, Christian endeavor is within the four lines, so to say, of this mixed parable. It enters into a good man's heart to publish good ideas or to assist useful reforms: he lectures in public and in private, he freely spends his time and his money in spreading the views and principles which he holds: he establishes schools and publishes literature, he lays himself out in every way to enlighten and benefit the public. Do you suppose that such a man will be allowed to go on without an enemy following him and sowing tares in the wheat-field of his noble and beneficent endeavor? He will be followed by the enemy, the enemy will awaken suspicions, he will question the man's motives, he will assail the man's reputation, he will throw doubt upon the man's integrity, in a thousand ways open to vicious ingenuity he will endeavor to thwart and baffle the purposes of the good man's heart. Is this true, or is it not—today? Is the good man living and is the enemy dead, buried, gone forever and forgotten? Do not the light and the shadow always go together? There is no ghostly mystery here: you cannot point to a wheat field in which no tares are sown.

Take your own *education.* Your father and your schoolmaster and your friends all have endeavored to sow the seeds of a good understanding in your mind and heart—yet what do we see in your life? Your very education turned to bad purposes, your very training made to add to your efficiency in doing that which is wrong. How came those tares into the field? Your mother did not sow them, nor your father, nor your teacher, nor your most loving friend—whence came those tares? An enemy hath done this.

Look at your *prosperity,* man of business: how riches have been showered upon you. When you were poor and little in your own eyes, men liked you because you were then gentle, sympathetic, approachable: you had a heart that could be approached, and that could show itself in all the tenderness of loving sympathy to those who were in circumstances requiring the remedy of your love and patient care—but with your riches there has come what men call presumption, or self-confidence, or haughtiness: you are no longer gentle, simple, tender, sympathetic, accessible. How did these tares come into the field? An enemy hath done this.

It is always the same. No man can *preach* without having the enemy at his heels; the enemy is as busy as the preacher; the enemy is now preaching to you as certainly as I am endeavoring to preach to you. Some of you are buying and selling, some of you are now wool-gathering, some of you are a thousand miles away, some of you are writing tomorrow's letters, doing tomorrow's business and answering tomorrow's questions, and when all is over you will awake as out of a confused dream that has a kind of religious haze about it. The enemy is working as well as the preacher, he is suggesting all kinds of doubts, difficulties, and suspicions, prompting all kinds of questions that will break in upon an implicit and loving and loyal obedience, directing your attention to little points and to transient accidents—the occasion rather than to its solemn purpose—which is to lift the soul into the light, and to gird it with the very strength of God. The enemy will entice you into considerations of place and color, of manner and length of service, and into a thousand little petty, frivolous discussions, and will succeed if he lure the mind away from the sovereign purpose of the occasion—which is to make you pray. And at the end of the whole, with broken mind, confused, bewildered head and heart, neither upward nor downward in its look, but halting, we may have to say, "An enemy hath done this." So the parable is not ghostly and magical, but has its base upon the lines of our common consciousness and experience, and as it is awfully true at the one end it may be equally true at the other.

The *inquiry* which was made by the servants is the inquiry which is made *today*. The servants of the householder came and said unto him, "Sir, didst thou not sow good seed in thy field? from whence; then hath it tares?" We have not gone beyond that inquiry; it is the puzzle of every honest mind how the tares came to be mixed up with our thinking and feelings, our motives and our service. It is sometimes a mystery to ourselves; we are puzzled to the point of intellectual and moral distraction by the problem of what we call the origin of evil. You cannot go up and down society without putting the very question which the servants of the householder put to their master. Go into an educated company, listen to the conversation, some parts of it bright, pure, noble, elevated—and then the bitter word, the unkind suggestion, the harsh aspersion, the uncharitable judgment, the biting or venomous criticism. You say, "Were not all these people educated and brought up well?" Yes. "Then, where did these tares come from?" Good question, indeed!

The same inquiry has its place in a higher region—we have precisely this experience in the Church. We are puzzled by the tares that are growing in our own hearts. I can see the tares in your life, and you can see the tares in mine—but there are tares in all human life, even of the very best kind, and the perplexing inquiry that brings with it a heartache and a burning agony, is—How did those tares come to be here? Sir, have not these people been to church? Sir, have not these people been bowing down at the altar? Sir, have not these people been to the holy sacrament? Where did these tares—of evil words and unkind deeds and movements and adventures and experiments and tricks of an ungodly kind—where did they come from? The two things do not harmonize.

"Sir, was not that man praying on Sunday?"

"Yes."

"Then how did he come to be doing dishonest deeds within twenty-four hours of his own Amen? Was that man not singing in the church?"

"Yes."

"Then why is he uttering all these words of discord, these dissonant, harsh-breaking tones of human speech, while yet the cadence of his own hymn is trembling and dying in the distant air?"

So this parable might have been written last night, and we might be reading it for the first time this morning. The teacher that can throw himself over the arch of nineteen hundred years thus, and talk to us in our own language, must have had at least great intellectual foresight and moral shrewdness and breadth enough of sympathy to be more than any man we have ever known. If Jesus of Nazareth were here today, he could not amend this parable in any of its facts and applications. Though nineteen hundred years old, it is not a day old; judged by the necessity of the occasion it is as new as our last action, it is as appropriate as the very last word of wisdom we ever uttered. In this sense is the Testament always new to me. I am not endeavoring to verify faded ink; I ask no chemist to help me to blacken this yellow fluid—'tis black enough, I can read every jot and tittle of it, and I say, if this Man is as sound in his higher reasoning which transcends my power to follow him in all the entirety of his sweep as he is in those parts which I do understand, verily he is the Revealer, the Builder, and the Glory of the Kingdom of Heaven amongst men.

So far, then, the parable fits human circumstances with exquisite delicacy and precision. Let us go further. The answer made by the householder is the only answer we have today about all vicious and unhappy results. "An enemy hath done this." That is our one and only reply. It goes to the root of the matter, it touches the difficulty on every side and at every point. Every man has his enemies, every man's work is watched, and every attempt will be made to mar it. There are men who love to do evil; they are not happy except in the work of destruction. It is easy to do evil—they have chosen the light end of the burden. It is easy to suggest doubts and difficulties about human character and purpose and motive: it is easy to sneer, it is easy to tempt. There are men who would spoil your business if they could; the enemy was on your track when you began the business of life; he tried to take away your clients and patrons, he depreciated your goods, he said he would crush you.

Tyndale's translation of this verse opens a new field of criticism. He reads, "An envious person hath done this." Instead of reading "an enemy," he reads "an envious person," and that seems to bring the text nearer and nearer to us, and to make it appallingly English. An envious person—beware of envy, it is cruel, it is the sister of jealousy, it is relentless, it will plague your life, it will rob every flower of its perfume, it will bar the light out of every window in your house, your dinner today will be no refreshment to you, but will leave your hunger still gnawing you, if you envy some other man's larger lot. And this is one of the last passions and vices to be overcome; who can fail to envy a fellow-tradesman who is doing better than he is doing? Who can fail to envy the preacher who is succeeding better than he himself is succeeding? And envy eats up its own victim; it does not hurt the person who is envied, but it eats like a canker the soul that indulges in it. You have no pleasure in your own house while you are envying another man's dwelling-place; all your gardens and fields and horses and estates and servants are nothing to you until you can get that little corner or patch of vineyard outside there, and the lack of that will make you a poor man forever, though you count your money by millions and speak of your lands in miles.

Thus again the parable becomes quite our own. The inquiry is ours, the reply is ours, the parable is true to circumstances as we ourselves know them; therefore it may be true in any *larger* application which the parabolist himself may attach to the meaning of his graphic similitude. An enemy hath done this. Here is a young man who had been deceived, tempted, led off into downward paths; both his feet are fastened in cruel snares, the disappointment of a lifetime culminates in him. What do you think about the case? An enemy hath done this. This is not the handiwork of a friend, there is no nobleness here, this is not the spirit that would save the world, this is enmity incarnate. An unsuspecting mind has been poisoned by some deceiver, its faith has been broken, its sweet and trustful prayer has been turned aside, a sinister bar has been drawn upon the medallion of its integrity, the old frankness has gone, the open face, the ringing voice that had no wrinkle in it, that was spread out in ingenuous and beauteous simplicity—all is changed. The very eye is altered, the tone is ambiguous, the movement is shuffling, the whole air throbs as if troubled. How do you account for it? In no words more incisive than these—an enemy has done this; it is bad work—you should know the character of the man who did it by the results he has brought about. It was no angel that gave the look to that eye that is now in it, it was no angel that altered that sweet tone of childhood into the muffled noise of a man who wants to utter a double meaning in every speech he makes. An enemy has done this!

Let us be frank with ourselves. He may come to us in the guise of a teacher, he may have come visored as a friend, but by his results let his true character be known. He was an enemy, his enmity is incurable—avoid him for the future. A generous soul has been dwarfed and impoverished of its noblest impulses, the soul that always had a frank "yes" broad as an opening day to every appeal made to his charity has become soured, suspicious—he asks questions now which never would have entered into his mind in earlier days; he calculates, he counts, and reckons and estimates and puts down. How do you account for this change? It is easy to *see* where the enemy has been working upon a man: the tares cannot be *hidden*. It is easy for me to know instantaneously whether a man is going down or going up—we *feel* it. There are some impressions too delicate for speech, but still they have their influence upon the mind. Let us be careful. It is a sight to cry over with rivers of tears to see the men we loved and all but worshiped grown all over with tares. They used to be so noble, kind, sympathetic, generous, helpful—the world could never be cold to us so long as they were in it. Day by day the tares grow in number and strength till we know not what the end will be.

So far the parable closely identifies itself with our consciousness and experience. Let us see if it continues this closeness to the very end. The *appeal* of the householder is the most solemn appeal which any man can make today under similar circumstances. What was the appeal of the householder? The servants said, "Shall we go and gather up the tares?" The householder said, "Not till the harvest." That appeal cannot be altered: it is magnificent in its sublimity, it is grand in its heroic patience. He will have no violence, he will not have the wheat injured. Let both grow together *till the harvest*. Indeed, there is a final day, there is an hour of separation, there is a crisis in which the good are separated from the bad, the sheep from the goats, the wheat from the tares. The confusion is not everlasting: the work will be given up to the holy angels, they cannot mistake the good for the bad, or the bad for the good: the discriminating process shall go on steadily until every tare is out and every grain of wheat shall be saved for heaven's garner.

Let us remit our case to the *harvest*. Do not be answering the fool and the enemy *now*, and thus wasting opportunities which ought to be usefully employed in endeavoring to do good, but wait till the harvest. Then shall all qualities be tested, then shall every man have his proper place and standing before God. It suits impatient men to be going to work now in this matter of discrimination. Our impatience is our littleness. It is the hindrance of every ministry, spiritual, moral, educational, and commercial—and there are fussy people who want to be *doing something* now, as they suppose their activity to be: they want to expel. O you fool, if I begin the work of expulsion, it will be by throwing you out from the uppermost window of the church. Expel? It is not mine to anathematize or excommunicate, or open the door that any man may go out. My appeal is—wait till the harvest. I am not a judge or an overseer invested with the responsibility of final criticism, I want to be a teacher, a friend, a helper, to see the very best side of every man, and to encourage that best side in continual and useful growth.

Leaving the parable for a moment, and not attempting to follow all its lines out, lest by mixture of metaphor I should fail of my immediate purpose, let me appeal to myself, and through myself to those who hear me, and who may need the appeal, to cultivate with a more ardent diligence the growth of the *wheat*. There is wheat in everyone of you. Take that road of hope. And every one of you has his enemies that want to sow tares in his soul. "What I say unto one I say unto all—Watch" [Mark 13:37]. And some of you by the grace of God have been too much for the enemy, too wakeful: you have disappointed him to a degree which inflicts upon him the most severe mortification. Some of you are nearly all wheat: I wish to God I were myself. Let there be no violence in your education, no forcing, no dragging out with a hand that is unaccustomed to the process, but let there be solemn, quiet waiting, knowing that the harvest will come, and God will do what is right in the end of the age.

twenty-six

THE GRAIN OF
MUSTARD SEED

Matthew 13:31

IS IT TRUE that there is a conquering force in *vitality*? Do really good things always *grow*, and in their expansion offer hospitality and defense to others? May what is here said of the kingdom of heaven be said of every other kingdom that is true, grand, pure, and beneficent? If so, then surely it may be said of the kingdom of heaven with infinitely multiplied force, and with infinitely extended meaning. First of all, therefore, let us grapple with the case as an earthly one, and then look forward to its heavenly bearings and applications.

Take, for example, the mustard seed of *liberty*; would it be wise and right for any great historian or poet to say the kingdom of liberty is like unto mustard seed which a man took and sowed in his field, which indeed is a little seed, but it so grows as to throw off all tyranny and oppression, and give the poorest man a status and a chance in life? Would that parable outrage any laws of intellectual conception or any laws of intellectual and patriotic expression? It would fit the case precisely, it would illustrate in picture one of the grandest doctrines that ever forced itself upon the attention of mankind. Liberty was the problem of parliaments, it has been the cause of wars; men have fought that other men might be kept in bondage, nations would not relax their grip upon the neck of millions of slaves—but the little mustard seed of liberty was sown, and whatever has in it vitality given it of God must grow. The little seed will take root, the root will expand, and growing roots will split rocks as certainly as they can be separated by gunpowder. That little root will never rest until it has broken up the huge rock—so the seed of liberty grew and extended itself with beneficent expansion in England and the

Americas and at the cost of millions of treasure and many lives human slavery was abolished as an iniquity and a curse.

What is true of England has been also true of other lands. Civil wars have been fought, intrigues have been entered into, the most desperate courses have been resorted to for the purpose of maintaining human slavery, but the little mustard seed of liberty has kept growing all the time, night and day, never ceasing to grow, and before its spreading roots the great stumbling-blocks have given way, and liberty is growing still! So far therefore the parable holds its place amongst purely human and political illustrations.

Take the mustard seed of *genuine force of character*, high quality of manhood—would he be a mere romanticist, who said, "The kingdom of noble, pure, heroic, character is like a grain of mustard seed, little to begin with, but it will grow and develop and strengthen until the men who despised it shall seek the hospitality of its shadow"? Any man saying these words would be speaking no poetry except the highest, which is fact and logic on fire, the poetry of truth—that this which is divine, simple, useful, beneficent, redeeming, must come to have the heathen for its inheritance and the uttermost parts of the earth for its possession. If you are a true man you cannot be kept down in the long run; if your character is right, it will in due time assert itself and claim its own. Men may proscribe you, condemn you, try to write you down, try to draw your clients, customers, patrons, and supporters from you, may indulge in every form of interference and unkind suppression known to the most mischievous genius, and yet not a hair of your head shall perish; no weapon formed against you shall prosper. Have we not seen this illustrated in countless instances—is it not the very blossom and glory of human history—is it not the confidence of all men who pray and wonder that the answer is long in coming? So far therefore the parable holds its own in purely human and social conditions; perhaps it may also hold its own in relation to that invisible, impalpable, immeasurable kingdom which we have come to know by the sweet name of heaven. Let us see.

Take the mustard seed of a truly meritorious *invention:* go even to that purely materialistic and mechanical side of life. Is it possible to keep down anything that is really *true* in mechanics? I have read the history of English manufactures to little purpose if I have not found that it has always been impossible to keep out of the mill and the factory and the place of mechanical operations any invention that was really good and really useful, and that completely answered the purpose for which it was put forward. If I go back to the north of England some thirty, forty, or fifty years and read the history of manufactures there, I shall find that machinery was burnt, that factories were burnt to the ground, that workmen were proscribed, that masters were slandered, and that opposition of every kind was offered to this or that particular mechanical invention. The working classes would not have it, great combinations of men were established for the purpose of putting it down, but where is it today? It was like a grain of mustard seed; it had mechanical truth, it had commercial reality in it, it was able to bless the very people that cursed it; and so, under the Divine Providence that takes care of all things true and pure and useful, and includes them all in the kingdom of heaven, we have seen that man's opposition has been turned aside, and that true things have grown to fulfill their purpose; and so it must be to the end of time.

We see, therefore, that there are enough illustrations of the doctrine that truth is mighty and must prevail. You cannot permanently keep down whatever is true in doctrine, in manhood, in science, or in politics. Water cannot drown it, fire cannot burn it, contempt cannot discourage it, and perdition cannot overcome it. This is not the case, you see then, with theology alone. A thing is true to me because it is true to my whole nature, and to the whole outlook and reality of life. If it shall come and separate itself wholly from everything known to my consciousness and my experience, it will bring with it its own difficulty which may prove to be insuperable, but if it connect itself with all that I know best and have established most thoroughly and confidently, then it may lead me on step by step to its own higher self and its own broader claim.

It is in this way that God comes to us. He does not strike upon the intellect like a great thunder blast that has no connection, reference, or illustration in any quarter of human consciousness, experience, or observation. He comes to establish himself in my confidence in this way, namely—"like as a father pitieth his children, so the Lord pitieth them that fear him" [Ps. 103:13]. As a nurse nourisheth and cherisheth her children, so the Lord. "If ye, being evil, know how to give good gifts unto your children, how much more shall your Father, which is in heaven, give the Holy Spirit unto them that ask him" [Luke 11:13]. The argument is cumulative; it begins in the human, the known, that which is fully ascertained and established, and then it proceeds to what we know as transcendental and supernatural heights, but we trust by that which we do know, and can test and prove, and we calmly, lovingly await the broader revelation; and in waiting we are inspired with noble hope, constrained to beneficent service, and are indulged with ineffable rewards.

This doctrine, therefore, is as true of medicine as it is of divinity, of mechanics as of the gospel, of navigation as of theology. Sometimes the full growth is long delayed; some men have to *die* as the price of their appreciation; some inventions and reforms have to flee into Egypt to escape the wrath of some angry Herod. Still the sovereign law holds good—that truth, in all departments of life, must come uppermost and sit securely on its appointed and inevitable throne. Let this be your confidence, men and brethren. If it be your confidence you can wait without murmuring—you can tarry without complaining; and when he comes who has been more misunderstood than you can possibly be, he will not forget his servant who has endeavored to represent in speech and life that which he has felt to be true.

In the light of these human, social illustrations, let us see how the parable fulfills all the conditions of things as they are clearly known by us, everyone. First of all, the kingdom of heaven is *not ashamed of small beginnings*. Herein it startles me very much. I should have thought that if the kingdom of heaven were coming amongst men it would have made for itself a great rift in the sky, and with blast of trumpets and rolling of thunder and flashing of lightning, amid the pomp of heaven's hierarchy and the whole muster of its angel crowd, it would have come down to the earth and dazzled and confounded men by its infinite blaze of glory. God does not come this way: he is not ashamed to illustrate his progress by the development of small and relatively contemptible things. He is as the dawning of the day, he is as the growing of the mustard seed: he begins in a whisper, he challenges one and then another, he works in the individual heart, setting up there a good conviction, kindling an unquenchable enthusiasm, nourishing and cherishing a holy purpose—then another is added and the plural thus begins, and the two go forth together to seek a third; and thus the kingdom grows, friend finding friend, the evangelist finding the prodigal and bringing him home, the hopeful soul speaking the word of cheer to the dejected spirit, and thus the kingdom grows.

Be rebuked then, O impatient man, who do want, with great demonstration and force of arms, to impose the kingdom of heaven upon men. Let it grow according to its own law. Despise not the day of small things. A little one may become a great nation, and a small one an immeasurable people. Believe in the truth, and not in its merely numerical and demonstrative force—have faith in anything that is true and good, because it is true and good, and deliver yourself from the miserable fallacy and most mischievous sophism that a crowd is necessary to success, and that multitudinousness is a proof of truth or of reality. All history condemns such violent reading, and all history confirms the sublime teaching that whatever is true may have a small beginning, but it must overturn, overturn, overturn, until all hindrances are leveled with the dust. Thus and thus God's kingdom comes and his will is done on earth as it is done in heaven [see Matt. 6:10].

In the next place the kingdom of heaven connects itself with the greatest law known amongst us—namely, the law of *growth*. It grows in the individual mind, it grows in the national mind, it grows from alphabetical form into broader substance and expression, and then away again from all that is formal and mechanical up into the purely spiritual regions wherein we are enabled to say, because we are enabled to see, that God is a Spirit.

If the kingdom of heaven is associated with the law of growth, then it must proceed *silently*. I know of no growths that are noisy; the great oak makes no noise as it strengthens itself with the growing years. So is it with the kingdom of heaven: it grows silently in the heart, yet men take knowledge of the enriched character of the expanded mind, of the nobler tone, of the broader generosity; and they say, "This is growth in grace." If it associates itself with growth, then the progress of the kingdom of heaven will often be invisible in its more minute movements. Whoever saw a flower grow from this point to that while waiting and looking on? This flower has nothing to show for any one moment of its existence; the flower or the tree is not to be reckoned up from day to day: leave it for a month, leave the tree for a year, for ten years, and then return and remember that all this accretion has been going on without a single created eye observing the increase. We like to see things grow. Sometimes the child takes a little spade and digs up the seed to see if it has begun to grow. Perhaps we have all done this, and have been proud to see how the little white life, or green life, was coming up out of the seed we sowed, and then we have put it back again; and again we have come back to observe the growing, and yet we have never seen the operation. We have seen the results, but how they came to be results is a mystery to us, and must be a lesson.

Ah, the mysteriousness of growth—who can understand it, who knows how much goes to the making up of it—the earth, the sun, the rain, the dew, the light, the wind—what chemical elements are set in motion, thrown into combination; what ejections, what absorptions, what strange and subtle combinations, and the whole thing moving on to express a purpose in the mind of the Creator? It has pleased God to say, while we are looking upon all the vegetable kingdom, "My heavenly kingdom, my larger kingdom, is just like that—as silent, as invisible, as mysterious, as certain, growing up to the full expression of the purpose which was in my heart when I created this great theater of the universe and sent man into it to fulfill his destiny."

Another thing is that the kingdom of heaven carries its greatness even when it is in its most *minute and microscopic form.* The greatness is in the *seed* itself: if we had instruments fine enough to look really into the seed, we would see the mustard tree in the mustard seed, the oak in the acorn, the great cedar in the seed out of which it grows. The cedar, the oak, any other tree or flower is not something added afterwards, but it is in reality in the root or seed which is in the earth. We are prevented seeing it simply because of our lack of natural or instrumental vision.[*] So it is with the kingdom of heaven. Men do not take on other selves and other manhoods as they advance in life, but they fulfill a writing and a destiny in themselves not only from the moment of their birth, but through eternity. Nothing happens as a surprise, nothing is written on the margin of the divine program as an afterthought; everything is fore-appointed, fore-ordained, elect, standing fast in the counsel of God, and is a surprise only to our weakness. So the kingdom of heaven is always great: great when you are teaching it in the Sunday school to a little child, when you are writing about it on the blackboard, when you are endeavoring to put its mysteries into words of one syllable, so as to lodge the truth in the little mind of the little hearer; it is the kingdom of heaven still, compressed, condensed, simplified, made easy, but carrying in it all the force that shall conquer creation, all the mystery that shall spread itself out before the admiring and grateful gaze of men as the revelation of God's mercy and love and grace in Christ Jesus. The planet is in the molecule; tell me the creation was made out of the molecule,

---

[*] Today we can observe the phenomena of seed-growth by use of a high speed camera. *Ed.*

and I find but the broader confirmation of the truth of my text in that statement. A molecule will do to begin with, but what a molecule, that has grown and split itself off into constellations and suns and universes, and which astronomy has no tape long enough to throw around to take the measure of the circumference thereof. What a mustard seed it must have been!

So with God's kingdom; it will grow until Christ shall have the heathen for his inheritance and the uttermost parts of the earth for his possession, and the handful of corn upon the top of the mountain shall grow until the harvest, waving in the south wind, goldened by all the suns of the universe, shall proclaim the fulfillment of the divine purpose, and angels shall gather it and sing the harvest home.

The last confirmatory point is that the kingdom of heaven is available for *other uses* than those which are sometimes thought to be distinctively religious—as with the mustard seed grown into a tree, the birds come and lodge in the branches of it; did the tree grow for the sake of the birds, or did the birds avail themselves of the hospitality of the tree? It is even so with the kingdom of heaven; whatever is true has a right to be in the Church, all art and science, all commerce and literature, all recreation and joy—do not banish these sacred birds from the branches of the Church tree, for they all are God's, and if they do not receive hospitality in the Church, they will find it elsewhere, and the Church will be the loser in the long run.

Take the broadest view of the Church; it should offer hospitality to all the birds of the air, to all creatures that need lodging and help, defense, education, strength—it should throw itself out in loving and mighty appeal in every direction and offer the hospitality of heaven to all the children of earth. Open your churches for music, open your pulpits for lectures, open your schoolrooms for amusements, open all your premises that you may spread a meal for the hungry and offer rest to the weary, and by-and-by men and women will say, "Where are we? This is a wondrous song, this is inspiring music, this is bread truly useful for us in the hunger of life—where are we? What is this building? There is something strange about it. What is that in which the man stands and from which he speaks—and what are those seats, and those books lying here and there?" And it may come to dawn upon them that they are in their Father's house, and they who came to hear the entertainment, or be fascinated for a moment by some transient enjoyment, may remain to pray. Do not drive the birds away, do not starve the birds: the church was not distinctively built for any of these outward or collateral purposes, but as the birds of the air came and lodged in the full-grown mustard tree, so may many birds, and men, and women, and little children, and outcasts, hopeless and heartless ones, come and find it warm in the Church and be drawn by its glow of charity still further, until at last they enter the sanctuary of its truth.

I am thankful for this suggestion of *growth*: it does not frighten me, it gives me the true law of judgment; night and day the kingdom grows, it makes no noise, it resorts to no violence, but quietly and sublimely and solemnly it comes to the perfectness and grandeur of God's purpose. Sometimes when we awake to an appreciation of summer growth we say, "The flowers, the trees, seem to have come out in the night time: what a change! How sudden!" Perhaps it will be thus with Messiah's kingdom. Today Herod is on the throne, today the sword is slaying the innocent, today he who is born Christ the King is taken away to Egypt, the upper hand seems to have been to those who devise evil purposes and carry out mischievous intentions—but still the kingdom moves, still the seed develops, still the growth expands; someday it may appear to us as if quite suddenly the consummation had been realized, and we shall say to one another, "This is none other than God's kingdom come, and the earth has been warmed by the summer of heaven."

To that end let us work, and let us, from that purpose, gather courage to speak the broader, bolder prayer at the throne of the heavenly grace.

twenty-seven

TREASURE AND PEARLS

Matthew 13:44–46

THESE PARABLES may be taken together, as expressing two sides of the same truth. "The kingdom of heaven is like unto treasure hid in a field." There were no banks in ancient times, such as we have now, and therefore persons possessed of property of a valuable kind were known to hide it in fields and in out-of-the-way places. The figure is that of a man who comes upon joy unexpectedly. He was not looking for treasure, but in digging his field he came upon it without anticipation, and therefore his joy was the greater. How far and in what sense do these parables correspond with what we know of life generally? Can we not confirm the doctrine that the joys of surprise are amongst the keenest of our delights? The joys that we anticipate are often dulled by the fact that we have discounted them: we knew that they were coming, we had often talked about them, imagination had set them in false lights and in preposterous relations, so that when they really did come they were less than our expectancy, and so they became disappointments rather than pleasures.

Understand, then, *the place of surprise* in the divine economy. We are to come upon things unexpectedly, we are not to wear them out before we handle them, their presence and their use and their value come to us instantaneously, and because we knew nothing about them our joy is the greater. If you expect your friend to leave you a large estate, and he leaves you something less than you had anticipated, the property actually brings dissatisfaction with it, but if you expected nothing, and he left you one green field, the bequest would occasion great joy in your heart, not altogether because of the value of the bequest, but because it came upon you without the slightest hint or expectation.

Now the kingdom of heaven is like unto treasure hid in a field: it is a continual surprise. God is able to do exceeding abundantly above all that we ask or think [Eph. 3:20]. Herein is our expectation itself foiled. We cannot raise our expectancy to the height of this heaven, but expectation is not forbidden herein in consequence of that solemn and glad fact. We dream of heaven, and talk of it, and set our poets to work to strike their harps to sweeter and higher strains and tones, because when we have formed our own heaven in the innermost and highest places of our fancy, it falls short of the reality only by infinity.

This is the testimony of every student of the Bible. Every page is a field in which there is hidden treasure—so say the men who have toiled longest in those holy fields. They are the men who are entitled to testify: such men are filled with amazement, new light startles them, unheard music holds their soul in glad enthrallment, presences rise before them and angels wrestle with them in power that is meant not to destroy but to save and to bless, so that the old man in closing his Bible says, "The last vision was the brightest, the last song was the sweetest"; says he, "I never knew what this Bible was until now. All the old passages glow with a new meaning, all the sweet and sacred promises come with a deeper significance and a more ineffable sweetness."

Are we able to follow this testimony, or is the Bible to us an exhausted book? It is an exhausted book only to the man who has never begun reading it. I desire to add my humble testimony to the deeper and bolder witness of men who are more qualified to attest, that every time I open the Bible it is as a field in which I find hidden treasure, and every time I conclude my exposition of any portion of holy Scripture, I find I have not even begun to touch its infinite meaning. So far, therefore, I feel no difficulty whatever in accepting the doctrine that the kingdom of heaven is like unto treasure hid in a field.

Now, in the next place, can we confirm the doctrine that *life is a search for goodly pearls?* Every man is at home in this truth. Examine yourselves, and you will find that your innermost motive is to find the choicest pearl. In business, in thinking, in literature, in preaching, in art, in music, everywhere—this is the innermost truth, that we are seeking for pearls of the greatest worth. "Who will show us any good?" is the cry of the anxious human heart. So, get what pearls you may upon the earth, there is always another Pearl beyond, larger, of a richer hue, of a higher value, and it is towards this that you stretch out your desire and your hand. Now this is the very motive, purpose, and ambition that the kingdom of heaven came to satisfy. Without this desire it would not have anything to lay hold upon. Here is the secret, mighty hold which Christian truth gets upon mankind: it addresses itself immediately and profoundly to the supreme desire of the heart. As light is adapted to the eye, as sound is adapted to the ear, as substance appeals to the touch, so this kingdom of heaven appeals to our highest sense, our spiritual necessity and receptivity. The kingdom of heaven is not something let down out of the skies, that has to be carried as a weight upon our head, for which we can give no reason, and of which we have no explanation; it is an appeal to something that is in us, it answers an interior voice, it offers to meet a felt necessity. Again examine yourselves and tell me if you are not seeking for goodly pearls. You want it in money, another man wants it in love; another man seeks for it in some larger definition of the term *life*; a fourth man seeks for it in books, a fifth in painting or in music, but every man here on this opening Sabbath of the year is seeking goodly pearls.

So I have no difficulty in accepting the parable when it says that the kingdom of heaven is like unto a merchantman seeking goodly pearls, not inferior ones, but the very best that could be found. This merchantman goes out over sea and land to find goodly pearls. It is recorded that the great Caesar was drawn to the shores of Britain because of the pearls that were cast upon them by the flowing tide. We too, little Caesars, soldiers, explorers, conquerors, have our eyes upon those seas that cast out of their depths the richest treasures. The kingdom of heaven comes to us, and says, "In me you will find the finest pearls."

In the third place, can we not confirm the doctrine that there are prizes for which one would *sacrifice all secondary enjoyments?* The merchantman, when he had found one pearl of great price, went and sold all that he had and bought it: has that any correspondence in our lives? Here is a student who has fixed his ambition upon certain honors; he gives up all ease, indulgence, quietness, and as much sleep as possible that he may lay his hand upon the supreme honor and be its happy owner evermore. You have talked to book collectors who have pointed out some one book for which they have given fifty other books. Being poor men in the matter of mere money, they gathered together books of inferior value, at least of inferior value in their own estimation, and they said to the possessor of the coveted treasure, "You shall have all the fifty for that one." We all have known men who have coveted some particular picture, and they have taken down all the other pictures on their walls and have said, "They shall all go if I can only get that piece of painting." So we also have experiences of this kind in our lives, and this is the very spring and force of life by which we always aim at that which is beyond. It is the *beyond* that allures us; it is the unattained that draws us by mighty spell and fascination onward and onward in our life course.

It is so with the kingdom of heaven. "Yea, doubtless," says Paul, "and I count all things but loss for the excellency of the knowledge of Christ Jesus, my Lord. What things were gain to me, those I counted loss for Christ" [Phil. 3:7, 8]. So he would have sold his ancestry, his pedigree, all that made him proud of the past, and would count it but as dung that he might win Christ. What is this but giving the very highest application to a principle which you have already affirmed in study, in the collection of books, and in the collection of works of art? And other men have sold all they had for the kingdom of heaven. They subdued kingdoms, wrought righteousness, obtained promises, stopped the mouths of lions, quenched the violence of fire, escaped the edge of the sword; others had trials of cruel mocking and scourging, yea, moreover of bonds and imprisonment; they were stoned, they were torn asunder, were tempted, were slain with the sword. They wandered about in sheepskins and goatskins, being destitute, afflicted, tormented—for what object? That they might win Christ, that they might have the pearl of great price as their supreme treasure. In doing so they are not acting the part of foolish men. The kingdom of heaven is like unto a merchantman. You believe in the common sense, in the energy, the prudence and the shrewdness of merchantmen; you glory in the strength of character and the sagacity of mind developed by business; this kingdom of heaven is not ashamed to say that it is like the best business man you have amongst you, with an eye as keen, with an ardor as intense, with a shrewdness as far-seeing as his, and having exhausted him, it multiplies itself by infinity.

This testimony, therefore, ought to come to you men and women of business with great force. The kingdom of heaven is not like unto a *dreamer* only, like unto a crazy *poet*, who makes jingling rhymes—the kingdom of heaven is like unto a *merchantman* who keeps his books, and lays his plans, and awakens his wit, and belabors his energy, and inspires his enthusiasm by daily conquest in daily toil. Wondrous kingdom: it will join any man in his daily toil, and say to him, insofar as he is a wise and honest workman, "I am just like you." It does not merely go into the studies of the artist, into the sanctum of the recluse, into the hermitage of the monk, into the high nest of the poet who loves to dwell in solitude, and say, "I am just like you, great men of imagination and of artistic sensibility and power," but it also comes down to the day laborer, and says, "This is what I do: I dig." It goes to the navigator, and says, "This is what I do: I have countless ships, and my meaning is to touch the uttermost parts of the earth with my beneficence and my light." It goes to the carpenter at the bench, and says, "I am just like you, I work all day and I work for a reward, a great prize." So here is a kingdom called the kingdom of heaven, that identifies itself with the business life of the land, and that reveals one shape of its supreme beauty through business, through merchandise.

While the kingdom of heaven so inspires a man as to lead him to throw off every fascination and inducement of a worldly kind, and to give himself wholly and absolutely to its worship and further pursuit, it may be said that all religions have this effect upon the human mind, which is only a proof that the strongest force which operates upon human intelligence, human inspiration, and human ambition is the religious force. Wherein, then, is the difference between the Christian kingdom and those other kingdoms of a religious kind which are not acknowledged by Christian theology? All religions compel devotion, all religions compel more or less a sacrifice—wherein, then, is the difference between them and this Christian kingdom of heaven? I will tell you. Jesus Christ came into competition with all the sovereign religions of the world; no religion of a sovereign and absolutely original kind has ventured to show its head since Jesus Christ was born. Let me give you time to lay hold of that suggestion; no great religion of this kind has been set up in the world since the birth of Jesus Christ. Judaism is a great religion, but it has not come into existence during the last eighteen hundred and eighty years. Buddhism, Confucianism, are great religions, but each of them is more than eighteen hundred and eighty years of age, a fact which throws into infinite significance the comparison which Christianity institutes, by which it claims to be "the pearl of great price," the one pearl which lowers the value of every other, and which trusts to its intrinsic value to save it from all competition, and to ensure its ultimate and universal appreciation.

It is something to remember that since the child was born in Bethlehem no great or sovereign religion (with the doubtful exception of Islam) has established itself upon the earth. Here we come upon historical ground, and are able to fight with the invincible weapon of fact. What independent religion, right or wrong, has arisen since the birth of Jesus Christ? What man has arisen of such boldness of conception, grandeur of character, purity and sublimity of purpose and originality of mind as to rival or eclipse the man of Nazareth. Negative religions enough, if they might be called religions, denials and criticisms are in abundance, which owe their temporary life to the very character which they assail — but no man can worship in the temple of *doubt*, no man can broadly, deeply, and permanently influence the world who has nothing to suggest but a *negation*; negatives can never ascend the highest seat and rule with dominating and beneficent supremacy. Where is the majestic personality, the profound philosophy, the heroic sacrifice, and the valiant propagandism of a new faith that claims the sovereignty of the world? I do not include perversions and corruptions so foul and obvious as are found in Islam; I ask for an independent, original, and sovereign competitor. The kingdom of heaven is like unto a pearl of great price; it holds itself up as such, and asks for all the other pearls to be brought, that they may be contrasted with its ineffable preciousness. No competing faith has been suggested with such breadth of suggestion as to get more than a moment's life in the estimation of mankind, and no such faith has embodied itself in any leader that the world has cared to arrest and crucify.

A great argument takes its inception here. Men have always looked for someone other than Christ, and no other has come with a single tittle of claim that could bear one moment's examination. Negations have no missions, no adventures, no audacities of a beneficent kind; they only live spasmodically and temporarily, they do not live in themselves and by themselves, of their own divinely created force. This faith of Jesus Christ knocks at every door, it thunders upon the door of India and China, and sends its ship in full sail to the islands of the sea, and the cry is:

> "I am a merchantman who has found a pearl of great price; examine it, test it, receive it — but in doing so all other pearls must be given up. If any man will be my disciple, let him deny himself and take up his cross daily and follow me [Luke 9:23]. He that loveth father or mother more than me is not worthy of me [Matt. 10:37]. Go, sell all thou hast and give to the poor, and come and follow me [see 19:21]. Strait is the gate and narrow is the way that leadeth unto life" [7:14].

What are all these quotations and references but so many expansions of the great doctrine of this text that the kingdom of heaven is as a merchantman, who, having seen a pearl more valuable and precious than all others, surrenders the life-gathered store that he may possess himself of this most precious of all pearls?

Where is your competing pearl, where is your competing Christ, where is your nobler love or your grander purpose? The air is troubled with doubts, the night is thick with skepticism, the Church is annoyed now and again with the arrow and the pestilence of ardent foes, but since the star glittered on Bethlehem no man has arisen to claim the heathen for an inheritance and the uttermost parts of the earth for a possession. Christianity makes this supreme claim to us all this morning; it asks us to lay our little pearls beside it, that it may show by self-revelation how little they are and poor compared with its magnitude, its quality, and its luster. Christianity is a comparative religion, a competitive faith; it asks to be looked at in the light of all that has gone before it, and a religion which comes before me with a claim so broad, so substantial, so manifestly profound in its common sense arrests my thoughts and demands my confidence.

twenty-eight

A DOUBLE ASPECT
OF THE KINGDOM

Matthew 13:33, 47–50

LET ME TRY to reveal the kingdom of heaven today under two aspects. It has already come before us under the image of the sower, the parable of the tares, the grain of mustard seed, the treasure hid in a field, the pearl of great price—by this time surely we ought to be well acquainted with this kingdom of heaven, yet it is the eternal mystery as surely as it is the eternal revelation, Jesus Christ now gives us two more opportunities of knowing still more clearly what his great kingdom is. He condescends to paint two more pictures, a woman hiding leaven in three measures of meal, and a man casting a net into the sea.

"The kingdom of heaven is like unto leaven which a woman took and hid in three measures of meal, till the whole was leavened." It follows then that the kingdom of heaven, like all other truth, is *penetrating in its influence.* It goes forward to its work little by little: it never rests—it cannot rest until it has covered the whole space of its opportunity. It can never give in—all things must go down before it, not violently, but certainly. No great or true idea can be in the human mind without penetrating that mind through and through, and passing on to other minds and completing the same subduing process there.

Not only is it penetrating, but it is *gradual* in its process and advancement. Great ideas do not seize the mind all at once and rule it with undisputed domination. One by one, little by little, a man here and a man there—such is the rule of this gradualness. But it never goes back, though appearances may seem sometimes to indicate the contrary. The movement of truth is always forward. The truth was never so fully, broadly, and benignly established in the human mind as it is this day.

211

You can quote a thousand instances to indicate the badness of the race, its love of error and its pursuit of corruption, and every instance that is quoted may be perfectly right, within its own limits. Nevertheless the kingdom moves, the penetrating influence gradually asserts itself. How long will it continue to assert itself? Till the whole is leavened. The time is fixed in the parable, the date is here marked down in plain figures, if we have eyes to read it. This is a dated promise, and the date is "till the whole is leavened."

Have we any parallels in our own life that will enable us to seize, more completely, the gracious and generous meaning of this parable? We have a parallel, certainly, *in the education of the mind.* No mind is educated in one day: education is not something thrust upon a man which he can seize in a moment and make his own without a long transaction. You cannot tell how you were educated: there is no specific day in our human life upon which we can say we were then educated, in any complete or final sense of the term. We may have vivid memories of certain days, but education is not a day's work, it is not a time work, it is an eternal process. How the light came upon the mind, how the new idea seemed to strike us with instancy and startling suddenness—yet when we came carefully to look into it we found that it was the culminating point of a long process, and that but for the process the culmination never could have supervened. Watch your child's progress in letter, and it will be impossible for you to indicate any time at which he became a scholar. Jesus Christ says, "Just the same in my kingdom: it is not one sermon, one book, one act of prayer, but the repetition of many a process through the whole space of the lifetime. It is not one shower that makes the summer, it is shower upon shower, baptism following baptism in gracious intermission and yet in gracious persistency." It is thus we grow.

We have a parallel not only in education, but in *the deepening and ripening of all great convictions.* If you will search into the history of your mind, you will find that some of your convictions have taken a long time to form: there were prejudices to be overcome, there were defects to be made up, there was information to be gained, there were experiments to be conducted—for a long time you wondered and hesitated, you oscillated between two opposite points, you knew not to which point you would at last gravitate and where you would "finally" settle, and yet there did come a point in your thinking and deliberation at which you said, "This is right, I see it at length, and forever I will take my stand here."

It was so in your appreciation of character, it was so in your decisions of a literary and commercial kind, it was so in the election of your companionships, it was so in the change of your most profound and solemn opinions; it was so, too, in that grandest act of life for which there is no better term than the old word *conversion*. You remember your being converted, turned around, set in a homeward direction, taken from the wrong road, and placed in the right one: without gibberish or whine or mocking pretense, you are not ashamed to say that you were converted.

You have a parallel also in *the formation of character*. No man makes a character in a day. He may destroy a character in a moment, but it takes a lifetime to build one. Many of you are in the time of blossom and of promise, but not of character. Many who now hear me are young, and they, as we say, shape well, but we do not pronounce anything like a final judgment upon them at this time. No young man can have such a character as is possible to old age if that old age has been reached by the right processes. It would be impertinence for thirty to compare itself with sixty or with seventy, if on the part of the elder there has been a lifelong endeavor after truth and purity and perfectness.

"Till the whole was leavened." Do not say that the right leaven is not in us because the end has not been reached. Judge nothing before the time. You complain of the unripeness and unmellowness, the superficiality of many a young character and the incompleteness and imperfection of many a young career. Consider and see how foolish you are in pronouncing such judgment. The leaven may just have been hid in the three measures of meal: the leaven has not yet had time to work: the leaven has been in you for half a century, but it has only been in your son for half a month or half a year—it would therefore be unwise on your part to condemn the young because of their imperfection, incompletion, immaturity. It is right for youth to be imperfect, but for you at your ripe age of seventy to be as childish, foolish, worldly as the youth of twenty, that would be double crime, redoubled, multiplied by many an aggravation, and carried up to a point of black blasphemy against every law of growth and right and divinity.

While I thus speak a word on your behalf, young hearers and young Christians, understand that you owe my defensive advocacy wholly to the fact that you are young. That which applies to you today will have no application whatever in twenty years. Then some other preacher must defend some other generation. Do not interrupt the working of this good ministry in your hearts: do not imagine that this ministry has completed itself in your life; you will expose yourself to just and bitter taunting if you give your elders the idea that the leaven of the gospel has worked out its whole influence in your spirit and career at a time when it has just begun to move in penetrating and subduing influence.

The kingdom of heaven is not only penetrating and gradual, it is *silent* in its ministry. The leaven makes no noise, it works quietly. Do not measure progress by violence: the kingdom of heaven comes not with observation. There is a subtle as well as an ostentatious working. You have got to learn the full scope and value of this most simple fact. A vulgar age talks as if aggressiveness had but one form and one method only as we are making a noise, organizing great bodies and forces, publishing programs in blood-red ink and beating a thousand drums; it is thought that we are making no announcement. My symbol of progress is neither a hammer nor a sword, it is the shining light, the growing seed, the coming summer: no crash of wheels, no blare of trumpets, no fluttering of banners driven by the wind, but silent, solemn, irresistible day, spreading its conquering light over all the spaces of darkness, awaking all living things to labor and to song, and leaving behind it a benediction that shall be no burden. Fussy, fussing little man, trumpeter and drummer, and gifted with making nothing but noises, learn from thy great parabolical Master this day that the kingdom of heaven is like unto leaven, which a woman took and hid in three measures of meal, till the whole was leavened—a penetrating, gradual, secret, silent process, but a process that never ended till the work was done.

On the other hand, let no man mistake the parable, and by a mischievous perversion of its teaching cover his own indifference and neglect. Do not say that you are silent because there is no virtue in silence itself; you must not be silent only, but penetrating, progressive. Not only is the figure negative, it is positive; *quietness* may be taken as the negative side, but *penetration* is the active and positive aspect.

What about your kingdom of heaven—is it a thing locked up in a safe, well shut in, deposited within an inner door, on which you turn twenty cunningly-formed keys? It is a kingdom, perhaps, but it is not the kingdom of heaven, it is not the divine thought, it is not the life that comes down from heaven; that life is not demonstrative, ostentatious, aggressive in any offensive sense of the term, but it is penetrating, subtle in its influence, always moving, always conquering, never resting till the whole is leavened. Be such influence yours and mine.

Take the next parable for one moment: "The kingdom of heaven is like unto a net that was cast into the sea and gathered of every kind." There was nothing discriminating in the net itself. The Church is a net that holds all sorts of people. Have we no parallels to this idea in our own courses of imperial, civil, and social action? Truly we have a thousand parallels. The kingdom of *patriotism* is like unto a net that was cast into the sea and gathered of every kind. Do you suppose that all who have gathered themselves together in the people's House of Parliament are patriots of the divine sort, men who have no ulterior motive of a selfish kind, men who have spent thousands upon thousands of pounds to go into Parliament, that they might die as pure martyrs on the altar of their country? Are you no further advanced in your study of human nature than to believe such to be the case? The House of Commons is as a net cast into the sea that has gathered of every kind. There are in all houses of government, all over the world, noble men, high-spirited patriots, incorruptible spirits that devote themselves to the noblest interests of their country; there are others who, perhaps, were never moved by a noble impulse in any direction, and to whom the country is nothing but a gigantic money producing machine. Shall we, therefore, revile patriotism, and run down great national institutions, and hurl indiscriminate epithets against forms of civilization to which we owe so much? It would be not only unwise and rash, but unjust and inexcusable.

The kingdom of *philanthropy* is also like a net cast into the sea, and which gathered of every kind. Do you suppose that all persons who wear the name of philanthropists are philanthropic in heart? There are men who make a trade of philanthropy; there are those who live upon the charitable dispositions of others; there are men who coin the tears of sympathy into wealth for their own using. On the other hand, there are philanthropists without whom the world would be poor, who have great broad, soft hands that lay upon the world's weakness a grip that helps it, and that give to the world's poverty donations which make it forget its destitution. But because there are all sorts of persons in the kingdom of philanthropy shall we say that there is no philanthropy of a pure and noble sort? He would be a foolish and an unjust man who would bring any such wild accusation against the philanthropic spirit of the age.

Then, again, the kingdom of *general society* is like a net cast into the sea, which gathered of every kind. When your house-parties gather, do you suppose that every man in the little crowd is a friend of yours, sincere, true, genuine, disinterested? You are not so weak. Do you judge men wholly by their clothes—because they have respectable coats, have they therefore respectable characters? Because they have had good schooling in the head, have they had a thorough education in the heart? You know the answer to these searching inquiries. Shall we, therefore, go around and condemn society, and regard all fellowship and communion as an organized lie? We shall stoop to no such folly.

It was *inevitable* that the kingdom of heaven should draw within itself every kind. The Church has its bad members as well as its good ones. I do not wonder—the Church is an excellent lodging. To be in the Church is to look well; to have a pew in church is to begin on the right list; to make a profession of the most popular religion is, at all events, to have a card of introduction to very large sections of honorable society. Shall we, therefore, say there is no kingdom of heaven because of the insincere, the unworthy, and the hypocritical? You would not allow me to say so about patriotism, philanthropy, and social institutions, and, therefore, faithful to your own wise reasoning, I must protest against any man's arising to bring a wild and indiscriminate accusation against what is known as the Christian Church.

Observe, Christ does not *hide the fact of a mixture*. Christ never hides any ugly facts; Christ makes more of his own failures than any other man could make of them. He cries over them, he drenches them with tears, he lifts up his voice and fills the whole space of the firmament with his moan. He acknowledges that he would, but the cities would not [see 23:37]. You will observe, also, that the bad is a testimony and compliment to the good. The children of this world are not unwise in their generation. They know where to cross the stream, they know the best form and attitude to assume in order to attract the friendly attention of the world; they are learned men in their own policies and methods, and if some of them have counterfeited the metal, it was because it was the metal of heaven that it was counterfeited.

And observe that the bad do not *succeed* in hiding themselves. There is no impenetrable secrecy in character. Every bad fish was found in the net and cast out. We may be in the visible church and not in the invisible. The Church is a mystical body. It is not important who was baptized with *water*, but who has been baptized with fire—this is the deciding question! The determining, penetrating question is not who preached with infinite eloquence, but who lived with *blameless consistency*. The rule of judgment will not be who professed, but who carried his profession out. But observe—and here with a sharp knife I cut off the pleasures of a thousand critics—it was the angels that had to perform the work of discrimination and separation, and not the fellow-members of the Church. It was not the good fish that expelled the bad; the angels came forth and severed the wicked from among the just. So shall it be at the end of the age, so shall it be with the tares and the wheat. The question was, "Shall we go and root out the tares?" and the answer was, "No, lest in pulling up the tares ye pull up the wheat also." It is not my business to find out your badness; it is not your business to find out my corruption. When one or the other becomes so exposed and evident and mischievous as to admit of no dispute and no palliation, I do not say that action may not be taken under such conclusive circumstances, but when the question is one of difficulty the decision should be one of charity. I would expel no man unless driven to it by evidence that not only convinced me, but that blinded me by its dazzling light. And why not expel any human soul? Because the good may be larger than the bad in that very soul. It would be easy for me to condemn any man who practices a sin for which I have no liking—but what about my own sin? Who are we that we shall judge one another, except nobly and hopefully? We shall be much deceived and disappointed in so doing; still it may be better for us to be disappointed and deceived in large applications of charitable criticism than to be confirmed, and to have our judgment approved, by some narrow, selfish, unworthy judgment.

twenty-nine

PARABLES TURNED
TO ACCOUNT

Matthew 13:51–58

JESUS CHRIST uttered a gospel which was meant to be *understood*. Do not create more mysteries than he himself created. Jesus Christ took his disciples, so to say, into co-partnery in divine teaching: this circumstance is never to be forgotten in estimating the value and force of the Christian argument. There is to be no needless mystery. Mystery comes as a necessity, and is not to be introduced by clever persons as a merely intellectual puzzle. This kingdom of heaven was meant to be understood, to be grasped by the human mind, and to be reproduced in human speech and in human life.

Observe, the disciples did not understand the parables until they went to Jesus Christ himself for an explanation. They followed him into the house, and said, "What did that parable mean?" The Parabolist became the Expositor. He is the same yesterday, today, and forever. In reading these parables, turn up the expectant heart after everyone of them, and say, "Lord, what is the meaning?" and he will withhold from your understanding nothing that is needful to the thorough illumination of every word he has spoken and that was intended for reduction to practical life.

Keep within the truth you do understand, if you would be mighty as speakers. That is the secret of impression and of consequences of the best and most enduring kind. It is not given to every man to understand equally the whole revealed word: one man has a gift of tongues and can speak all languages in the sanctuary; another man has a parable, in the interpretation of which he is almost a genius; a third is a speaker of consolations, his face was meant to represent them, and his voice, itself a mystery, was intended to convey solaces to the heart with all the witchery of celestial music.

This is the rule in all life, pulpit life, market-place life, theological, commercial, literary, artistic, musical—*keep within the limits of your understanding;* do not let the sparrow try to fly as high as the eagle, and do not let the child's little paper-boat go far out upon the sea, if ever it is meant to be brought home again. There are portions of this Bible which none of us understand: there are whole pages and books here that I can make nothing of. To some, perhaps, it may have been given—but I have not had time to inquire into their credentials—to expound the mysterious prophecies of the word; to others it may have been given to follow its typology with such intelligence as to be able to write under every type exactly what it signifies. I have not been conducted into those remote schools, I cannot tell you anything about prophecies and dates, and the interpretation of beasts and vials and trumpetings and apocalyptic signs—but this one thing I know, that Jesus Christ is the Savior and Teacher and Hope of the world. Within that limit do we range here, and if we have gone in and out and found pasture abundant, the praise be his who made the pasture so luxuriant and bade us to the enjoyment of his hospitality.

Having understood these mysteries so far, what was to be done? No sooner did the disciples answer, "Yea, Lord," than he said unto them, "Therefore—" This man's words come one after the other in most gracious and logical continuity. They no sooner admitted their understanding than out of that admission he struck the spark of a final parable. He was the Life, to touch him anywhere was to extract virtue from his being. The intellect that had conceived these parables, so varied, so resplendent, so exact in all their adaptations to circumstances, was not tired. Omnipotence cannot be tired, omniscience cannot be exhausted. So when the disciples said, "Yea, Lord," their very admission was turned into another parable. "Therefore the kingdom of heaven is like unto a man that is an householder," a parable after the parables, a sermon after the sermons. There was no ending to this man's teaching, the word was not its measure: after every word there followed an infinite ghostliness of possibility and suggestion. Let us look at this final parable.

"Therefore every scribe which is instructed unto the kingdom of heaven is like unto a man that is an householder, which bringeth forth out of his treasure things new and old." A householder who has treasure:

Jesus Christ claims for all the scribes of his following substantial truth. They do not utter mere phrases of their own making or utter sentiments which are the measure of their own sighing and desire only. In the God's Church there is a positive quantity, a subjective truth, a content that, so to say, can be seen, handled, felt, known, as a personal possession, an individual inheritance. Look at this circumstance most carefully, those of you who are anxious to know what Christianity really comprehends and purports to be. It is not a sigh, it is not a sentiment, it is not a rhapsody—there is nothing of the nature of mere fantasy in it. It has solid doctrines, grand conceptions of the divine being, broad and luminous revelations respecting human nature, great, solid, massive gospels as to the redemption of the race from the presence, power, tyranny, and torment of sin, and infinite hope which it can only indicate by words not earthly, but which fall infinitely short of the reality as God himself understands it. But a word has been given us which overpasses earth, time, death, tomb, shadow, and shines yonder as heaven.

So there is range enough in this divine revelation. If viewed poetically only, it is a grand and complete conception. It is not a broken arc, it is not a segment that mourns a loss which it can neither define nor fill up—it is a great complete circle, equally strong, and equally luminous at every point of its infinite circumference. So the Word of God is called bread: it is known amongst men as the water of life, of which, if a man drink, he shall thirst no more. The result of the appropriation of Christian truth and blessing is rest—rest in the soul, peace in the mind, calm in the heart, and no man within my knowledge has ever tasted the value of this treasure, and entered with conscious joy into its proprietorship, that has owned to one pang of disappointment. "Ho, everyone that thirsteth, come ye to the waters. . . . and as for your hunger, let your soul delight itself in fatness" [see Is. 55:1, 2].

Not only is the scribe like unto a man that is a householder, with treasure in his possession, but he is a householder who dispenses his treasure. He brings forth out of his treasure things new and old. The wise man holds nothing for himself alone: we are trustees, we are stewards, who act on behalf and in the interest of others. Every idea which I may have is yours, every idea which you may have is mine. We help one another by the friction of mind, the communion of heart, the mutual reciprocation of life, idea, thought, and purpose. The Church is a commonwealth—no one man is lord or king in it, except by natural rights and proofs which no other would for a moment dispute, but the humblest has a right to the ideas of the wisest.

This is the difficulty of the Christian Church throughout the world today. The door of the church is open, the front door and the back door and the side door, and above every open door is written, "Welcome" to the humblest, poorest, sickliest of the population. If any church is acting upon other lines than these, that church seems to me to fall below its high vocation in Christ Jesus. I know nothing of your narrow exclusiveness, I know nothing of what is known as your closed communion; I would not be a party to any communion that is closed, I believe in the infinite breadth, height, depth of these divine Gospels and all their practical meaning. This is my Father's house, and no man has a right to label it, or number it, so that it shall exclude the very poorest human creature that crawls upon the earth this day.

Understand that you cannot grasp the whole treasure. It is not within your power to consume the whole banquet, that is no reason why you should not satisfy your hunger at this table. To one man is given five talents, to another two, and to another one—to every man according to his unique ability, and every man has it in his power to lay hold of Christ somewhere. Know where your fingers were meant to lay their loving grip, and hold fast according to the divine purpose.

As for those of you who have the divine treasure, *do not keep it to yourselves.* "Go ye into all the world and preach the gospel to every creature" [Mark 16:15]. In proportion as power is given unto you "go ye and teach all nations" [Matt. 28:19]. That is the only true and most beneficent use of power. How is this to be done? Why, this householder showed genius in the distribution of his treasure—he brought forth out of his treasure things new and old. Surely this was a proof of his instruction. I would not listen to one sermon that was all new; in every discourse concerning the gospel which I hear there must be the boom, the infinite sounding of eternity; then may come the new parable, the bright suggestion, the flash of immediate wit, the kindling of sudden lights and the unbreaking of subtle and surprising music. But underneath every flower of human genius I must find the rocks of divine wisdom.

This is the true method, as it is also the true purpose of all teaching. In the school, in the nursery, at the fireside, in the church—to give everybody to feel the venerableness, the indestructibility of truth, and to lure them to its study and love and appropriation, by new hints, by novel adaptations, it may be sometimes even by eccentric uses of facts and thoughts—things new and old; old time—new summers: old light—new mornings; old eternities—newborn time; everlasting duration—transient days. So must things be intermingled and allied in any utterance that is philosophical, profound, sympathetic, and immediately useful in this kingdom of heaven.

Now Jesus seems to come down from the mountain once more, as he did after his great sermon. In its own way this sermon is as great as the first: the sermon so strong in doctrine was followed by the sermon so brilliant in imagination. Over the wheat field is spread the glory of a gleaming and many-colored sky: out of that sky indeed the wheat field came, and without it the wheat field could neither be sown nor reaped. We must not exclude *imagination* from the treasure of the Church: it is the highest faculty which can be used, it is the inner eye, it is that divine vision which sees more than is penetrable by scholarship. This is the difference between one man and another. One man knows the letter, is absolutely faultless in all the uses of grammar, yet there may never come one syllable of fire or one drop of dew from his philological lips. People listen, but are never thrilled with glad responses. Another man holds the divine secret and breathes it over our life at his will, and makes the heart leap with sudden joy and cry out because of glad surprise.

Some do not know what imagination is: they think if they are good at description they are strong in imagination: this is the absurdity, this the mischievous sophism—when you have mentioned all the seven colors you have painted nothing: if you were to paint a tree exactly as it is, you would not have painted it at all. That is a mystery and a fact; the trunk is the same height, the branches are the same in number, and all the dimensions are exact, all the leaves have been counted, and you tell me that the tree upon the canvas is not the same as the tree in the wood? Certainly, they have no connection with one another; you had not the eye that saw the inner tree—that is not the tree standing in the wood, that is the body; the spiritual tree is inside that, and you must get it out and translate it, idealize it. So the man standing there is not the man: that is his house of clay, his tabernacle of dust—the man is inside; you must see that inner light and describe that mysterious man. So the letter of the gospel may be a letter only, unless I have that vision and faculty divine which can penetrate the inner sanctuary of the thought and bring forth things new and old with the honesty of a steward and the energy of a genius.

Have ye understood these things? Not—have ye heard the letter? Not—can you recite the parables one by one? Not—have they fallen upon your outer ear and made a noise there? Have ye understood these things, have they entered into the very tissue and substance of your brain, do they fall into musical accord with all the springs and issues of your purest and noblest thinking? When you relate them, will you recite them as lessons which you have learned, or will you breathe them as part of the very life that is in you? When we can answer "Yes" to Jesus Christ's questions, he will follow our admission with a pungent and practical exhortation.

Now comes the inevitable *criticism*, the mean and low-minded attack which even the Son of God could not escape. "Whence hath this man this wisdom and these mighty works? Is not this the carpenter's Son? Is not his mother called Mary? and his brethren James and Joses and Simon and Judas? and his sisters, are they not all with us? Whence then hath this man all these things?" The inevitable criticism, the inevitable sneer, the inevitable profanation of every sanctuary God has built upon the earth! How is this? How can it be that men can say these things, acknowledging their reality, power, and splendor, and can in the same breath say "This man," with a covert sneer? This impossibility *we* are performing ourselves everyday! Instead of fixing our attention upon these mighty works and all this wisdom, and availing ourselves of the substantial revelation, we fall foul upon the poor instrument through whom the revelation was granted, we hurl at him every reminiscence we can gather up, and we disparage his personality that we may blunt the force of his appeal. Do not mourn such ingratitude and baseness, as if it were the Jewish property only: Jesus Christ was not hated and crucified by the Jews, he was despised and rejected of men.

I was recently rebuked upon this point with a rare piquancy and most pathetic simplicity. An educated man followed me after the discourse, and, speaking with a strong German accent, he assured himself and me in the same breath that what he was about to say was well intended. Then said he, "I was with you on the occasion of your five hundredth noonday service. I am the preacher in such and such London synagogue, and," said he, "if you will excuse me, there was one line in the carol which gave me pain." Bringing the carol under my eyes, he said, "See—'the wicked Jews'—why did you sing that in your church about the wicked

Jews?" Within the lines of a narrow history the carol was right, but within the true boundary the carol was wrong. They were not the Jews that killed him, mocked him, spurned him, threw his earthly ancestry in his face; it was man—every man. We crucified the Son of God, *we* Gentiles had our share in that foul tragedy. Do not teach your children in the school and at the fireside that some wicked people called Jews did this to Jesus Christ, and express yourselves in horror about the Jews as if you had *nothing* to do with it. The truth is this—*we were all there,* we all cut the accursed tree out of the forest and planted it and nailed to it the Son of God, and as he hangs there tell all the world that this was not a geographical incident or a mere point in passing history—that this crucifixion was the work of the whole race, and that every eye must look upon it and every heart mourn it as its own cruel deed.

This is the *worst* they can say about the Son of God. Let us read it again. "Whence hath this man"—covert sneer—"this wisdom and these mighty works? We cannot deny either the one or the other, but is not this the carpenter's son?" What an awful accusation. "Is not his mother called Mary?" What a distressing indictment against any man! "And his brethren, James and Joses and Simon and Judas? and his sisters, are they not all with us?" Well, suppose we say, "Yes, they are"—now what then? I am glad they say this; there was *nothing more* to be said, they would have said it if they could, yea, they would have dreamed a lie and imagined it true if they could.

Christian man, Christian inquirer, hear me. This is the indictment brought against him in whose name you were baptized—does it alarm, does it frighten you, does it bring with it any sense of oppressive humiliation? He was the carpenter's son, he was the carpenter, his mother's name was Mary, such and such were his social surroundings—now, when the little tale has been told, what remains? Hear the great thunder-burst of music and eloquence rolling down the mountain, and then listen to this little piping scorn, and tell me on which side do you stand? I will stand with Christ, the carpenter's Son, the Son of Mary.

thirty

A REVIEW OF MATTHEW 13

Matthew 13

THE SUBJECT of this chapter is the kingdom of heaven. Connect this circumstance with the fact that Jesus Christ came into the world to save sinners, and ask yourselves what is the connection between a kingdom and salvation. The kingdom of heaven has a great part to play in the work of evangelizing the nations. A purpose that goes out to take hold of kingdoms must itself be a kingdom. You cannot lay hold of worlds with a weak hand. You may affect the immediate surrounding by trifling circumstances, but if you are going to lay your grasp upon all the kingdoms of the world and the glory of them you must have a force equal to the occasion. Jesus Christ proposes to take hold of all kingdoms and to transform them into his own excellence, and fill them with the glory of his own excellent name. The kingdom of heaven, therefore, is a royal truth; it is a royal power; it is not one among many competitors, it stands alone and must absorb and sanctify all rivalries. Do not lower the occasion; realize its grandeur and rise to its appeal.

In this chapter Jesus Christ gives the word "kingdom" a new meaning and application. Up to this time it was an imperial term only or a geographical expression. Kingdom was a quantity bounded and named by the consent of other powers or held against them by superior force. It was a mere term in geography, in government, in statesmanship; in Jesus Christ's hands it becomes a heavenly claim, a divine power, a sacred sovereignty of impulses, thoughts, and purposes, so that all that is merely geographical drops off, and all that is heavenly clothes the royal word.

So far I could go well. I am stopped just there by an unusual punctuation, the discrepancy between the *speaker* and the *subject*. A *peasant*

227

talking about a *kingdom*—the rhyme is broken! A homeless wanderer using the highest terms in human speech—who can account for the discrepancy? I am not troubled by the discrepancy which the critics find in dates and places and small incidents, but a discrepancy like this may well take the rest out of my heart, and fill that heart with a grievous discontent. The world was too big for the speaker: he did not, from a human point of view, look a king until he was looked at the second time, and watched the clock round, and the year round, and not until the spirit was instructed in the mysteries of his truth did his personality take upon it its wondrous visage and color. Why, really, it is no discrepancy at all: the discrepancy was in me and not in Christ. I find that this is an eternal truth; that evermore the speaker is to be nothing, and the subject is to fill the heavens. Why, herein is the very glory of Christianity—that it absorbs all other little piping eloquence in the infinite redundance of its own thunder, and that our personality as revealers of the kingdom is nothing as compared with the majesty and glory of the thing that is revealed. Unhappily, even Jesus Christ himself, as you see at the end of the chapter, was not able so to control the thinking of the people who heard him as to fix it upon the subject. They, little creatures, could rise no higher than the speaker, and they mocked him because of the discrepancy that was in reality an argument and a vindication.

In reading this chapter as a whole I am struck with four things. First of all, from the nature of the kingdom of heaven you may learn, without a single word being said upon the subject, the nature of the kingdom of darkness. It is not necessary to describe the kingdom of darkness: what you and I, as Christian teachers, have to do, is to describe the kingdom of light. This was Christ's most wise and subtle method of teaching—not to paint hell—to refer to it in great graphic sentences as if in haste to be done with it, but with great elaboration and pomp of simplicity to reveal the infinite kingdom of God's truth and light and purity. Every parable that is spoken here admits of being turned in the directly opposite quarter, so as to reveal that about which it says nothing. Thus—the kingdom of heaven is like unto a man who sowed good seed. Then the kingdom of darkness is like unto a man who sowed bad seed, seeds of death, seeds of unhealthiness, seeds of disease, seeds of error. Learn thus from the kingdom of heaven what the opposing kingdom is.

Again—the kingdom of heaven is like unto treasure. Then the kingdom of darkness is like unto a bubble in the air. It is just the opposite of the kingdom of heaven. If the kingdom of heaven is treasure, the kingdom of darkness is an empty though gilded bubble, floating on the quiet breeze. Snatched, it is destroyed; there is nothing in it. It is lacking in substance, in positive and applicable value, it does not enrich life, it is weight without gravity, a burden without value, a kingdom truly, but a kingdom of disappointment.

Again—the kingdom of heaven is as leaven which a woman took and hid in three measures of meal. Then the kingdom of darkness is as poison which a man took and secretly injected into the veins of a sleeper until the whole was poisoned. The kingdom of heaven is a great force that secretly and silently works out the soul's regeneration: the kingdom of darkness is as the sting of the tsetse fly; the tsetse fly seizes the ox, stings the noble brute, and in due course of time the flesh swells and discolors, the skin falls off, and the strong one is thrown down in weakness and in death. The kingdom of darkness, therefore, is not a weak power, it is not an ineffective ministry: it also works, often silently and secretly, but it is working out the soul's destruction.

Or thus—the kingdom of heaven is like unto a net cast into the sea and gathers of every kind. The kingdom of darkness is as a net thrown into the sea and gathers its own kind only—a narrow kingdom, debasing whatever it touches, catching for the purpose of holding in vile captivity, netting and ensnaring that it may slay. Thus the parable is more than it seems to be. It teaches by contrasts; it has a far-spreading edge of meaning. In describing truth you need not describe falsehood: insofar as your description of truth is correct, you are really, in the most suggestive and graphic manner, describing that which is false.

This subtle influence of color was often felt in Christ's ministry. He used sometimes to speak as if he were addressing an absent congregation. Subtle speaker, wise assailant, he was addressing the absentees, they thought, till they thought again, and then suddenly they said, "He means us." He told them about a man who had property in the distance, and sent his servant to gather the fruits or the revenues, and the servant was not received well, and another servant was sent, and another, and last of all he sent his son also, and then he said, "What will he do to those husbandmen"; and they, thinking that the husbandmen were a thousand miles away, said, "He will slay them," and suddenly it burst upon their obtuse minds that all the while he was talking about them. That is the best use to make of the absentees.

On another occasion he was speaking his great truth, letting it fall where it might be applicable, and a man at the other end of the table said, "Take care: in speaking thus thou revilest us also," and the man having seized the hot iron, had more of it than he covenanted. It was thrust into him, for Christ turned and said, "Woe unto you also, ye lawyers" [see Luke 11:45, 46], and in that also he stretched a band and caught another set of offenders within its righteous captivity.

Let us learn from our great Prototype, our divine Master. We shall fall into some kind of dislike and criticism perhaps, still let us diligently and lovingly put our feet into his footsteps, and we shall come to the same desirable ends as to our great spiritual mission and teaching.

The next thing that strikes me in reading this chapter is that the great teacher did good rather by *revelation* than by *criticism*. He did not spend his time merely in denunciation. You must have a higher kingdom to offer, if you want to make a profound and permanent impression upon the age. It is not enough to provoke mere antagonism: I do not go out to deny any man's propositions or contentions, and rest myself in so doing: if I cannot reveal as well as criticize, I am as a bird with one wing. Christianity is a revelation, a surprise, a great offer. If any man have a gift at argument, and be blest or burdened with the genius of contradiction or debate, and have a keen desire to meet people whom it would be well to avoid, so far as mere social contact is concerned, then let him go out with his denials and contentions and continue his debate night after night. He is a greater teacher who has a kingdom to reveal, a positive and distinct offer of grace to make to men. We shall be unjust to the genius of Christianity if we treat Christian doctrine as a mere denial of some other doctrine rather than as a positive and grand doctrine of itself.

As a Church what have we to offer? With what do you seek to lure and satisfy human nature? It is the glory of Christ that he makes the largest offer ever made to the nature of man. His offer goes further, addresses more faculties, satisfies more aspirations, promises greater assistance, than any competitive doctrine known to men. Consider the wholeness of his kingdom, how it spreads itself over all the life, leaving no part or day untouched and unblest. He begins with childhood and writes "Kingdom of Heaven" on the fair brow of the little one. He follows the wanderer out, though the night be ever so dark. I never knew darkness to keep him at home, or wildness of weather, depth of snow, or keenness of frosty wind. The moment the front door opened, and the prodigal vanished, he says,

"I must leave you and go out after that which is lost, till I find it," and when that door opens again, it will open to let in two men, the Seeker and the man who was found.

Christ comes into the house when the sickness is there; be the sickness ever so vile; nothing keeps him away. Though the poor family be all crowded, ten in number, in one room, he comes in to make the eleventh, and though the room be high up on the roof yonder, he finds his way into the solitude and secrecy of poverty. He comes in the market-place and writes codes of laws for merchantmen: he stands behind the counter and writes with that wondrous finger the great laws of the best economy. When it becomes a question of the last wrestle, the challenge to the final conflict, he says, "Fear thou not, for I am with thee" [Is. 41:10].

This is the offer which Christ makes to us all; the largest, most ample, minute, detailed, comprehensive offer that was ever made. Other creeds meet me here and there, other kingdoms are partial in their revelations and applications, clever men merely address my intellect, sentimental men address my heart, nearly every teacher has some little thing to offer, a chain of two links to put into my hand, but Jesus Christ alone has undertaken to deal with every part, section, phase, and issue of my being, and I am bound to respect the grandeur of his challenge and to respond to the magnificence of his kingdom, though it be a kingdom at present but in word and in high poetry. Entering it, accepting it, living in it a life of citizenship, I come to understand that it is indeed poetry, because it is truth, without which there can be no poetry.

In the third place, see how with all this enchanting and startling originality of form, Jesus Christ declared eternal truth. These are no hot-house plants; these are not mushrooms a night old. Hear Jesus Christ's explanation of the parables. He spake unto the multitude in parables that it might be fulfilled which was spoken by the prophet, saying, "I will open my mouth in parables, I will utter things which have been kept secret from the foundation of the world" [see Ps. 49:4; 78:2]. These are no new lights, these are no new inventions: the form is new, the doctrine is old. This is not the favorite of a transient age; it begins with the unbeginning, it covers the infinite spaces, it antedates and postdates all human history, Alpha, Omega, the first, the last, which is and was and is to come, lifting up all time into a burning present. This is the secret and the glory of Christ's teaching; flowers are grown upon earth under which are the everlasting rocks.

So with every great and true deliverance and revelation of truth: it must be old as well as new. Make as many parables as you please, but do not trifle with the kingdom. The parables reveal the kingdom, the kingdom is older than the parables, and admits of all kinds of pictorial illustration and graphic description, and to the end of the ages the forms under which we present the truth will change, but the truth itself, like its living Lord, is the same yesterday, today, and forever.

Might I speak a word on behalf of the rising ministry, and of men who do not put the truth in its old forms, and may I ask you to believe that it is possible to change the parable without changing the integrity of the kingdom? We do not preach as Goodwin and Baxter and Bunyan and Owen and Howe preached, as to mere form, but we try, with another accent and with another range of illustration, not better than theirs, but simply other, to set forth the same truth, the same sin, the same cross, the same blood. The ministry is one, the parables are a million in number multiplied by ten, but the kingdom remains, illustrated by the advancing culture and the quickened genius of ages, itself venerable as eternity, its manifestations new, glittering, and gleaming as the dew of the morning. Do not, therefore, be harsh with your young men who are rising to preach the gospel in new forms and in new words that may look to you new-fangled and eccentric. The great fact is, the kingdom is the same, and the illustrations show not that we are divided about it, but that we are simply bewildered by the infinite fertility of its suggestion.

You know what all this means in the lower walks of progress. The steam-engine was in the world from the very moment of the world's existing — not mechanically, but elementally — and the elements lay there age after age, until a man combined them and made a parable of them, and that parable was reduced, from an invention and a flash of genius, into a fast-flying locomotive. The iron was in Eden, and the water was in Eden, and the fire was in Eden, but the combination and interrelation of these had to be realized long ages after Eden was lost. So with the telegraph and the telephone and all your modern and yesterday inventions; elementally they were all there when God laid the foundation of the earth and looked upon the little globe and said in heaven concerning it, "It is very good." The ages have come and perused the writing, searched into the treasure, found the operation of the leaven, and now the ages are rich; the inventions are new, but the elements which they apply and combine are as old as the ribs of the earth and the central fire of the planet.

So with all your music. You remember that John Stuart Mill was afraid that the time would come by-and-by when there would be no more music in the world, that the seven sisters would have done all they could for the world, but the wondrous seven still go on; there is no end to the innovation of which they are capable as to number and variety. Yet they are but seven; so they might sing with Wordsworth's little girl—only they never part company, they never die, they suit themselves to all the suggestions of the fertile brain of the musician. They are but seven, yet they stretch themselves around the whole sky, and sing night and day, and will shut themselves up in the prison of any instrument, to be liberated by any Moses sent of God to emancipate them from their silence and secrecy. The tune is new, the notes are quite old; they were heard in the plash of the first rain, in the concussion of the first lightning and thunderstorm, and in the song of the first bird that sung. So they come on and on, a gospel infinite and endless in adaptation, and so is the kingdom of heaven typified by all these parables. The kingdom, let me repeat, is eternal, it is the parable only that is changed.

And now, in the fourth place, observe how the most astounding revelation of wisdom and power cannot save the revealer from the *sneers of graceless critics*. My friend, there is no protection for thee; no angel can hide himself from the strife of tongues. There is no pavilion upon the earth in which you can hide yourself from the crudeness of those who are determined to misrepresent and abuse you. You cannot fight with prejudice, you cannot answer a whim; no argument can get itself thoroughly around a merely personal dislike. If you have made up your minds not to receive a revelation from a man, if that man be God himself incarnate, it lies within the compass of human malignity to nail him to the cross. If you, therefore, are speaking for human applause, you will be wounded in the house of your friends. If you suppose that the grandeur of your subject will protect you from the meanness of your assailants, you have made a most unwise and unfounded calculation. Is a servant more than a master? If they have called the master of the house Beelzebub, how much more they that are of his household? Why, in little and insignificant ways we are ourselves subject to all these misrepresentations, and are the victims of all these unreasoning and cruel prejudices. There cannot be any one of you who has a message and an individuality of his own that is not put to such torture as lies within the power of such critics to inflict. What did Jesus do? He went straight on with his work, he spake not a parable the less, did not a good deed the fewer, patiently went the round of his ministry, taking with him life, light, bread, water, comfort, hope, redemption, making his great grand offer in broad, human, divine language to the sons of men.

I close this chapter with regret; I entered it with great misgiving. I feared these parables, but as I entered into the cloud I heard a voice saying, "Fear not; this is my beloved Son, hear ye him." I leave it now as a man might leave good company and high fellowship. It is a gallery of divinely-painted pictures, it is a panorama of infinite wonders, it is intellectual as the fifteenth chapter of Luke is moral. I feel as if we were coming down a mountain; and whoever left a mountaintop but with reluctance? "It is good for us to be here; let us build three tabernacles," but he says, "No, this is not the place to build; if you have caught the oxygen, if it has got into your blood and reddened it, if you feel the mountain air stirring your pulses and lifting up your life to a new vigor, go down into the valleys and use your new life for the good of others."

thirty-one

HEROD HEARS OF CHRIST

Matthew 14:1-14

IT MUST NOT be supposed that Herod had not heard of Jesus Christ until this time, but at this particular juncture the fame of Jesus made a new impression upon the ruler's mind. There are some hours that are historical, although the very things we remember in those hours have not been unknown to us or even unfamiliar to us aforetime. Notice the kind of fame which Herod heard of Jesus. Was it the fame of his eloquence or the fame of his spirituality? Was the governor struck by the breadth and grandeur of the spiritual conceptions of the new teacher? Probably not. What struck him most, and therein showed the worldliness of his nature, was the miracles. Some men are more fascinated by lightning than by light. Herod heard of mighty works, grand wonders and astounding signs, but it is not said that he had heard of the beatitudes and reveled in sympathetic appreciation as he listened to the dripping music, the sweet pensive words which fell from the lips of the Teacher on the mountain.

It is even so today: we do not see men in their grandest point; it is some little incidental and transient thing that attracts our crude attention, some trick of manner, or tone of voice, or method of assault: but what of the intellectual view, the spiritual unction, the groping after the infinite, the passion of love, the redeeming care, the eternal patience? No reference is made to the higher qualities of men until long after their ascension. At first we talk about their miracles, their prodigies, signs and tokens, and not a word do we say about the subtle process that has in it ten thousand miracles of insight and sympathy and eloquence of the heart.

Mark the wisdom of Jesus Christ in this matter, he knew how the world must be approached, he understood the value of collateral helps such

235

as miracles; Jesus Christ never intended the miracles to be continuous in the Church, because he knew they would soon drop into commonplace. Man has a wonderful capacity for absorbing miracles, of forgetting the last wonder, and of asking for another. Yet miracles have their place; they are great trumpets that call attention, flashing, dazzling signs that awaken men and make them look, and while they are looking, the great Teacher seizes his opportunity to touch and bless the inner nature.

What have we been in these matters? Mere starers, wrought upon by fancy, the victims of our own wonder? Why, what is this but worshiping idols of our own making, bowing down before worldly things of our own fashioning? The call to us is to the inner sanctuary, the upper chamber, the place where the Shekinah shines. We are stunned by miracles; we are saved by truth.

Given a mighty thought and a mighty deed, to know which will soonest win the attention of the world and secure its paltry fame, and the deed will outrun the thought. A man who goes into a dangerous place or takes a daring leap, or does some act of romantic madness, is known across a wider horizon than the man who has the divine gift of prayer, and who can work the all but infinite miracle of opening the door of the kingdom of heaven. Who heeds thoughts or cares for sympathy, or adds up in positive value the tears that flow in commiseration over human distress? The world is a ready reckoner, quick at great batches of figures, totaling them into millions that fill the mouth and daze the imagination where miracles are concerned. But where thoughts, feelings, impulses, inspirations, beatitudes, commendations of virtue are concerned, where is the ready reckoning? We shall learn better by-and-by. Keep in the school of Jesus, and you will learn that there is an arithmetic that is valueless but for momentary convenience, and that the true riches are within—that the ornament of a meek and a quiet spirit is in the sight of God of great price, that miracles of the ordinary kind, such as are found in the gospels, are but introductory, when rightly used, to the light that is meant to shine upon the mind, and to lead the heart upward into the great mysteries of truth and fellowship with God.

Herod, having heard of the fame of Jesus, even upon the comparatively low ground of miracles, gave an explanation of what he heard. I cannot tell how many hours of silence preceded the utterance, but the utterance itself came with the suddenness of an unexpected shock.

Herod said with startling abruptness, "This is John the Baptist." We thought his name had been forgotten. No storied marble stood above the headless body to remind the tetrarch, no brass memorial was to be found on all the walls of Herod's palace to remind him of the death. How was it that he knew so distinctly the name of the murdered man? Is there a recording angel, are there invisible presences dogging our steps and whispering to us unwelcome words now and again, even while the wine is halfway to the livid lips with thirst for its fire? Immeasurable life, mysterious life, accursed memory! Cain took to city building, he will fill his head with masonry; still the dead man looks at him from every foundation he lays. He will build high, but the red blood reddens the uppermost mortar, and oozes upward to remind him of what he once did.

Some say Herod was a Sadducee, and we know that the Sadducees say that there is no resurrection. If Herod was a Sadducee, this is a startling instance of the power of truth and fact to override our speculative creeds, tear them to pieces, and make us poor indeed. We shall know the value of our creed when the last pressure is put upon it. It is one thing to have a creed over a foaming glass of wine and in the midst of a steaming feast when gaiety fills the house and loud rough laughter is the music of the moment, and another thing to have a creed that will go with us through every hour of the day, through every wilderness, up every steep and rocky place, that will clutch our hand in the dark and say, "You are all right; walk on, and I will take you into the morning." Herod's, if he was a Sadducee, was a speculative creed, a thing that pleased the mere intellect for the time being, a piece of rationalism that seemed to fit the occasion. When this great tragedy asserted itself in all those bitter, cruel memories he forgot his Sadduceeism in the presence of an accusing conscience.

Search your creeds through and through, and see if they are faiths that will carry you across the whole bound and scheme of life, or whether they are little transient pleasures, butterflies that live in the sunshine, ephemera that die in the beam that created them. My own experience deepening everyday, growing painful in richness, is this: no faith will go with a man up every hill, through every valley, into every pain and every darkness, and through all the light and joy of life, but the faith that Jesus Christ is the Son of God and the only Savior of the world. Other faiths please me intellectually more, for a little time suggestions coming from other masters give me some delight within given limits, but the theology of Jesus Christ alone fills the whole horizon, and is equally strong at every point. As a personal experience let this go for what it is worth; if your experience coincides with it, insofar as it does let us add our testimony together until the witness becomes in itself a second gospel, not a gospel of revelation, but a confirming gospel, setting to the gospel of revelation this seal, that we have proved it in actual experience.

Herod felt the pressure of the eternal law of righteousness. There was one sermon he did remember—brief as a lightning flash, but so memorable that recollection could never throw it off. Men remember different kinds of sermons. There are some sermons we try to forget, and fail to do so. Sometimes the sermon is in one sentence: it is not at all necessary that you should approve of every sentence in the sermon, or like the sermon as a whole, any more than it is necessary for the man who sits down at the table to consume the luxuries with which it is loaded—he may refuse this, or dislike that, but there is enough to satisfy his hunger, and in that satisfaction his contentment should find its pleasure.

If you had interrogated Herod as to the scope of the ministry of John the Baptist—in what relation he stood to the ancient prophets and in what precise relation he stood to the coming Messenger, to the Lord himself—probably Herod could have given you but lame and imperfect answers. But if you had asked Herod if he could recall one thing that John had ever said, he would have recalled something that was not addressed to the multitude, but that was shot into his own bad heart. He never quoted that sermon but to himself. To himself he preached it probably everyday.

The impression made upon Herod's mind was the deeper because John was known to him as a good man and just. Our sermons derive force from our character. The solid noble character gives weight to the weakest words. A lofty and pure consistency utters what might, from a literary point of view, be of the most imperfect sort, with an accent that makes it eloquent. The grim ascetic, the stern child of the wilderness, draped in camel's hair and fed on locusts and wild honey—he on whom there rested no spot of shame, of foulness or suspicion—said, "It is not lawful for thee to have Herodias as thy wife." Who dares interfere with such things now? No man of my acquaintance. What preacher dares interfere with the family life of his congregation? Not one. Are there not families that would absorb whole libraries of consolation who would resent the faintest approach towards rebuke? If the preacher sees that you are going to marry the wrong man or the wrong woman, dare he interfere? Only at the expense of his head. The law is the same in all ages. Sympathy at a high price, judgment and rebuke at the price of loss, neglect, persecution, martyrdom. If I were to interfere with your marriages, because of their kinship, because of their lack of adaptation and proper coincidence and rhythm, what would be your retort? Imprisonment, decapitation. Not in their physical forms—thank God we have outlived that lack of refinement, but where is there a man who dare ask if the weights are just and the balances equal, or if an enemy has not snipped off part of the yard measure? No man dare interfere with such things now.

The martyrdom having been committed, we come to the twelfth verse, which reads like the bitter music of despair, ending in one troubled hope. Almost every word of the twelfth verse throbs with pathetic suggestion. "And his disciples came"—with heavy feet, with heavy hearts, with tearful eyes, with great groaning, with wonder that might at any moment turn into impiety and hard talking against Heaven's justness. "And took up the body." A heavy load, yet a precious burden; took it up tenderly, lifted it with care, a body that had never known the meaning of luxury, self-care, indulgence; a body whipped, scourged, mutilated, held in most severe discipline, every member of it a slave, a gospel in itself of abstention, discipline, severe and inexorable control. Took up the body—the lips gone, the eyes gone, who can tell what was being done with that head? When the head of the eloquent Cicero got into the hands of Fulvia, the woman against whom that eloquent tongue had thundered, she pierced the tongue with sharp instruments, that she might avenge herself upon the eloquence she could not answer.

"Took up the body." It was all that was left them. They buried it—they had nothing else to do: they must needs hide it away. Give me a place that I may bury my dead out of my sight. We think we will keep the dear body forever, but a law, higher and more inexorable than our desire in such matters, says, "The time will come when you will say—'Take it out of my sight.'"

Now for the note of a troubled hope. "They went and told Jesus." He was always hearing calamitous news. When did anybody go to him with news that made his face broaden and brighten and glow with new joy? Whenever the door of the house was battered by an importunate hand it was that some sadder tale than ever might be poured into the ear of Jesus. If you saw a woman speaking to his bent ear, she was pouring into it some tale of woe. If you saw a man accosting him, it was that the man might tell Jesus of some bitter distress at home. We could not do without that hearing ear.

"They told Jesus." To tell our grief is something: to put our distress into words is to get relief. We can tell the Savior everything; we keep back no syllable of the tale. You would be lighter of heart if you would tell the Savior everything that is giving you distress. He is our priest, and to him we must confess. Tell him about your difficulty at home, your trouble with your child, your perplexity in business, the distresses for which there are no words—these you can sigh and hint at in your suggestive and eloquent tears. Let there be no lack of confidence between you and your Lord. It is not enough that he knows by his omniscience. He asks us to tell him as if he knew nothing. Herein is the mystery and the grace and the satisfaction of prayer. Though the Lord knows everything we are going to say, he entreats us to say it, knowing that in the prayer itself is often hidden the contentment of its own answer.

What effect was produced upon Jesus Christ? "When Jesus Christ heard of it he departed thence by ship into a desert place apart." It was most natural. There are some occurrences that simply make us quiet. There are shocks we can only answer by eloquent dumbness. He departed and went into a wilderness: it was better to be among the barren sands than amongst murderers and most cruel-minded men. There are times when we are all but inclined to give up our work. Our rain is lost, our dews fall in stony places, our best endeavors are returned to us without echo or answer of joy and gratitude, and we sigh for a lodge in some vast wilderness, some boundless contiguity of shade. This will be only for a while, however, in the case of Jesus Christ. "When he went forth and saw great multitudes he was moved with compassion towards them, and he healed their sick." He was bound to come back again: the sickness would have a greater effect upon him than the murder. He will not relinquish his work because of instances that might have shocked him with fatal distress. He looks upon the multitudinous man and not only upon the individual mischief-doer and murderer. He was the Son of Man, Jesus Christ always took the broad and inclusive view, and this held him to his work when individual instances might have driven him away from it and afflicted him with fatal discouragement.

It is even so we must look at our work, great or small. If we were to be determined by the action of this man or that, we should soon abandon the work and have nothing more to do with it. We have not to look at the individual stumbling-block, at the personal fault-finder and heart-breaker, we have to look upon the multitude, the sum-total of things, we have to listen for the universal human cry, and so long as we hold ourselves to universals rather than to particulars we shall be found steadily in our work. Now and again we may be in the wilderness for a while, shocked and distressed, mourning with a great sorrow some unlooked-for calamity, but as upon the air of the wilderness there comes the moan and sigh and wail of the world's sorrow we shall go out again and be found faithful servants, working to the last limit of our strength, and working till the last glint dies out of the fading day.

To this Jesus let us cling, to this Jesus let us evermore go. Withhold nothing from the Lamb of God. The bitterer our tale the sweeter his reply, the more agony there is in our prayer the greater grace will be in his answer.

thirty-two

MAKING SUGGESTIONS TO CHRIST

Matthew 14:15–21

ONE CANNOT but be struck by the infinite ludicrousness of the situation. It is sadly comical. Jesus Christ did not receive much help in the way of suggestion from his disciples; and when they had come forward for the purpose of making propositions, I know not of any figures more strikingly grotesque and pitiable. We, however, have been in the same position with the disciples sometimes. In those hours when lucky ideas have occurred to us, and very bright suggestions have been welcomed as if they were angels from heaven, we have gone to supreme minds, to the great burning and leading intellects of the age, and have laid before them our neat little plans for meeting urgent circumstances, and to our humiliation and bitterness we have found that the suggestions which we considered startling in their originality were dismissed twenty years ago as fables that would not bear looking into. It is dangerous to meddle with some minds. It is a very fearful thing to fall into the hands of the living God. It is infinitely impertinent to make suggestions to Omniscience.

Look at the disciples. A happy idea has occurred to them, and their faces are flushed by its fire. They are benevolent men, they have been measuring the situation with their calculating eyes, they have seen the sun setting, they have felt the evening chill in the wind, and they have thought very kindly of the numerous people who were in the desert place, and as if their Master had been absorbed in contemplations supernal, having in them nothing of care for the present life, they go up and tell him what to do. They will be snubbed. I wonder what his answer will be: certainly it will turn their counsel upside down, whatever it be.

243

What was the proposition of the benevolent men? Surely they spoke one word for the multitude and twenty for themselves. It was evening, and they, perhaps, were getting tired, and they thought to hide their desire for rest under pitying sympathy for the weariness of other men. Now they take the case into their hands what will they do? Let us hear them. Perhaps they may speak revelations. "Send the multitudes away into the villages that they may buy themselves victuals." That is the world's benevolence, that is the conception of charity in many cases and in nearly all cases in the absence of the inspiration of the love of Christ. Pause awhile. Look at these benevolent men; admire their extraordinary benevolence and kindness of heart. We are glad to hear them speak now and again: when they do speak they make history. They spake about the children, and said, "Send them away"; and Jesus said, "Suffer the little children to come unto me." Hear them speak about the multitudes, and they say, "Send them away." This—O, hear it—this is the grand suggestion of the servant: what will the command of the Master be? O, little moth, silly, silly moth, take care of the candle or thy wings will be scorched. Theological suggestors and preaching men, and persons who have theories to propound, be careful lest the Master overhear you and account you the children of folly.

How much better to have gone to him and have left the case in his hands. It is always wise to trust Omniscience. It is a continual mistake to be making suggestions to Divine Providence. Remain where you are: Jesus knows when the sun is going down, and when your hunger becomes a distress. I will not leave the ground until he bid me go. In his presence I have no hunger, no pain, no weariness: I stand here till he says, "It is now time to arise and go hence." I pray you, with a beseeching of the heart, not to be making suggestions to Divine Providence, but to remain in your situations, houses, businesses, and present relations until he give the sign to go. Let us be thankful that we are not left to the devices of the disciples: let us gladden ourselves with the holy and inspiring thought that the Master still lives.

How will Jesus receive this suggestion? Deferentially? He never did receive a suggestion from the disciples with the slightest token of respect. Once one of them said to him, "This be far from thee, Lord," and he said, "Get thee behind me, Satan" [Matt. 16:22, 23]. Another time they said, "Take the children away," and he said, "Suffer the little children to come unto me" [Mark 10:14]. Now they say, "Send the multitude away, that they may buy victuals for themselves in the villages," and he says, "They need not depart—give ye them to eat." How musical his voice sounds after their rough tones. Put the two expressions together, and see the infinite discrepancy. "Send the multitude away, that they may go into the villages and buy themselves victuals." It is not a suggestion, it is the rudest proposition that the lowest and coarsest minds could have made. Now hear the voice that holds in it all heaven's music—"They need not depart." That was the revelation, and that is true of human life in all its points, aspects, bearings, and necessities.

You need not go out of the Church for anything that is really good for you. When will the Church arise to this conception of her responsibility, and to this realization of her unsearchable riches? The idea which presses itself upon us as a trouble is that people imagine the Church is a measurable quantity, set up for the purpose of dealing out a specific article. Is there bread in the Church? There is bread enough and to spare. Has the Church a music hall, a picture gallery—does the Church afford opportunities for recreation, for intellectual culture, for social progress, for the consideration of ethical commerce? If the Church fail in these particulars it is because the Church has been misread, not because the Master occupies a solitary point and leaves the rest of his universe to be occupied by other persons.

What do you need most? I will find it for you in the Church. You need not depart from Christ, for whatever you want he has the key of the library, he keeps a great bread-house, he knows how he has made you, your love of art, your passion for music, your delights and your comforts, every one of them he is accountable for, as to their control and supply. Let me, therefore, protest against any theory that would narrow the Church and dwarf it into one amongst many, instead of making it many in one. I am aware that we have driven away so many people from the Church into the villages to buy victuals for themselves that we shall have a good deal to do to get back terms and phrases which ought never to have been divorced from the altar, and when they do come back they will be so distorted in image, and so vitiated in use, that for a long time some persons will protest against their being used within the walls of the sanctuary.

Where are our hosts of young people now? We have sent them into the villages to buy bread. Where are those that were weak and faithless of heart, weak and trembling in soul, doubtful, troubled by infinite unrest of heart? We have sent them into the villages to buy bread. We were only too glad to get clear of them. Jesus never sent them away: as they were going he said, "You need not depart." The Church, therefore, must stir herself to a realization of her true call of God. I want the Church to have many mansions. If you please, the mansions need not, so to speak, overlap one another, or encroach upon each other's position and special meaning—but in my Father's house there should be many mansions, and no man should be allowed to go away because there is not enough for him at home. Build the church ten times the size, stretch its hospitable roof over all things that can feed the best nature, and charm the noblest instincts and impulses of human nature, and do not narrow and impoverish and dwarf yourselves.

You are called upon, Christian churches, to supply all the necessities of the world. We may have to alter old habits and modernize ancient methods and do a great many things that appear to be revolutionary, but I would write upon every church front, as an appeal to the whole public, these sacred words—"Ye need not depart." Everything that man can need for his healthy instruction, edification, culture, and perfecting is within the boundaries of Christ's conception of his own Church. The time will come when we shall not need to modify any of the great grand words ever spoken by Jesus Christ. The mischief is that a cold age wants to drag down the reading to its own coldness. I say concerning this Book of marvels and most astounding miracles—let every line stand. There are coming men who can read the Book in all its apocalyptic wondrousness of suggestion, color, pomp, and music. We may not be able to read it; our ears are filled with unholy noises, our eyes are divided so that we cannot focalize our vision and fix it with intensity enough upon the object to see its real beauty, but in the coming time there are generations that will be able to read the Book in all its breadth, and we must not spoil it for their using. Fear not, the Lion of the tribe of Judah has power to open the Book [see Rev. 5:2–9], and in an infinitely less degree, but not lacking in healthy and noble suggestion, is it true that hearts are coming, brighter minds, nobler souls, who will be able to open the Book in its true sense and read it with all its magic and power and grandeur of suggestion.

Do not drag down the Book to your present coldness. Do not imagine that the Book is about to accommodate itself to the impoverishment which you have inflicted upon yourselves. The miracles stun us because we have lost the power of grasping them, but when materialism goes down and faith rises to its proper position, then the miracles will be easy reading to all believing souls. You must enlarge the idea of the Church.

"They need not depart—give ye them to eat." You never know how much you have till you begin to give. The thing given with the right spirit grows in the giving. You will find after you have withdrawn some donation from your store, with a good motive and a right intent, that when you go back again to the store it will have returned, and in your secrecy you will say, "What mystery is this, when I have given the money? It was taken out to be given, but I must have forgotten to convey it." This is the ministry of the angels, to go to the secret drawer and put the money back, to watch your face when you return to count what you expected to be the diminished amount. We have proven this: we must not be accounted foolish men by those who have not entered into the same experience. If I were my own treasurer I should be poor in a month: I would not know what had been done with the money. But taking it always from him in the act of giving it to him it grows in the giving.

Let us hear those wonderful men talk again. And they say unto him, "We have here but five loaves and two fishes." Did they tell the truth? No. Did they distort the acts? No. Is it possible to state a fact and yet to keep back the truth? Perfectly possible, and done every day. Let us hear how much they had. Five loaves and two fishes—and no more. Sure? What had the fools forgotten? What we forget in all our miscalculating. Give me the inventory of their property, will you; it will then read thus: "We have here but five loaves and two fishes, and God and Christ, and the Miracle-worker and the Creator." What poor inventories we return. The stationer could give us paper enough for our inventories ten thousand times over. We give the material side only when we add up our riches; we put down the loaves and the fishes, and the water and the gold, and the silver and the stones—but what about ideas, impulses, thoughts, purposes, burning desires, imperishable capacities? What about the immortality that stirs within us? With such omissions your inventory is not worth the paper it is written upon. When you reckon up your little stock tonight do not forget to add at the foot of the roll—"and Christ, and Providence, and my Father in heaven," and you will lay down your weary head as a millionaire, multiplied by innumerable millions as to store and value.

Jesus said, "Bring them hither to me." He was not disturbed by the number, as the disciples were. In their hands the loaves would have been only five and the fishes would have been only two, but in Christ's hands the stock will be multiplied into a great feast. It is the same with everything we have. Let us take up our two talents to Christ—we shall bring them back two hundred. Let us take up our resources to Christ, and we shall come back multiplied into an army that cannot lose a battle. This accounts for your non-success, my friends: you are using your little store without passing it through the all-multiplying fingers: if you were more religious you would be more successful.

Now this is a miracle which does not appeal to the imagination. Sometimes the rationalists have told us that the people upon whom the miracle was wrought were simply operated upon by a magnetic will, by a higher power of mind than their own, and they for the time being became the happy subjects of a kind of magnetic action. I imagine the bread had no imagination to be wrought upon: it would appear to me that the five loaves and the two fishes were not subjects for the operation of any magical art. Moreover, the whole story is so constructed as to make it sternly literal. "Jesus commanded the multitude to sit down on the grass, and took the five loaves and the two fishes, and looking up to heaven, he blessed and brake, and gave the loaves to his disciples, and the disciples to the multitude." Jesus did not personally give the bread to the multitude—he passed it, as he passes all his bread, through the medium of ministries and servants of his own appointing.

It was more than a mere miracle: it was a sacrament. He made a religious feast of it. He never did anything secularly, as we use that cold term—his whole life was religious, his very breath was a prayer, the opening of his eyes was a revelation. He did nothing without his Father. We should have larger comforts if we had more religion in the using of them. Your unblest bread will soon be done. If you eat like an animal you will be choked, if you eat sacramentally you will have "bread enough and to spare" [Luke 15:17]. Eat with contentment of heart, with a sense of gratitude and thankfulness to God, as the guest of God, and the host will see that you have enough. Do not spread an atheist's table that you may put upon it venison and wines of all famed vineyards: you will only get up a glutton and an alcoholic, flushed with a bad heat and satisfied but for an hour. On the poorest meal, on the simplest engagement of life, ask the heavenly blessing—secretly or audibly, but mean it—and sitting down to your little table, say "I am here as God's guest: he asked me to sit here," and the feast will be a holy sacrament.

There are eternal meanings in this bread-giving. This is the miracle of the ages. It is the only miracle which all the evangelists have told, and there may be a purpose in this unanimity of record, for this is the miracle we must all partake of or we cannot live—we must eat the flesh and drink the blood of the Son of God. "Except a man eat my flesh and drink my blood he hath no life in him" [see John 6:53]. This is the true bread which cometh down from heaven, of which if a man eat he will hunger no more. Now we come with our little dwarfing expositions, and take all the sap, the juice, the wine out of his holy growth. We will ask little questions about transubstantiation, and we will set up little enigmas and miserable riddles which are unworthy of the Christian imagination, and our religious liberties and privileges. This is not a question of transubstantiation: the bread does not pass into any other body or substance: the wine is wine at the last as at the first, and no magic can change its nature. And yet as in the letter I feel the spirit, so in these elements of bread and wine my heart feels that it is feasting upon the living Lord. Do not ask for this gospel to be reduced to words: I ask you to enlarge your words to receive this gospel.

Have you eaten of the bread sent down from heaven—have you drunk of the blood of the Son of God? If not, you have no life abiding in you. Lord, evermore give us this bread. This is the bread that endures unto life everlasting [see John 6:27]. In my Father's house is bread enough and to spare [Luke 15:17], and I perish with hunger: I will arise and go to my Father, and I will say unto him, "Father, I have sinned against heaven and in thy sight, and am no more worthy to be called thy son" [Luke 15:21]. Have you challenged him with a speech so eloquent in contrition? He will shake the heavens that he may reply to you with the enthusiasm of his whole house; his angels and his first-born will consider it no humiliation to gather around you and clothe you and make you rich with all heaven's wealth.

Return, return, hungry wanderer in the wilderness: you need not depart: in your Father's house are all mansions [John 14:2], and there is a resting place even for you!

thirty-three

REVELATION BY NIGHT AND DAY

Matthew 14:22–36

IN THE CASE of feeding the multitude the disciples rashly undertook to give advice to the Master; they rushed in to sacred and forbidden places. Out of their urgent cleverness, they had evolved the suggestion which pleased them like a new toy. We have seen how Jesus Christ treated the smart ignorance of his shallow counselors, and with what infinite beneficence he confounded the notion of sending anybody away from himself to find anything that could do human life the very least good.

Now the scene quite turns. Jesus Christ leaves the disciples to manage their ship, just to show them how cleverly they can do without him. They wanted to take the bigger case into their own hands, and he would not allow them so to do, but to meet them by gracious compromise he gives them a ship to take care of, with what upshot we have seen. Thus he always rebukes clever meddlers with his administration; he gives them something to do by their own skill and power, and shows them by many a disaster what it is to take life away from its divine center, and to conduct life on a wrong principle. He allows us to make little experiments—well for us if he be looking on even from a mountain top while we make them. It would be the death of us if he turned his back away and looked elsewhere. He is gracious, and allows us to work our own cleverness on a small scale, that we may see how frail we are, and how hollow and utterly lacking in all comprehensive and grave wisdom, and how true it is "without me ye can do nothing" [John 15:5]. He is allowing you now to conduct that small enterprise of yours in business. You will come to him presently, all broken in pieces, and ask him to reconstruct you. Well will it be for you if he is looking on from a mountain top—he will gather you together again with a great redeeming grace and gently rebuke you for undertaking to do anything by yourself alone.

Jesus went up into a mountain apart to pray. We wonder how a grand outward ministry can be sustained. The answer is simple in its sublimity. Every outward ministry that is life-taxing, so to say blood-drinking in its fierce demands upon the ministry, is sustained by mountain climbing, solitary communion with God, the nursing of old gentle mother Nature, and soul-fellowship with the Father of all life. The inward man must be renewed day by day: we must deepen the soil, if we would enrich the crop. If the Master could not do without lonely prayer, the servant surely cannot dispense with secret devotion. It is not enough to pray aloud, nor is it sufficient to pray in company in the language of common prayer: we must know the agony, which is joy, of speechless communion, and the exquisitely tender gladness of secret fellowship. We must be closeted with God. "Come up to the top of the mountain," said the Almighty to Moses, "be ready in the morning" [Ex. 34:2]; and while the dew was sparkling in the hardly risen sun, they held great speech together, sublime as music. O, those dewy hours, those opening moments of the day— what conquests may then be won; when our first interview is with God, we cannot fear the face of man. Let us look at the scene until it live before the eyes of our heart forever.

He went up into a mountain. Not one traveler accompanied him, no seething multitude made the air hot by pressure and noise. The great wide sky—how wide it can be, let the poet tell me—opened before him like a door into the central heaven, where the throne is, and where the Shekinah burned as if glad to see him back again, poor without him, owing all its blue and light and tenderness to his presence.

Away went the traveler—the breezes breathing upon him like blessings beforehand, and though every shadow formed itself into the suggestion of the cross, the light beyond was a prophecy of triumph and glory. Always look to the light as well as to the shadow. Christ's back was bent as if by a burden invisible, yet he lifted his head with kingly dignity and moved upward like one who had an appointment with God. He went up into a mountain apart to pray. Not alone to recruit his bodily strength, not to view the varied and enchanting scenery. He went to church, he sought the sanctuary, he yearned for the infinite. If he could not do without going to church, who am I that I can dispense with attendance upon the sanctuary? I am but a fool with cap and bells, pleased with the jingling of my own metal, if I do not go to church to fill up the emptiness which nothing else can satisfy.

We must have sanctuary hours, Sabbatic times. Herein is the wondrousness of that word—"Remember the Sabbath day to keep it holy" [Ex. 20:8]. The word *holy* there cannot mean anything of the nature of spiritual sanctification: a man cannot remember any one day to keep it holy unless he keep the whole time holy. You might as well say, "Be truthful one day out of seven, be honest one day out of seven, be high-minded and pure one day out of seven." It cannot be done. Holiness is not an entry upon a register: a man cannot look at his calendar and say, "The time has come around for me to be holy." So with this church-going. You cannot go to church on Sunday with any deep and living appreciation of its opportunities and privileges unless you are in church all the week long. The church is not a separate building you can enter upon particular days: if so at all, it is so only to those who do not enter into the spirit and genius of the occasion. The whole world is sacred, and the church is quiet. We must have quietness as well as sacredness. If we enter church in this spirit, we shall be alone, yet not alone, for the Father will be with us.

Jesus Christ could not live within the boundaries that could be touched: he yearned for the infinite, and must in his life have an outlet towards the eternal. Man, I will not discourage or lay upon you one straw's weight of disapprobation: if it is in your heart to grip the bigger earth, the larger place, the broader liberty, the unnameable quantity—you are not far from the kingdom of heaven.

In Jesus Christ's prayer we do not find what is usually known as asking, or petition, in the ordinary sense of the term. That is the very smallest portion of prayer. Prayer was communion with God—in the case of Jesus Christ, identification with the Father, absorption in him, communion with the spring of all being and might. The begging attitude becomes us well, but we must not abide in that posture of petition, it is the poorest notion of prayer to beg, to ask, to desire that the right hand may be filled and the left hand be filled and the head and the heart be filled—it is the meanest begging. We should seek to be one with God, we should enlarge prayer from petition into fellowship, communion, sympathy—then may we hold long talks with God, have all day speeches with him, and be impatient because the darkness threatens to punctuate with its too hasty period the eloquence of his communications. Rest in the

Lord, wait on the Lord, put your hope in God—these are the terms which express the most complete joy of prayer.

When the even was come, he was there alone. He was often alone, he was always alone—he never could be dualized. When in the crowd he was alone, he trod the winepress alone. He was with us, yet in a sense not of us: he sat down beside us, and yet the universe separated between the points. Yet in one sense, limited by convenience, he was alone on the mountain, though all the angels were with him. The evening before, five thousand men crowded upon him, and their appeals were like five thousand arrows quivering in his heart. He was then the center of humanity, now he stands alone upon the mountain, and is the center of creation, alone as he was before the world began, alone, gathering strength by rest, alone because solitude is needful to the completeness of the souls, education, and he must teach us this by example.

Jesus Christ went up into the mountain for our sakes: if he taught us to pray, he taught us how to pray, where to pray, when to pray. We must have our times of withdrawment if we would get a strong hold of life and be master of its vexing details. Do not always be in the crowded streets or in the rush and noise of tumultuous throngs. Five minutes every day alone with God would make us more than conquerors in the day of battle. Fear yourselves if you dare not be alone: probe into causes, when you dare not take a lonely walk—all the day long from the morning until the evening; your brain is unhealthy, your heart is unsound or your circumstances are of a nature to be pitied, if you are afraid to go up a mountain alone and be there all day without speaking to any human creature. Solitude, religiously used, chastens the soul, fills the heart with heavenly peace, and opens the mind to the daily revelation which God makes to those who love him. We have times for eating, times for sleeping, times for recreation, why not have times for communion with God and reading deeply the mysteries of his Word? Time spent with God lengthens and gladdens all other time. No man ever lost a customer by being at church with the right motive and with the right spirit. No man ever found twenty-three hours in any day of which one hour was given to the worship of the Father of spirits.

Turning now our attention to the disciples, we find that their management of the ship was a poor management. The ship was now in the midst of the sea, tossed with waves, for the wind was contrary. They who were going to manage the multitude, were unable to manage their own ship. Our helplessness ought to be the basis of our best education. If we cannot manage the little how can we manage the great? Thus light is let in upon the administration of the universe. If we are in trouble with one little ship, how then can we control all the ships of the sea, all the star-vessels that sail through the infinite firmament, all the hosts of men that gather on the face of the earth, all the legions of angels that populate the cities above, all the forces that burn and throb in every line of the immeasurable universe? We may see how great the Lord is by seeing how little we are ourselves. The infinite discrepancy should drive us to the use and security of prayer.

On the fourth watch of the night Jesus went unto them, walking on the sea. They could not come to him, so he went to them. They must know what it was to be away from Christ; still the eyes of watchful pity were upon them, they were seen from the mountain, they were in an enforced and undesirable loneliness—

> Alone on a wide, wide sea—
> So lone it was, that God himself
> Scarce seemed there to be.

No such loneliness was ever uttered by Samuel Taylor Coleridge in worthy terms. That was not solitude, it was vacancy. Distinguish between those terms. They were not alone with God, they were alone without God. That is not solitude, it is emptiness.

How did Jesus Christ view the tossing vessel and the fear-smitten disciples? With something of amusement, knowing how near his own hand was, and how adequate his strength? Did he think of what had occurred a few hours ago, when those blundering navigators proposed to deal with a great question of political necessity in the wilderness? Did he say, "This will show them how little they are and how unworthy to meddle with the administration of vast concerns"? We cannot tell what were his intellectual processes, but his heart was always at the front, his beneficence seemed to outrun his judgment—so he went unto the panic-driven disciples when they were tossed on the sea.

Jesus went unto them walking on the water. If this act stood alone, it might frighten us. Do not read the miracles as if they were unconnected events—any one miracle will terrify you. You must read every miracle as part of some greater wonder; then it will come to you not with violent and mighty shock, and overthrow you by irresistible collision, it will fall into the rhythmic march of a life that could never be measured by the figured lines of human arithmeticians. Yet all past miracles are lost upon us: we must have a present miracle. The disciples therefore could not live upon the miracles of yesterday, they must have the miracle of that present hour. So must it be with ourselves—we cannot live upon historical wonders, we can only be nourished by daily revelations of divine power and continual manifestations of divine care and love. We cannot be saved by a cross nearly two thousand years old, viewed in the mere light of history; we are saved by a cross older than the foundations of the earth, yet new as the sin of this present evil moment. Jesus Christ must be the Lamb slain from before the foundation of the world, and slain every day to our consciousness, our helplessness, our burning contrition and our penitence which cannot answer its own bitter prayers. Life is a continual miracle. The bread we eat is always broken by divine hands. We have so confused and huddled events as to forget their right succession: we are too frequently content to stop at intermediate causes and present agencies—were we to search back the bread that is in our hand every day as to its history and its origin, we should find that it was broken by divine, all-blessing hands, and is itself a miracle.

The disciples were afraid when they saw this figure, and cried out, saying, "It is a spirit." How we are frightened by a spirit! Whoever was quite comfortable even with a supposed ghost? Whoever was just where he would like to be when in the middle of a haunted house, without a man within a mile of him? Yet God is a spirit: we who would be afraid to go into a reputedly haunted room and stop there alone one night, cry out sometimes in unbelief and foolish questioning, "Why does not God show himself?" God is a spirit. It is not enough to see the figure: the sight is often misleading: so the ear must be charmed—the voice can do what the eye fails to accomplish. So Jesus said, "Be of good cheer, it is I, be not afraid." You cannot read the sermon—you must hear it. Some of us cannot read the Bible, we must hear it read by a sympathetic voice every tone of which is a subtle suggestion or a profound exposition. The eye is a deceiver, and is deceived every day, and there is no more mischievous an absurdity than the proverb "Seeing is believing." So it may be, but what is seeing?

The ministry of the human voice is of God's appointment. It charms itself into ineffable coloring, apocalyptic variety and suggestion, it booms, it whispers, it commands, it soothes, it thunders with strength, it prays with piteousness of sympathy. The gospel therefore is given in charge to the human voice. Preach the gospel—it never can be read, but in a secondary and introductory sense it must be heard. The voice of Jesus was recognized when his figure was indistinguishable.

Now comes the great *if*, that always lay in Christ's road like a preliminary cross. Peter answered the Lord and said, "*If* it be thou." That was the old "if"—it occurs in the story of the temptation, early in this same gospel. When the tempter came to him, he said, "*If* thou be the Son of God, command that these stones be made loaves." Now the senior disciple says, "*If* it be thou, bid me come unto thee on the water." Beware of the doubting *if*. Every man has his own test of deity. Peter had his little test. It was accepted, and Peter shows us here instinctively what is shown in every day's history of human life, properly read, that men when they have their tests accepted, are made afraid of their own tests, and sink in the very water they wanted to walk upon. Beware of setting tests for God; be on your guard against yielding to your own cleverness in setting traps for deity. Sometimes the Lord may accommodate himself to our absurdities of conception and desire. In this case, when Jesus said "Come," the proposition was Peter's, the test was Peter's, the failure was Peter's: he was afraid by the very manifestation of his own proofs, and ran away from his own test, like a man surprised in guilt.

What will Jesus do? He will save the doubter as well as the despairer. He saved the whole body of the disciples in their despair, he will save the single disciple in his doubting. So he must save us every day. Every day he plucks me from the yawning abyss, every day I have the same common coward's prayer to offer, "Lord, save me, or I perish," and he has the same great lordly reply of the outstretched and all-redeeming hand. That is the image of human life, that is the symbolism of our daily experience, our continual discipline, crying in the bitterness of despair, being answered out of the fullness of infinite love.

Then the result—"Of a truth thou art the Son of God." So we are converted every day, and every day we sin. In the morning we write a great "if," in the evening we write a great creed. We never read last night's creed, we always begin with the morning's great *if*.

We may include the remaining three verses of the chapter, and say, in doing so—see how Jesus Christ goes to work again. He entered into the land of Gennesaret. The men soon had knowledge of him, and they sent out into all that country, and brought unto him all that were diseased, and besought him that they might only touch the hem of his garment, and as many as touched were made perfectly whole. Back to work again, on the mountain and in the city—these were the points between which that heart oscillated—longing for the mountain, drawn to the city, yearning for communion, yet devoted to beneficence, every day needing fellowship higher than the relations of earth could supply, and every day going down the mountain again to pick up the lonely one, to help the helpless, and to redeem with mighty heart, even with outflowing of sacrificial blood, every son of Adam.

thirty-four

DEFILEMENT SPIRITUAL, NOT CEREMONIAL

Matthew 15:1–20

NOT OFTEN did Jesus Christ lose his patience, but when that circumstance did occur, it was marked by the utterance of very memorable words. We are sometimes warned not to provoke quiet men. Nor was this loss of patience in the case of Jesus Christ in any sense one of mere irritation or peevishness — it was rather a sense of moral indignation. The answer which he made to the Scribes and Pharisees who came from the metropolis was an instance of high, noble, moral resentment: it was not anger of a merely personal and selfish kind, it was a grave and solemn judgment. That the leading men of the day, the scholars and the clerks of the time, should be putting such trivial questions, should be mocking the spirit of progress by such frivolous inquiries, should be making such mountains out of such molehills, roused the most divine anger of an earnest soul.

Consider how this answer of the Savior carries with it some profound suggestion of the supreme purpose of his life. He had not come down to make nice things, to arrange a ritual, to propose encroachments upon a ceremonial descended from the seniors — he came to save the world. Hence his flashing anger, his burning, scorching retort upon men who wanted to bind down his attention to the basest frivolities that could engage the attention of the basest intellects. Always learn from his answers to his opponents something of Jesus Christ's main object in life.

The difference between the Scribes and Christ was that they lived in ceremony, and he lived in truth. Their religion was a trick in ritual — all religious observances and duties had been reduced to a mechanical standard and arrangement. With the Son of God religion was life, spirit, it was a vital principle, a divine inspiration, a continual drawing down from heaven of the energy and the grace needful for the work and the suffering of life. Observe therefore that the difference between them was not literal and measurable in words; it was vital, final, and indestructible.

This is what Jesus Christ has to say to all opposing parties. He does not come as one of many, saying, "Let us see where the exact point of rest is, as between us, controversialists as we are, each entitled to an equal hearing with the other." He holds no parley, he has no rivals, he makes no compromises—never does he approach any opponent in the spirit of reconciliation. Everything must go before the spirituality and the splendor of his kingdom. The Scribes and Pharisees proposed a *quasi* friendly conversation upon differences. They say:

> We do thus, and thy disciples do so; why should there be this striking difference in our ritualistic practices? Can we not arrange matters better than they at present stand? We have the seal and the sanction of the elders, and surely something is due to seniority in the Church and in the ages. The disciples are guilty of what appears to us to be a violent encroachment upon old usages—let us talk the matter over.

Jesus Christ never talked matters over upon equal terms. Remember this in considering the sovereignty and the completeness of the claim which he laid to the attention and the confidence of the world. How Jesus Christ might have popularized himself by compromise, by gracious approach, by an attitude of conciliation, by suggesting that he was not infallible, nor was he above receiving a hint from those who had been in the world before him. He dominated *in* men, and therefore *over* men. No other domination is worth having. To rule over men may be a transient supremacy; the true rule, the everlasting primacy, is that of ruling *in* a man, in his thoughts, feelings, convictions, and in the whole range of his noblest nature.

If Jesus Christ were with us today, he would alter the religious standpoint of many men, and thunder upon their closed ears the solemn words that Christianity is not an affair of meats and drinks, of bell-ringing and magic, of church-going and hymn-singing, but of life, love, pure-ness, sanctity of heart and completeness of consecration. Cheap indeed is the religion of hand washing. Who would not wash his hands all day long as the price of heaven? "A man," says Jesus Christ, "may wash his hands all day long, and in every act of purification he may be adding new guilt to his heart." So with our solemn exercises today—they go for nothing except according to the inspiration which directs and ennobles them. We may go to church and yet not be there at all in spirit, sympathy, fervent and vehement desire after God. Men can sing a hymn, and in the singing of it can add a crueler wrath to their hate. Men can pay pew-rent, that they may have room to grumble in. "What doth the Lord thy God require of thee, O man, but to do justly, to love mercy, and to walk humbly with God?" [Mic. 6:8]. This is not an affair of hand-washing, hair-combing, clothes-wearing, attitude, mechanism or manual service. The religion of the kingdom of heaven is a condition of the heart. What a man's heart is, that is also the man himself. As a man thinks in his heart, so is he [see Prov. 23:7].

Does Jesus Christ then do away with all outward observances, with church-going and with hymn-singing, with religious engagements and duties of various kinds? Most certainly not! He approves them every one, if kept in their right place. The Savior is saying to them:

> You must understand that religion is not an affair of mechanism but of spirit, and that it is possible to do everything that is written upon the register with puristic punctuality and completeness, and yet not to have a heart filled with the spirit of sacrifice. Where the heart is not so filled and ruled, all your bead-counting, your Paternosters and Ave Marias go for nothing—they beat themselves against the ceiling under which they are breathed: they never touch God's distant sky.

We must have our Church framework. We are exhorted not to forsake the assembling of ourselves together [see Heb. 10:25]. We have the distinct promise that where two or three are gathered together, Christ is there to bless them [Matt. 18:20]. We have Christ's own example for holy rest and honest searching of the Scriptures, to give mutual fellowship in all godly concerns, but unless the whole of these come out of the heart and with the heart's meaning upon them, however good relatively, they are worthless intrinsically.

262 • *Matthew 15:1–20*

Well for the Church, even a day of triumph and coronation, when nothing more can be said against it than the metropolitan Scribes and Pharisees said against the disciples. Is this their noble impeachment? Does their charge sharpen itself into this piercing question? What a mighty assault—what a tremendous burst of feebleness. Why do thy disciples transgress the tradition of the elders, for they wash not their hands when they eat bread? Have the Scribes and the Pharisees, metropolitan and provincial, of our own day, anything graver to bring against us? Some charges answer themselves by their own absurdity, and require no greater confusion than is brought upon them by their palpable feebleness. How is it with the Church just now?

Mark the strength of the Savior's reply. This man brings his answers from afar: in his arm is an infinite leverage—when he strikes, all things fall before the fist of his almightiness. Hear the piping voice of the metropolitan critics—"Why do ye also transgress the commandment of God?" Now the issue is sharply joined. That is exactly how the Church ought to stand in all ages. The world may be able to bring against the Church the charge of not attending to ancient usages and peculiar ceremonies, but the Church ought always to have it in its power justly to hurl back the accusation in the tremendous inquiry—"While we may not have washed our hands, you have steeped and soaked your hearts in the devil's pollution." We must not use the words in the absence of solemn proof. We are only now indicating the ideal state of things and the real state of relations, if we speak of Jesus Christ rather than of Jesus Christ's nominal Church. Whosoever says to Jesus, "I think I find an omission in thy teaching and practice," will have for his answer all this thunder and lightning of personal accusation of the gravest guilt. That we might be able to return such a *tu quoque*, such a "You also" should be the burden of incessant prayer.

Consider the condition of the metropolitan Scribes and Pharisees, when they heard Jesus Christ's answer. People who find fault must expect to have fault found with them. That is the one thing which the critic always forgets; the critic always forgets that he exposes himself to criticism. How is it that the critic always forgets this? He sits at his desk, he reclines in his pew, he rests on his pillow, he walks his garden paths, he sits under the shadow of his broad trees, and shakes his head in sober judgment upon all other men, forgetting that all other men, should they think it worth their while, might find a thousand faults where he could supply a thousand actions. It never occurred to the Scribes and Pharisees from the metropolis that there could be any answer to them. Everybody had always yielded to their criticism and judgment, and had gone, probably with secret fee, to find out what they ought to do, from the great interpreters of the law. Here is a Man who confronts them and challenges their purity. They thought they had found a weak place in the armor of the disciples, and having pointed to the open crevice, and looked as only such critics could look, Jesus also put forth his hand and said, "Is this your breast-plate?" "Yes." "Why, 'tis a rag of tinder; if I touch it, it crumbles into black dust." They ought to have very strong and complete armor, who point out the weak places in the panoply of other people.

This instance illustrates the law of declension. There is an inward collapse first—a reinstallation of the spirit of selfishness; and then there is an attempt to find in framework what only can be found in spiritual reality and completeness. Men keep up the framework of appearances to the last: the anxiety of many minds is to save appearances. Jesus Christ never attempted to save appearance at the expense of truth. Are we endeavoring to keep up appearances by church-going, by continuance in customary ways, by habits and usages for which we have really no heart, but which we must appear to respect, or other people will begin to imagine the real state of our spirit? The Lord's lightning smite all mere appearances and pretenses. We are killed by our pretensions, when they are not supported by an inward reality. What are we in our heart—what is our meaning, what is our purpose? These are the vital questions which men must put to themselves and answer, if they would have real depth of life and healthiness and enjoyment of being.

This answer was indeed a long thunderstorm. The clouds were, so to say, gathered from distant skies. Not content with merely accusing them of violating the commandment of God, he said, "Well did Isaiah prophesy of you." There are men who are anxious to find out when prophecy terminated: they are most eager to discover the precise points upon which the prophecy took effect, and was accomplished, and became like a gate shut because the king had passed on. Jesus Christ gave terrific applications of prophecy again and again. Turning upon the leading men of his age he said, "You are meant when Isaiah said, 'This people draweth nigh unto me with their mouth and honoreth me with their lips, but their heart is far from me.'" When we are searching into apocalyptic visions and suggestions, and are digging deeply into prophetic mines and are wishing to know when times and seasons accomplish themselves, it may be well to remind our own hearts that probably Jesus would fix the great moral accusations of prophecy upon us. While we are seeking to read some difficult hieroglyphic and to apply some marvelous suggestion or combination of dates to some pope or king or mighty warrior, Jesus might lay his hand upon us and say, "You fool, when the prophet thunders against wrong, all his thunders beat upon your own head."

Surely this plan would give us a new scheme of Bible reading, and instead of making enigmas and finding Napoleon the Greats and mighty popes distant, some dead and some coming a thousand years from now, we should feel that the prophets foresaw our day, and laid up for our guilt, the judgments of God.

"Ye hypocrites." Other men called them Scribes and Pharisees, Rabbi, Lord, Master, Great One, Prince. Looking at them as only he could look, he said, "Ye hypocrites." That was plain speaking. Jesus Christ could make no progress in society unless he spoke with the utmost plainness of words, which nobody could possibly misunderstand. We make no advancement because we are the victims of euphemism—that is, a style of speaking which calls things by their wrong names—bad things by good definitions, and which covers over the evil with a handful of stolen flowers. You must get at the very core of the disease if you are to make any progress. Not that we are to call one another hypocrites, for that would only lead to mutual recrimination of the most severe and most unprofitable kind—no man can call his brother a hypocrite without possibly exposing himself to a just retort, but we are to remember that God sees us as we are: we are to be faithful with ourselves: instead of calling other people bad names, we are to attach the right label to our own actions and not to shrink from the solemn fact that our life is often based on a lie and directed to the consummation of the hypocrisy. When men talk thus, it may be roughly, but with solemn, urgent plainness, to themselves, we may have some hope that, feeling the acuteness of the disease, they may be impelled to cry to heaven for the remedy.

Jesus Christ does not change the subject when he proceeds to tell the multitude what the true law of defilement is. He found the age imagining that what a man took into him defiled him: Jesus Christ said, "That is not the law of pollution"—Jesus Christ laid down this grand law, that no man can defile another; every man defiles himself. He would say:

Away then with your trumpery excuses, as to circumstances and conditions and contagious surroundings.
That law will bear amplification into the fuller law that no
man can injure another permanently; it is the man alone
who injures himself. As no man can defile you, so no man
can injure you in any profound, vital, and lasting sense.
You may indeed have much thrown at you that is of a nature most disagreeable—you may be defiled outwardly—
so you may be encountered by misrepresentations, sneers,
harsh criticisms, untrue and vile aspersions of every kind—
but they do not touch the man. When you are really injured, you have injured yourself. There is no case of
man-slaughter, in the higher region of interpretation,
but there are innumerable cases of suicide. You are not defiled by your circumstances, by the conversation you
hear, by the duties you may be compelled to undertake,
you are defiled when you have in you an impure thought,
a bad desire, an ignoble impulse, a motive that will not bear
the scrutiny of light.

Cheer up, then! Fear not any assault and battery, any fierce assault
by which others would seek to drag you down: it is as the beat of a bird's
wing against the eternal granite. A man may be wrong in opinion yet
right in heart. When this doctrine is accepted, the Church will enter
upon a new era of influence. I am not, of course, speaking of moral opinion, but of opinion of a speculative kind, even speculative opinion
upon speculative subjects. The Church too eagerly embarks in speculative controversy, and cannot support her conduct by our quotation from
her Lord. Even speculative opinion is not to be undervalued. So long
as it is held as opinion and not forced upon men as final dogma or infallible proposition, it may be held with advantage.

As to moral questions, there must be no light assumption of opinion.
There must not indeed be two opinions upon moral questions—there
our understanding must with one another be unanimous, complete, without hesitation or reservation of any kind whatever, but upon those
questions which are speculative, doubtful, let us have charity one with
another. Let us take care that no wrong uses are made of speculative opinion: it may be made a standard of orthodoxy and unorthodoxy, and men
may be ostracized and condemned and undervalued and suspected, and
may be open to all kinds of social disaster because of their speculative

opinions upon purely speculative questions. I would wish my own course to be this: to have a heart thoroughly at one with itself as to God's moral requirements, the hideousness of sin, the abominableness of iniquity, the beauty of righteousness, the necessity of sanctity of heart. Upon all such questions there must be no dispute, no compromise, no trifling or tampering. When I enter into other regions of the Holy Book, I desire to be quiet where I cannot speak wisely, to accept with modesty where I cannot explain with a luminousness equal to the mystery I undertake to elucidate. God allows me to ask questions, to make propositions, and to change my mind often in the course of one day respecting opinions and matters which are either speculative or are too high for me. He judges me by the condition of my heart: where it is broken, contrite, penitential, he will not rebuke me because of the poverty or the erroneousness of my speculative opinions. Were Jesus Christ amongst us now, he would surely set a fire upon all those controversies which divide men, about things as relatively unimportant to his central purpose as was the washing of hands to the commandment of God.

Now comes the solemn question, vital, final, all-inclusive. Seeing that Jesus Christ attached such value to the condition of the heart, how is the heart to become such as he will accept? He himself must do the whole work herein. The cleansing of the heart is from on high, and is by the mysterious process of blood. Do not think of blood in any low, common, or merely physical sense of the term. The blood of Christ means more than the mere blood of the body: that was its needful symbol; without that shedding of blood we could have got no hint of the higher meaning of the great and tragic type of its quality and reality. We are saved by blood, we are redeemed by blood; without the shedding of blood there is no remission [Heb. 9:22]. We have erred in the life, and only by life can we be saved. Life for life, blood for blood. We made the tragedy necessary: had we sinned skin deep, some skin deep remedy would have been found for us, but having sinned in the soul, having collapsed in the inner sanctuary of the nature, having done wrong with the innermost thoughts of our heart, nothing can meet the infinite collapse but God's sacrifice of himself in his Son. You are not saved because you can explain this, but because you believe it. I am not asked how I account for my salvation, I am saved because of my faith in the Son of God. If it has pleased God to make this revelation of the method of acceptance as between himself and me, it is not for me to find critical fault with the terms, or to make a metaphysical puzzle of a grand moral proposal, but to fall into his hands, and to await the explanation as the ages of eternity unfold themselves, and give opportunity for a more profound study of divine things.

The disciples were not as the master. They came to him and said—so typical of them, for even his disciples formed part of his disfigurement and humiliation: he was betrayed by the very men whom he elected to the discipleship—they were to drag him down, they were to form the elements and materials of some of the most bitter mockery that was ever heaped upon him. They came and said, "Knowest thou that the Pharisees were offended after they heard this saying?" Just what is said to faithful ministers today. Who does not hear that offense was given, that this man or that woman was never coming to church again because of this saying or of that? What does the poor minister do? I would that we might follow the Lord, who said, when he heard about the offended Pharisees, "Every plant which my Heavenly Father hath not planted shall be rooted up. Let them alone: they be blind leaders of the blind, and if the blind lead the blind, both shall fall into the ditch." He had given offense, and when told about it, he calmly stood upon the rock of the divine election, and found peace in the sanctuary of the divine defense.

thirty-five

CHRIST SURPRISED BY FAITH

Matthew 15:21–31

OUR LORD is now touching upon half-heathen countries, and about to give forecasts of his universal empire. Up to this time he has moved within given geographical limits, now he looks, and almost steps, over the dividing lines. It belonged to the religious genius of Matthew in particular to see beyond Hebrew boundaries, and to note every sign of the universality of the kingdom of Jesus Christ. It was Matthew who brought the Magi from the far east with their presents of gold and frankincense and myrrh. A man like Matthew could not have omitted that incident from his story, though the other evangelists take no notice of it. Not Luke but Matthew notes the case of the Canaanitish woman. Matthew is a silent man; there was next to nothing said about him: again and again he shows us in his noble Gospel how great and noble were the thoughts that moved and ruled his mind. There is nothing little in Matthew's conception of the kingdom of heaven. He does not beat off the men from the far east, saying, "You have nothing to do with this birth"; nor does he rebuke the Canaanitish woman—he rather rejoices in those openings which show him light through their welcome crevasses, and Matthew says in effect, "This Master of mine shall rule from the east to the west, from the north to the south, and his house shall be large as his universe." Who knows but that as Mary was the mother of Jesus in the sense of bringing him into the world, so this Canaanitish woman may be the mother of Christ as introducing him into Gentile lands?

It is thus that individual names are lifted up in importance, and that small events are charged with infinite meaning. We know not what shall be the limit of the Amen to this prayer of hers. This supplication

269

may mark the agony of a birth time. Jesus Christ is now very near the dividing lines: will this Canaanitish woman succeed in taking him over the boundary, and bringing to Gentile necessity, and sin, and pain, all the sweet gospel of heaven? Let us see.

The woman was both right and wrong, in her simple prayer. That indeed may be said about all our prayers—mostly wrong, however, in many instances. Her prayer was conceived in the wrong name, in this instance arising no doubt from her courteous recognition of historical facts, but she appealed to the Son of David. By no such narrow name can Jesus enter into Gentile lands. If Christ was not more than the Son of David, he have no message to heathen countries. Notice, therefore, how the story develops the life and purpose of the Holy Christ. How keenly the Savior listens to every word that is addressed to him, and note how he will not answer prayers in the lump and gross, and how he will come to the human heart, along certain defined lines. There is no roughness in his method, there is no tumultuousness in the plan of this all-redeeming and all-healing Christ. When addressed by a Gentile suppliant as "Son of David," he is deaf. In other instances Jesus Christ had readily answered prayers that were addressed to him as Son of David, but the prayers in those instances were spoken by Jews. A Gentile, as such, knows nothing about the Son of David; some greater, broader name must be found, and what do you know but that now he will take upon him, in some sense previously not adequately realized, a name that shall enter into every language, and be at home in the prayers of the whole world?

Jesus Christ answered the woman not a word. In truth she had not spoken a word to him in his proper capacity. There were some things which Jesus Christ could not do in his hereditary capacity or merely local and ancestral name. There were divisions of kingdoms and properties which he could not attend to. Men must be brought to learn the exact scope and purpose of the mission of Jesus Christ in the world. We know what it is amongst ourselves for men to be limited in their official capacity: they can do certain things for us in their personal capacity which they could not do in their official function. As officers they cannot speak to us, whereas in their capacity as fellow-citizens and sympathizers, they could address us the whole day long, and spare nothing of the language and music of their pitying and full love. When we address Jesus Christ as "Son of David," we must not rest there. To that local and limited title we must add some designation worthy of the purposes of his heart. We belong to the Gentile race. From the house of David we are excluded: Abraham knows us not: we must not therefore walk up Jewish staircases to these heavenly heights, but other ways must be found, and other ways have been opened for us, and as Gentiles we must move to the cross by methods which have been indicated from heaven.

In the light of these suggestions read our Savior's reply—"I am not sent but to the lost sheep of the house of Israel, as the Son of David." In other words—"If this woman addresses me as the Son of David I have nothing to say to her. If that is all she knows about me, if she comes to me as a great Jew and a great descendant of an illustrious sire, I have no reply to make to her plea." Whether there is any other way of coming, we shall see.

The bitterness of her trial gives the right tone to the woman's prayer. She prayed a second time. Jesus Christ himself amended his own prayer upon one memorable occasion. He allows us to amend, enlarge, simplify our supplications. Then came she and worshiped him, saying, "Lord, help me." Sorrow abbreviates our prayers, sorrow teaches us true eloquence. When the heart is in the grip of a deadly agony, it knows how to pray. In our ordinary, and more or less conventional public worship, we must have order and method, by which the public can be guided. Beyond all such arrangements there lie the innumerable plans and methods of approach to heaven, known only to the heart in its keenest pangs. There are times in which no man can teach another how to pray. Bursting out of his throbbing heart will fly the great desire, in appropriate speech and tone. Unless we have had experience of that kind we are not in a proper mood to discuss the possible prevalence of prayer: questions to which this inquiry respecting prayer belongs, are not to be discussed with cold intellectualism. When your child has been grievously vexed with a devil, when the last hope of your life has been blown out by a sudden and most cruel wind, when you are climbing up steep places and the loose stones are giving way in your hand, you will know whether prayer is a necessity of life or a recreation of the religious fancy.

Our prayers are forced out of us, and being forced out of us by some mighty impulse which cannot be adequately described in words, they seem to take the Kingdom of Heaven by violence. When men feel the bitterness of sin, they will find right names for Christ. Understand more and more clearly that Jesus Christ is not to be approached as an intellectual or historical problem with any hope of solving the great enigma to the content of the mind. Herein is much time wasted, and temper often greatly exasperated, that men think they can subject the Son of God to arbitrary vivisection. We see him only now and then. We may speak about him in the deepest sense and with proper tone only occasionally. He is with us always as a vision of the heart and an inspiration of the will, but for the purposes of explanation in words to others, it is only seldom in a lifetime that a man has the responsibility of such an occasion. We must feel Christ rather than understand him, we must wait for his coming rather than surprise him by our intellectual agility and resoluteness. When we feel the bitterness and the burden of sin, we see the cross, as in the darkness we see the stars. No man should speak about Christ except from the point of earnest conviction of sin and an impelling necessity of the soul to find out who he is and what he can do. He is not a subject for essays and for deliberate and clever discussions; he cannot be subjected to the scrutiny of criticism to which historical characters of another kind easily yield themselves. Christ is the angel that comes to the heart, the Messenger that finds his way to us along the intricacies and difficulties of our sorrow, the Savior that visits us in the midnight of our hopeless guilt.

He is always born in the night-time. Under the pressure of penitence and broken-heartedness you will know by what names to address Jesus Christ—then you will know whether he is God or Man; you will never be able to settle that question by dry intellectual processes, but when the heart wants him, cries for him, must die without him, it will dictate to the head the appellation which is worthy of his dignity and his power. All these mighty cries of blind men, troubled souls, needy women, show what kind of man is expected in one who claims to be the King. Jesus Christ was promised as a King, a Ruler and a Mighty One, who should have the nations under his feet and sway them with omnipotent majesty. When he came along the common lines of human history, entering into cities and habitations, men who were in great need and distress, showed by their prayers what a true king must be. He must bring with him something more than a crown, something more than royal regalia, something more than court and pomp: he must bring help. A king is an irony if he be not beneficent above all other men. A king mocks our social helplessness and our social poverty if he be not the princeliest giver, the man whose heart is a great treasure-house, out of which are handed, night and day, donations to make life richer and gladder. Thus do we learn from sorrow what we never could learn from mere genius. The world felt the kingship of Jesus before it could assign that royalty its technical name. Early in the pages of his history, the lame, the crippled, the maimed, the blind, the deaf, the dumb, were crowding around him, saying in mute eloquence, "A king must help, or he is not a king." So is sorrow an expositor, and so is agony one of the world's greatest preachers.

Jesus Christ abased this Canaanitish woman, but we never find him subjecting any human creature to abasement without his disclosing a gracious purpose of exaltation. Jesus answered, "It is not meet to take the children's bread and to cast it to dogs." This is one of the passages which no criticism can explain. We ought to have heard the tone in which Jesus Christ himself delivered the words. To feel their import properly, we should have seen the expression of his face when he uttered the rugged and severe reply. The printed page is poor when it undertakes to make representations of this kind—the illuminating smile, the explanatory tone, the subtle music, the step towards, the help nearly given—what can the printed page make of these? Was he quoting a proverb, was he reminding the woman of one of her own sayings, was he bringing to her memory something she had said about other people? It is thus that Christ takes the sword out of our hand, and gives us to feel the sharpness of its point. Happily, though we cannot enter into the whole atmosphere of the reply, and thus find out its mitigations, we know what happened immediately afterwards, and that subsequent action must be taken as the light and exposition of all that went before.

How will the woman reply? She will stand upon her dignity. No heart that is filled with agony has any dignity of a petty kind to stand upon. She will be offended. She might have been if her child had not been grievously vexed with a devil, but love keeps the temper sweet. She will be struck dumb, having no reply to words so clear and final. We look from Christ to the woman, wondering what she can possibly reply. Her answer is before us, and is it possible for any answer to be keener in its wit, tenderer in its pathos, more hopeful in its sentiment? She said, "Truth, Lord: yet the dogs eat of the crumbs which fall from their Master's table." He inspired that answer himself: that eloquent reply was part of the exaltation which he meant to assure and confirm. No grander answer was ever returned by human lips. There is nothing in the eloquence of Christ himself superior to this flash of the heart's wit. This illustrates what is meant by inspiration.

How did Jesus Christ reply to this method of putting the case? He replied instantly, with the whole gospel in his tone, with all the love of his heart beaming, burning in his transfigured face, "O woman, great is thy faith." He always recognized the operation of faith in human life. Nothing seemed to surprise the Son of God so much as the exercise of faith. We cannot define faith in any adequate terms: it is not a dictionary word. Faith is the sixth sense, faith is the religious faculty, faith is the power that takes all other senses and glorifies them, faith is the step into the invisible which the soul takes in its supreme moments of inspiration. We have lowered the word faith by trying to intellectualize it: it has come within the purpose of some men to attempt to explain faith—the explanation had better have been left alone, for it does but spoil what it attempts to illumine. We know what faith is when the heart is in the right condition. "With the heart man believeth unto righteousness" [Rom. 10:10]. This is not merely an intellectual process, and does not therefore come under the laws of merely intellectual inquiry or anatomy. Faith is the supreme act of the heart, and is not to be explained until after it has been done. When a man has given himself wholly to the Son of God in some great passion of sacrifice, the minister it may be, or a friend, stands near him and says, "Now, that is faith."

It is a word that comes after the action and not before it. Wit is a partial gift, eloquence belongs to but a few, poets are born, not made—but faith is the universal possibility. Herein is the one word which belongs to all languages. Believe on the Lord Jesus Christ, and thou shalt be saved. Men are saved by faith that is in Christ. ". . . The life which I now live in the flesh, I live by faith on the Son of God, who loved me and gave himself for me" [Gal. 2:20]. "Lord, increase our faith" [Luke 17:5]. "Lord, I believe; help thou mine unbelief" [Mark 9:24].

Can we believe for others? Is there an operation of proxy in the kingdom of heaven? This woman is not praying for herself alone, she is principally praying for her absent child who is grievously vexed with a devil. Where the child cannot herself believe, does the Lord Jesus accept the mother's faith as the child's act? Into questions so difficult we cannot enter with any hope of complete illumination—still the heart says that we can almost believe for other people. Your mother wants to stretch her godly faith around your blasphemy, so that you may be saved. Your father wants to include you within the amplitude of his faith, for he calls your unbelief a devil, and in many a secret prayer to heaven he says, "My son is grievously vexed with the demon of unbelief." It is impossible to resist the operation of this law of inclusion: we cannot question that we all receive benefits from heaven because of the religion of other people. Ten righteous men spare the city [Gen. 18:32], the house of Potiphar is blessed for Joseph's sake [Gen. 39], the ship tossed upon the sea is spared because of the prisoner Paul who is on board [Acts 27], and many of us are today reaping the crops which our fathers sowed in seed. Pray for your child: be yours the big faith that surprises God—then who can tell what answers may be returned?—for Jesus answered and said unto the Canaanitish woman, "Be it unto thee even as thou wilt." He gave her the keys of the kingdom and said, "Use them after thy liking."

Then he passed on, and came nigh unto the sea of Galilee, and went up into a mountain and sat there. And the people allowed him to sit there, combining ease with dignity, taking rest, and contemplating the city with all its sin and pain, from a distance. It is not so that the tragic story reads. No sooner had he sat down than great multitudes came to him, having with them those that were lame, blind, dumb, maimed, and many others, and cast them down at the feet of Jesus. We belong to him most when we are in our deepest, most abject helplessness. He does not say, "Take away these burdens and leave the mountain free for my enjoyment"—no, he was king, and a king must give, a king must identify himself with his subjects, royalty must sympathize. And Jesus healed them, so that they who were borne up the mountain as burdens, left it with agility and delight and thankfulness. Then was there great rejoicing among the multitude: they could not deny the wonderful works that had been done. When we see dumb men speaking, lame men walking, maimed men whole, and the blind seeing, it is surely impossible for us to engage ourselves to some sorry intellectual explanation of these marvelous and astounding disclosures of power. The people yielded to the natural instinct, and the mountain throbbed again with the resounding song and shout and jubilance of those who beheld the revelation of the kingdom of gracious power.

Jesus Christ is doing greater works today, and today the world should be filled with the music of praise and thanksgiving unto God. Were not some of us blind and do we not now see? How few years separate between our present condition and one that we dare scarcely recall because of its humiliation. We were as sheep going astray, but we are now returned unto the Shepherd and Bishop of our souls. We were defiled and unclean and polluted and corrupt, but now we are washed, we are cleansed, we are sanctified. If it is a great thing—and no man would question its greatness—to see the maimed made whole, and the dumb made to speak, it is a greater thing to see a bad heart turned to righteousness, and to hear blaspheming lips opened in loyal prayer. Such are the continual miracles of the grace of Christ.

thirty-six

CHRIST THE SATISFACTION OF HUNGER

Matthew 15:32–39

ALL ORTHODOX CRITICS regard this miracle as totally distinct from the strikingly similar one recorded in the fourteenth chapter. There can, indeed, be no doubt about it, if we believe what Jesus Christ himself is reported to have said in the sixteenth chapter, wherein he asks the people if they have forgotten the five loaves of the five thousand, and the seven loaves of the four thousand. This is one of the repetitions which are necessary in beneficent life. We must not find fault with the miracles because we have experienced something very like them before. Our life is a continual miracle; repetitions ought not to be monotonous to us, our love ought to be so intelligent and lively as to discern in every repeated miracle some new phase and tone of the divine mind and purpose.

Amidst all his thinking, which must have been of the most trying nature, Jesus Christ's acute and passionate sympathy was never suppressed. With such problems pressing for solution, with the purposes of eternity about to accomplish themselves in his agony and death, with the cross daily acquiring new definiteness of outline and weight, who could wonder if all that was merely sympathetic should be forgotten or suspended? Are we not absorbed in the solution of our intellectual problems, are we not sometimes so taken up with great questions, that we cannot attend to domestic affairs, or household anxieties, or to the so-called petty troubles of our passing life? Here is a man who was slain from before the foundation of the world, who is now to be seen in heaven by faith's vision, as a lamb slain, who was a Man of sorrows and acquainted with grief always, who had the wall of salvation pressing upon his attention and crushing the strength of his heart, and yet he has time to bestow attention upon the hunger and thirst of the multitude. Wherein then is our reasoning wrong, when we think that great intellectual and moral considerations might have excluded the action of sympathy? It is wrong in the fact that we do not understand the real nature and scope of sympathy, when properly interpreted and understood. But for his sympathy the cross would have been an impossibility; intellect cowered before it, love took it up and bore it onward until its very gloom was carried into glory.

So shall it be with all crosses that are rightly borne. If we carry our crosses in Christ's spirit and according to the measure of Christ's will, we shall force our troubles beyond the dark point at which they would bind us down, and make those troubles contribute to the very satisfaction which they were meant to destroy. Intellect soon drops its crosses, love bears them on to the happy consummation. We are too impatient with our crosses: we try to cut them down; we should let them alone until they take root and blossom and bear fruit for our soul's satisfaction. Herein is the lesson of Christ broad and gracious to us in all its application of wisdom and of comfort. You want to cut the cross into small pieces of wood and to burn them in the fire and so destroy the tree of crucifixion: Jesus Christ shows us how we are to treat the cross—we are to carry it forward from step to step until we cause the extreme of trouble to touch the beginning of joy. Let us consider then the High Priest of our profession, "Let us run with patience the race that is set before us, looking unto Jesus the author and finisher of our faith, who for the joy that was set before him, endured the cross, despising the shame, and is set down at the right hand of God" [Heb. 12:1, 2]. The joy that is beyond should give strength to bear the cross which is the immediate portion of the passing day. If we omit from our recollection the coming, the necessary joy, then there should be no wonder if our souls are cast down as under the pressure of an intolerable burden. Our light affliction is but for a moment, while we look not at the things which are seen, but at the things which are not seen. We are to be constrained to nobler heroism of endurance and sweeter gentleness of patience, by the power of an endless life. Take in more field, cast your eyes abroad upon a bolder horizon, recognize the ulterior purpose and the sure consummation of divine love, and then the cross will begin to bud, and to have upon it green leaves, and then colored blossoms, and then rich sweet fruit; and the soul will know that it was a glad time when that rough cross was planted in the soil of the life.

Hear this sweet music, which rises with the might of gentleness, in the desert. It comes upon us suddenly, and yet there ought not to be any suddenness in such a strain. Jesus says, "I have compassion." This is the key word of the Savior's life, the surname of Christ is *compassion*. Why should such a speech startle one? He refers to his compassion as if it were a new feature in the day's proceedings: he indicates the rising of compassion as though it were a new emotion of his life. What was the Savior doing all the time but having compassion? The feeling never ceased: it touched with its own gentleness everything that Christ did—he might have prefaced every day's work with "I have compassion," he might every night have fallen asleep to the music of his own words, "I have compassion." It gave a wondrous expression to his eyes, caused the subtlest tones to enter into his gentle yet all-pervasive and all-penetrating voice, it lifted him up above his burdens and made him face the devil with a new energy—it was the secret and the very inspiration of his life and ministry.

If you read the life of Jesus Christ under this suggestion that compassion is the key-word of it all, you will find everything Jesus Christ did taking on a new color and bearing a new attitude and general relation to all history and to all providence. When Jesus preached, he preached as one who had compassion, and preaching without compassion is not preaching the gospel in a gospel tone. He who would preach Christ must preach him yearningly, tearfully—there must throughout his sermons be great gushes of tenderest desire for the souls of men. This is the secret of apostolic power: Paul besought those who heard him night and day with tears; the apostle punctuated some of his letters with weeping. Jesus Christ was a preacher whose words were steeped in feeling; every sermon therefore came from his heart, belonged to his heart, expressed his heart's uppermost feeling and purpose. When Jesus Christ denounced, he denounced in the spirit of compassion, his curses were the emphasis of his pity and his love, not in relation to those on whom they fell like thunderbolts, but in relation to those on whose behalf he poured out the malediction of his righteous and solemn anger. When he denounced the Pharisees because they would not touch the burdens they laid upon men with so much as the tips of their fingers, it was because he had compassion upon those who were oppressed by the tyranny of those who sought to over-ride and over-drive them. When he called men hypocrites, liars, actors, it was because they were deluding and misleading people, and because he had compassion upon the dupes and victims of priestly cunning and wicked purpose.

Why then should we be surprised when Jesus Christ says "I have compassion"? Sometimes he had to express his compassion in the very lowest and commonest forms. He accommodated himself to human weakness in the ways in which he made his revelations. We ought to have known that his very cunning was the expression of a passionate feeling, we ought to have heard tones of compassion in every beatitude he pronounced and in every thunder of denunciation which he launched, but seeing that we were not spiritually sympathetic enough to do so, he had to actually come down and express his compassion to us in the feeding of our physical hunger. He has, so to say, to force himself by basest miracle upon the rude stupidity of those who cannot follow the more subtle music and more divine passages of his ministry. Not until he clothes some of us do we understand that he cares about us. He has, so to say, to build up, brick by brick, our very houses, and not until he has roofed them in and furnished them and made them glow with comfort do we begin to see that possibly there may be a Father and a Savior in the universe. When our spiritual education is more advanced, when our sympathies are more eager and sensitive and are illuminated with divine intelligence, we shall see God in other directions and in other relations, and shall not need the miracle of bread to convince us that the very hairs of our head are all numbered and the very beatings of our heart are heard in heaven. Meanwhile we are rude, coarse, impervious, and he has to treat us according to the impenetrability of our moral condition.

"I have compassion." How did he say that word? With what richness of tone, how broadly yet penetratingly he pronounced the word. He expounded it in its very enunciation, it warmed the wilderness when he uttered it, a new glow of hope pervading the breasts of all who heard that ineffable music. The compassionate man is the one whom we need longest and most often. The clever man amuses us for a moment, the entertaining man comes happily into the life now and again on sundry numerable occasions, the argumentative man troubles and vexes the intellect with many a hard proposition which he labors to solve and settle according to his own conceptions, but we tire of them all—we cannot live upon cleverness, entertainment sates its dupes, argumentativeness wears the brain which it challenges to high controversy, but pity, gentle compassion, noble all-including sympathy—it is the everlasting necessity, it is the most divine expression of interest.

This is Christ's power over the world—not the splendor of his intellect, not the witchery and fascination of his simple crystal eloquence, but his love, care, pity, patience, hopefulness, the heavenly way he has of stooping down to us and reconstructing our life when it has been shattered by rude blows, by whispering into our ear the word of hope which we dare not whisper to ourselves lest we should provoke the sword of conscience or bring to bear upon our souls the sting of outraged memory. By his love he wins, by his compassion he stands foremost among the world's redeemers, not one of many but one alone, and they are broken parts of him.

In such miracles as this we see how Jesus Christ includes the whole life in his view and intent, and how nothing is too lowly for him to do that will bring into our hearts quietness and rest and satisfaction. The clever man will abandon you when you enter the chamber of affliction: his voice would be harsh there. The entertaining man cannot go with you into the sanctuary of sorrow: his laughter would offend the genius of the place, his jokes would be blasphemies in that solemn place. The argumentative man would even vex the soul by his many problems and propositions, his hypotheses and clever conjectures, when the soul is ill at ease and is the subject of such afflictions as can be known only by those who have been transfixed by the accusations of God's law.

Who then can enter the chamber or be at home in the great darkness or take up the speech of the new land and utter it so that the soul can understand its whole meaning? He only who trod the winepress, who sweat, as it were, great drops of blood, who spake seven times on the accursed tree, who said, "Father, forgive them, for they know not what they do," and who added, "It is finished" [Luke 23:34; John 19:30]. He goes with us everywhere, he is with us at the wedding feast, he will find enough wine for the guests. Wherever he goes he takes the wine of gladness with him, and when we come to die, he will be the principal guest in the chamber, and will then give us the same wine, the wedding wine. He only goes everywhere and is equally strong at every point.

Now we come to a point which forever separates Jesus Christ from all other men, even the most tender-hearted and compassionate. It can be said of Christ alone that his resources were equal to his compassion. Our compassion outruns our resources: we are so often utterly helpless we might as well have no senses at all. What we would do, if we could: we would lift up the sick and the weary and make them well in a moment if it lay within our power to do so. We would take up the languishing and the death-stricken and make them glad in the summer light, and cause them to laugh with new energy, and because of new earthly hopes. We would cover up the grave, filling it with flowers, and smooth down the green face of the earth, so that it would be a shame to rip it up again for the purpose of hiding away the life of man. But though this would be the expression of our ignorant compassion, we are left without resource.

Jesus Christ always startled his disciples by the completeness of his proposals. "Feed the multitude," said he, and the disciples instantly answered "How?" "Go ye into all the world and preach the gospel to every creature" [Mark 16:15]—the same completeness and the same compassion, the same determination to meet the necessity of the whole case; and truly, from a human point of view, there is a little apparently in the one case as in the other—that is to say, in the case of preaching the gospel to every creature, and feeding the multitude with a few loaves and small fishes. What is there in this gospel to preach to every creature? What is there of sufficiency to meet the needs of the human family in all lands in all times? Yet it grows as it is spoken: this message never ends: it hesitates for a moment to accommodate the weakness of the speaker, but it waits for him, it makes the air throb and burn until he returns to his work, itself is never expressed in final speech. Let those testify to the sufficiency of the gospel to meet every need, who have known the gospel longest.

Notice the reason which Jesus Christ gives for his action—"lest they faint in the way." Here is the preventive ministry of the Savior: he does not wait until the people do faint, he will run before them to prevent them from fainting. Who can estimate this aspect of the Savior's ministry amongst us? We know the accidents which actually occur, and we magnify them into tragedies, but who knows the accidents which we narrowly escape, the accidents, so to say, which might have happened, the perils which surround us on the right hand and on the left and yet which do not express themselves in their ultimate form? The physiologists tell us that everyday we have ten thousand narrow escapes from death: you do not know how near you were dying five minutes ago—death, so to say, brushed you, and there was not room for a breath between the monster and the possible victim. We only know the rude accident, the actual fainting fit, but the accidents from which we are spared, the fainting fits that are kept off, the perils that are commanded to stand aside, who can estimate all these? Yet in this instance Jesus Christ invites our attention to his broadly preventive ministry; the action in which he goes before us to make ready against every contingency that could give us trouble.

"I go that I may prepare a place for you" [John 14:2]. He is always running before: if he goes away, he says, when we cling to him as if we would detain him on the earth, "It is expedient for you that I go away" [John 16:7]. He never did anything for himself; he saved others, himself he could not save. Today he is pleading for us, making our poor prayers, into great prevalent intercessions, lifting up our little ministry of supplication into his own broad and grand priesthood, and giving gifts unto men as the answers to his own great prayers. We do not know all that Jesus is doing for us, we do not even know all that the summer does. Add up and tell me in plain speech what the summer does. You will speak of gardens and meadows, blossoms, foliage of a thousand tints, ripening fruits, singing-birds, great breadths of blue sky, height on height, an infinite immensity—is that all? You do not tell me how the summer climbed up into the poor man's one-paned window and looked at him and told him he should be well again. You do not tell me how the summer subtly affected the souls of men who were depressed, and caused them to believe that even yet they would have a few cheerful hours before they passed away and were no more. You cannot follow all the ministry of light; it is always speaking, always working miracles, always recalling hope, always showing ways out of difficulties—light, a word of one syllable, but of all syllables in one.

Christ did not say that he wished to perform a miracle; Jesus Christ had no wish to show signs and wonders, and to display mere power. Had the bread been equal to the compassion, no miracle would have been performed. Compassion is the secret of every miracle; there are no instances of Jesus Christ exerting mere power for the sake of its display: he never sought to do anything by the exhibition of mere omnipotence. Read the miracles in the light of this suggestion, and you will find that every miracle is, so to say, the expression of his tears, the utterance of his love, the form of his compassion. Think of all his healing, and see in all the wondrous cures which he wrought, how he had compassion on the multitude. See him raising the dead, and as the dead rise in obedience to his word, hear him say, "I have compassion on the living because they are so lonely and cold in the absence of the loved one." See him walking on the sea, and hear him saying to the cold night wind, roused into storms that frightened the poor voyagers, "I have compassion on the storm-tossed disciples because they are alone and know not what to do." And hear him say on the cross, "I have compassion on the multitude."

thirty-seven

READERS OF THE OUTSIDE

Matthew 16:1–12

THE PHARISEES and the Sadducees had looked upon the whole demonstration of evidence applied by Jesus Christ in the course of his varied and exciting ministry, and were exactly in the same condition of unbelief and disguised or avowed hostility as before. No impression had been made upon them of a vital kind. They had been dazed and stunned by a succession of miracles, but had not been convinced. Allowing that great and wonderful cures had been performed, they were piously anxious that now some sign should be shown to them from heaven. You can understand the unction with which they pronounced that sacred word. They would now change the field of proof: a token from heaven would be exactly after the temper of their pious and noble minds. They had observed the wonderful deeds which had been done, which were of a material and sensational kind, and which were adapted in a kind of broad manner to a certain low type of mind—but they desired a sign from heaven. The earth had been enough, and now they, wrapping their religious cloaks closely around them, desired a sign from heaven. Pious, sweet-souled, godly men, who were alive on the heavenly side of their nature and who would accept any hint or claim that came from the sky, in infinite preference to the cures of the leprous, the dumb, the deaf, the blind, and the maimed.

This is a common and holy trick in all corrupt churches. Give them what you may, they always want miracles of another kind. Their hearts are determined in unbelief, therefore do their minds affect to find fault with the evidence, or if not to find direct fault with it, to suggest supplementary demonstration of a totally different kind, and the corrupt

Church is never so near its total damnation as when it affects its most unctuous piety and wants a sign from heaven.

We want sermons of another kind, when the devil is twisting his fingers further and further around us. We admire the sermons that are delivered, but we want to see a sermon from heaven. Such people grant the intellect but they affect to pine for the feeling. They do not deny the genius but they desire more spirituality. They do not doubt that good has been done in certain cases and to a certain class of minds, but they desire to see good of another kind done. This is a stock temptation of the old serpent. He says, "What you have to eat is all very good, but you ought to ask for something if not better, yet different. You cannot deny that notable miracles have been done, and that wonderful doctrine has been propounded. Admit all that: appear ever to be generous in your concessions, but ask for something different, play the pious trick." Old serpent, cunning—and yet his cunning ought now to be so transparent that we should mock it and reject it with bitter scorn.

How did Jesus Christ treat this pious inquiry, this high spiritualism of desire? The answer which he returned was itself a sign from heaven had they who received it but have understood its scope and its purport. It was a two-edged sword—no other man in all human history could have made that reply. Observe its moral discernment. "O ye hypocrites." Unhappily we have only the cold ink to represent that word: we miss the atmosphere of its utterance, the emphasis which carried it straight into the guilty heart. "O ye hypocrites." Was not their pious speech about heaven, was not their question simple and direct, is there any one word in it that could give reasonable offense, did they not belong to the spiritual section of the Church, the sighing, crying and sky-desiring section of the great family of human students and religious inquirers? "O ye hypocrites,"—that was a sign from heaven, to know them through their disguises, to accost the devil when he wore an angel's livery, to take him with mocking familiarity by the face and call him devil, notwithstanding his clothes—that was a sign from heaven.

In the case of Jesus Christ we must always judge the question by the answer which he returns. We do not say everything in words: the big lie is in the heart and not in the speech. Christ answers the question we want to ask, and not merely the inquiry which we actually put in words. Was not this penetration of character a sign from heaven? Was he ever much grander and nobler than when he faced the Pharisees and Sadducees and answered the question about heaven by a charge of personal and unmixed hypocrisy? Did this Man palter with his age, did this Man pay a high price for popularity? Was this the way to increase his fame and his comfort? Would it not have been better for him to have taken the Pharisees and Sadducees into some quiet and sacred place and shown them tricks from heaven? Mark the stern and invincible consistency of this Man: he will have no compromise with hypocrisy. He will not enter into partnership on forbidden terms and with forbidden people. This is the eternal miracle of truth: it pierces us, being sharper than any two-edged sword. This is the proof of its inspiration which the Bible always gives. Do not find its inspiration in its literary conscientiousness, in its mechanical consistency, in its artistic finish—find whether it is inspired or not by its moral penetration, moral omniscience, moral authority. In any right reading of this Book we stand in a holy place, cut off from everything else, made solemn by an unspeakable quietness, so quiet that a whisper is as thunder, so holy that a sigh may pollute the awful sanctity. So come to the question of the inspiration of Christ, and the inspiration of the Scriptures. Understand what the Bible is in its moral tone and moral claim, and as it warns off all generations of vipers and broods of serpents, and will have nothing to do with hypocrites and masked men and visored faces, learn that it is the very judgment of God amongst men, no more to be trifled with than is fire.

The moral discernment of Christ's answer justified the judicial tone by which he mocked the hypocritical inquirers. "When it is evening, ye say it will be fair weather, for the sky is red, and in the morning, it will be foul weather today, for the sky is red and lowring." They were weather-wise, and nothing more, they mistook the sky for heaven, and the weather for a revelation. This is the perpetual mistake of men who have no inward and spiritual life. The temptation of today is that men should study the barometer. Such study has attained almost the dignity of a science—the barometer is now a Bible. Jesus Christ does not condemn this study of the weather, he says it makes a man foolish if he can only do so much and do no more. A man's knowledge may itself be an argument against him if it stops short of wisdom; if the light that is in a man be darkness, how great is that darkness! Jesus allows that they who questioned him could read the face of the sky, but he charges them with inability to discern the signs of the times.

What would you say about a man who knew all the letters of the alphabet, but could not put them into words? How would you estimate the claim of any man to wisdom who knew every word in the English language, and yet never could arrange those words into sentences? It looks as if a man were certainly learned when he knows instantly every letter of the alphabet—what more can any man know? He can repeat the alphabet backwards forwards, onward from any given letter—what more can be desired? Yet as there are those who know the letters but cannot shape them into words, so are there men who can count upon their fingers the great dogmas of Christianity but cannot run them into musical utterance, or mass them into grand practical argument, or translate them into noble and beneficent life. They are weather-wise, letter-wise, but nothing else beyond that. Herein is the great difficulty of all-expanding revelation, and all-broadening and ever-enlarging and enlightening ministries amongst men. We cannot get them to understand that it is one thing to know the letters of the alphabet and a totally different thing to run those letters into words and those words into ample and eloquent sentences.

Jesus allows a certain amount of knowledge on the part of his interrogators and then he mocks them as being only learned in the weather, skilled in the clouds, but having no eye to read the writing of the heavens. When you look upon the clouds you do not look upon the sky, when you look upon the sky you do not see into heaven, when you read letters you do not form words, when you pick out individual words you do not construct tuneful and inspiring sentences. Stop not short in your education, but get away from the letter to the word, from the word to the sentence, from the sentence to the meaning, from the meaning to the music, from the music to the Musician—God.

Jesus Christ's answer was more than a mockery, it was also a revelation of the great fact that we are surrounded by legible and visible providence in human affairs. "Can ye not discern the signs of the times?" We should not need miracles if we could rightly read events—that seems to be the spiritual doctrine of Jesus Christ: he teaches us that we have a sign from heaven every day, and that we only need the seeing eye to behold its luster and beauty. It is thus that the Son of God lays his claim upon our attention and confidence by the breadth and moral nobleness of his teaching. While we with blatant curiosity and affected piety are wanting new signs and new tokens from heaven, he says, "God is revealing himself in all the processes of the age, in all the developments of civilization: you should read these things more carefully, and you would not be pining and sighing for other proofs and demonstrations of the divine finger."

Facts are lamps by which we should see God. The rapid and startling combination of events surprising the crafty by new conjectures and appalling the strong by unknown energies, are signs of a power as beneficent as it is unlimited. Ye can discern the face of the sky, but can ye not discern the signs of the times? The little that we can do is mocked by the great which we cannot do — or a more cheering view is that the little we can do should be the stimulus to our attempts to still loftier and nobler discoveries. Can ye not discern the signs of the times? This question is a challenge and not a rebuke. Christianity always calls us to an interpretation of the events that make up the history of our own day. Daily journalism should be daily preaching: men who keep diaries should know that they are writing revelations from heaven. The legendary John Wesley was known to say that he read the newspapers to see how God was governing the world. When journalism is honest without being pious, real and healthy without being sentimental, it will show us every day in its broad sheet a thousand signs from heaven.

Christianity therefore is a call to present day thinking. Venerable as it is with the colors of old time, it is yet modern in its sympathy with human aspiration and its control over human motive and purpose. Not ancient history but modern activity comes within the claim and sovereignty of Christian faith. The Church must modernize itself, and forever be the youngest as well as the oldest of human institutions.

Jesus Christ in closing, which he today practically does, the great series of miracles with which we have now become familiar, and in pointing to the signs of the times as God's revelations and tokens amongst us, takes his stand upon the broadest and most indestructible ground. This is a noble finish to the miracles. Again and again we shall see in further reading, a wonderful work here and there, but practically as to their massiveness and consecutiveness, the miracles are closed in this reading. Jesus Christ in retiring from a series of mighty works says, "If you want more miracles, more signs from heaven, look at events, study the history of your own time, from a religious standpoint survey the great march of civilization, the conflict of interests, the battle of truth against error, light against darkness, and he who reads the signs of the times correctly will need no more miracles of the kind now closed, for his own life will be a wonder, every event upon earth will be an interposition from heaven."

This is healthy teaching, this is robust, masculine talk. The man who took this attitude was not afraid of his religion suffering from contact with material civilization and with public conflicts of all kinds. He was not only a God distant, infinite, impalpable and unnameable, but a Father in the household, watching all the family life, interposing in its succession of daily events, and asserting himself with all the processes and developments of individual, social, and national life. This is a grand farewell. He is now about to be taken up from us into a loftier region of teaching, and before this intermediate ascension he says to us in broad noble speech, "Read the signs of the times, consider the events that are passing around you, and you will have no further need for miracles and wonders of a kind to which you have now been long accustomed."

Let us learn then from Christ's answer that the events of the day are signs. The sign is always more than itself: the sign points to the thing signified. And let us also learn that these signs were meant to be studied. Jesus Christ would never refer us to unauthorized sources of thought and expression. God means his providence to be searched into, compared one with another, set in proper relation and succession. Have we the seeing eye? There is a shape in events; circumstances, occurrences, transactions are not unrelated stories, but they were meant to be put together to grow up into a holy temple unto the Lord, from the foundation to the loftiest pinnacle. Do not suppose that time is chaotic, look for the shape—when you cannot see the shape, look for the shadow. Your affliction means something, your disappointments have a purpose, your successes have a divine meaning, your opportunities are doors opened by divine fingers. Fool is he who thinks that every event is but a laden vehicle that turns out its contents every night, and passes on to bring other contents and to throw them into the same shapeless heap.

Read the signs of your own life. Throw the memory of the heart back to the time when you were young, little, poor, unknown, misunderstood, misjudged, assailed, nearly ruined, often sick, sometimes friendless. How doors opened, how friends came, how unexpected voices broke in upon the solitude of your despair, how little gleams and glints of light stirred in upon the darkness of your dejection—let the whole scene pass before your inner vision, and you will need no miracles of a sensational, external, and striking kind. You yourself will be the miracle, and unless a man feels himself to be a miracle, all written and historical miracles will be but so many stumbling-blocks to his faith.

If we preach the miracles only along the line of merely intellectual inquiry, all nature will seem to be against us, great laws of continuity will assail our faith in every approach it makes towards the conclusion, but if we ourselves, being miracles, preach the consideration of Christ's wonderful works, they will seem to be part of himself, almost parts of ourselves, and we will know them by a masonry of the heart which has no words which can adequately express the subtlety of its penetration or the grasp of its power.

Though the written revelation has closed and no more ink can be added to God's Bible, living revelation is continual. Woe unto that man who takes his ink-horn and dips his pen, with the hope of adding anything to the Book to which God himself has added the grand Amen, but joy to that heart, a Sabbath every day, light upon light till the whole life burns with a sacred luster, who sees God in Providence, reads him in daily events, hears his going in every click of the telegraph, sees him walking upon the waters, and watches him bringing chaos into order, tumult into peace and music.

A small event occurred afterward, a scene of blundering stupidity on the part of men who were nearest to him, and who ought to have heard the beating of his heart more clearly than others, but as we ourselves are making the same blunder every day, mistaking the letter for the spirit, the loaf for the doctrine, mixing up sacred and secular, and not able to distinguish the one from the other—we had better not rebuke their stupidity in terms too severe, lest we inflict fatal wounds upon our own sagacity.